# The Everyday Life of Urban Inequality

# Culture, Humanity, and Urban Life

***Series Editors:*** Jessica Bodoh-Creed (California State University) and Melissa King (San Bernardino Valley College)

## Mission Statement

How are urban processes entangled with human experiences? In the *Culture, Humanity, and Urban Life* series, scholarly monographs and edited volumes explore this question and illuminate diverse forms of such entanglement through empirically based research. This series emphasizes anthropological approaches to the study of human life in relation to the urban. It seeks to illuminate experiences and effects of urban cultures and situate specific cases in a comparative set. By exploring the intricacies of human-urban relations, this series contributes to better understanding of the ways that humans particularly conceive of and experience nature, personhood, ethics, culture, and social life.

## Books in Series

*The Everyday Life of Urban Inequality: Ethnographic Case Studies of Global Cities*, edited by Angela D. Storey, Megan Sheehan, and Jessica Bodoh-Creed

*Urban Mountain Beings: History, Indigeneity, and Geographies of Time in Quito, Ecuador*, by Kathleen S. Fine-Dare

# The Everyday Life of Urban Inequality

## Ethnographic Case Studies of Global Cities

Edited by
Angela D. Storey, Megan Sheehan,
and Jessica Bodoh-Creed

LEXINGTON BOOKS
*Lanham • Boulder • New York • London*

Published by Lexington Books
An imprint of The Rowman & Littlefield Publishing Group, Inc.
4501 Forbes Boulevard, Suite 200, Lanham, Maryland 20706
www.rowman.com

6 Tinworth Street, London SE11 5AL, United Kingdom



British Library Cataloguing in Publication Information Available

**Library of Congress Cataloging-in-Publication Data**

Names: Storey, Angela, editor. | Sheehan, Megan, editor. | Bodoh-Creed, Jessica, editor.
Title: The everyday life of urban inequality : ethnographic case studies of global cities / edited by Angela Storey, Megan Sheehan, and Jessica Bodoh-Creed.
Description: Lanham : Lexington Books, [2020] | Series: Culture, humanity, and urban life | Includes bibliographical references and index.
Identifiers: LCCN 2020010240 (print) | LCCN 2020010241 (ebook) | ISBN 9781793610645 (cloth) | ISBN 9781793610652 (epub)
Subjects: LCSH: Urbanization—Social aspects. | Urban poor—Social conditions. | Sociology, Urban. | Equality.
Classification: LCC HT151 .E836 2020 (print) | LCC HT151 (ebook) | DDC 307.76—dc23
LC record available at https://lccn.loc.gov/2020010240
LC ebook record available at https://lccn.loc.gov/2020010241

∞™ The paper used in this publication meets the minimum requirements of American National Standard for Information Sciences—Permanence of Paper for Printed Library Materials, ANSI/NISO Z39.48-1992.

# Contents

# List of Figures

# Acknowledgments

This volume came together with the invaluable support of many individuals. First and foremost, we are grateful to Jessica Bodoh-Creed who envisioned this collection and brought together a group of international scholars. Thank you to series editor Melissa King for support throughout, and sincere gratitude to our editor at Lexington Press, Kasey Beduhn, for guidance and patience as we navigated this process.

Our revisions were aided by the helpful feedback of an anonymous reviewer. We also benefited from the opportunity to present a subset of these chapters at a panel at the 2019 American Anthropological Association's annual meeting. The conversations with Ben Chappell, Lucero Radonic, and Seng-Guan Yeoh were helpful in the final editing process. In particular, we would like to thank Anru Lee, who offered constructive insights as the panel discussant. For inspiration in collegial collaboration, our thanks to Tad Park and Jim Greenberg.

We have great appreciation for our family and friends who traveled this editorial road with us, especially to Shachaf Polakow for the use of his photograph on the cover of this volume and his profound support.

Finally, as ethnographers, we owe a debt of gratitude to the people who graciously allowed us into their homes and lives, sharing their perspectives, stories, and insights with us. For everyone who helped guide us in our research, thank you! We hope that we have done service to your stories, struggles, and communities.

A.D.S & M.A.S.
January 2020

# Introduction

## *The Everyday Life of Urban Inequality*

Megan Sheehan and Angela D. Storey

Steadily increasing inequality and the spectacular pace of urbanization frame the experiences of city dwellers across the world. As individuals struggle to navigate disparities and make a home in the city, their stories and frustrations often escape notice. Yet, when more readily visible collective actions or public protests emerge, they are frequently rooted in broader experiences of inequality. On October 18, 2019, after weeks of dispersed actions, high school students in Santiago, Chile, used social media to coordinate a city-wide movement. Groups jumped turnstiles at subway stations across the city, bringing transit to a halt and drawing the attention of international media. The protests coincided with the roll-out of a 30-peso (US 4-cent) fare increase for mass transit riders, and press coverage largely positioned the actions as a response to the fare increase (Bartlett, 2019; Londoño, 2019). Protesters quickly responded, "It's not 30 pesos, it's 30 years," a motto critiquing the impacts of Chile's now-entrenched experiment with neoliberalism, and this maxim circulated widely in social media. Forceful state repression of the protests galvanized widespread support. One week later, 1.2 million protesters—nearly 20 percent of Santiago's population—took to the streets to voice discontent with a slate of state policies and their impacts on everyday life: the privatization of pensions, the high cost of living and low wages, underfunded education and health-care systems, and growing disparities between the rich and the poor.

Chile's mass mobilizations denouncing neoliberal state policies and rising inequality are not isolated events. In the same month, protests in cities around the world called attention to local iterations of global socioeconomic shifts. In Quito, Ecuador, residents took a forceful stance against austerity measures, calling for economic and political reforms to address widening inequalities. In Lebanon, proposals to tax gasoline, tobacco, and WhatsApp calls drew people to the streets in Beirut and many other cities. In Haiti, the end to fuel subsidies, misappropriation of development funds, and scarcity of basic goods spurred near-daily rallies in Port-au-Prince. In Iraq, people protested high unemployment and a lack of economic opportunity in Baghdad. And in France, the yellow vest movement took to the streets of Paris to mark a year of actions demanding economic reforms. Lived disparities, limited access to resources, and perceptions of insufficient state responses to social and economic inequalities garner passionate debates and move people to action in each of these cities.

The price of gasoline, taxes on WhatsApp calls, and privatization of pensions are issues that resonate deeply with urban inhabitants. These movements, and others like them, point to the necessity of understanding the overlapping inequalities that shape daily life and ground collective action, the likes of which were seen profoundly in October 2019 mobilizations. In response, we ask: What does it mean to live within a city defined by myriad visible and invisible inequalities? What everyday worlds, meanings, or exclusions are concealed by city aspirations to development, to capital, and to a mode of globalization shaped largely by neoliberal ideologies?

This volume draws from situated ethnographies to explore what it means to live within cities marked by both entrenched and emerging inequalities. Each author engages broad questions about the reproduction of poverty, the creation of political marginality, and the destruction of communities by examining quotidian lives and spaces. We prioritize the voices of urban residents whose concerns often go unheard in decision-making—those being ushered out by gentrification, rehoused without their input, or forced into unsafe transit on long commutes. Using the tools of ethnography, these geographically diverse case studies speak to the ongoing rise of urban inequality by situating daily life at the intersection between global processes and local histories. As a whole, this volume considers tensions between development and displacement, belonging and contestation, and difference and proximity as key axes along which urban inequalities are wrought, contested, and remade within everyday experience.

## THE GLOBAL RISE OF URBAN INEQUALITY

The growing gap between the wealthy and the poor can be seen in the expansion of income inequality. In 2016, the top 1 percent of the global income bracket earned 21 percent of all income, while the bottom 50 percent—half of all people in the world—earned just 10 percent of global income (Alvaredo, Chancel, Piketty, Saez, & Zucman, 2018, p. 13). This increasing disparity exists alongside the global reduction of extreme poverty. As of 2015, less than 10 percent of the world population lived on US$1.90 per day, down from 29 percent in 1999 (World Bank, n.d.). These seemingly opposite trends emphasize the need for more detailed understanding of the daily life behind such statistics.

In 2010, the Oxford Poverty and Human Development Initiative developed a measure for poverty that considers access to education, health care, and basic utilities. This Multidimensional Poverty Index suggests that, as of 2019, 1.3 billion people—23 percent of the world population—live in poverty (OPHI & UN, 2019). This more nuanced measure indicates that global poverty has remained entrenched, even as incomes climb. Instead of demonstrating that inequality is inescapable, economists argue that such disparities are the result of specific policies, pointing toward markedly different growth rates of income inequality that correlate to differing national policy approaches (Alvaredo et al., 2018).[1] Indeed, while inequality is a global phenomenon, the chapters in this volume highlight the ways in which socioeconomic inequality results not merely from universal processes but from particular intersections of history, politics, and economic decisions.

Inequalities are often vividly manifest in metropolitan areas across the world, becoming ever more consequential as the pace of urbanization continues to accelerate. The world population became predominantly urban in 2007, and by 2050 more than two-thirds of all people will be based in cities, with most urban growth centered in Asia and Africa (UN, 2018). A growing number of these sites are megacities—metropolitan areas with over 10 million inhabitants (Van Mead, 2019). As urban areas become home to more residents and take on greater importance in national and global economies, the challenges of urban inequalities are more pronounced. The striking speed and scale of urbanization requires massive investments in developing housing, infrastructure, and institutions such as education and health care required by city residents. Even as national governments, international organizations, and other stakeholders attempt to meet the need of current city residents, nearly 1 billion urban inhabitants experience substandard living conditions, with limited access to potable water, sanitation, or residences constructed from solid materials, and without sufficient space to accommodate the household unit (UN, 2018). These basic needs will continue to present challenges for urban development and will increasingly become markers of urban inequality.

Across disciplines, social scientists have examined the myriad ways in which inequalities manifest within and between social groups. Considerations of inequality often begin by analyzing economic and resource stratification through largely quantitative and historical approaches (Hoffman & Centeno, 2003; c.f. Gootenberg, 2010; Lin, 2000; Stiglitz, 2012). Scholars emphasize the complexity of inequality and argue that analyses need to include perspectives beyond those afforded by data-driven statistical analyses

(Grusky, 2007). McGill argues that ethnographers are well situated to analyze how global relationships—often articulations of a neoliberal economic order—are made meaningful in local sites (2016). He goes on to argue that inequalities often stem from global relationships, and situated research can lay bare the multiple, overlapping, and self-reinforcing processes through which inequalities are produced (McGill, 2016). Cities have long been a focus of scholarship on inequality (c.f. Park, Burgess, & McKenzie, 1925; Wirth, 1928), and they remain at the center of significant debates about the reproduction of marginalities, exclusions, and resistance (Bayat, 2013; De Genova, 2005; Holston, 2008; Mitchell, 2003; Roy & Ong, 2011).

Each contribution in this volume analyzes the experiences of urban residents in order to show the multifaceted ways in which inequality is produced. Contributors chart how urban inequalities take root historically, linking current experiences with the colonial, neoliberal, and development policies that shape modern urban lives. Authors draw from detailed experiences such as finding housing, securing access to basic services, and engaging in cultural traditions to demonstrate how each permutation of lived inequality results from overlapping structural factors and the ordinary strategies that individuals employ to make-do amid disparity. The authors also make clear the power imbalances between urban inhabitants and the forces of capital, of legal jurisdiction, and of the long shadows of colonialism. Each chapter offer examples of individuals, families, and communities making the city their home and crafting spaces of belonging in the context of exclusions. As urbanization quickens in pace, state-led development initiatives appear incapable of fully provisioning the basic needs of burgeoning urban populations. In this environment, sharing the creativity of grassroots approaches and voices from the urban margins becomes increasingly vital.

## WHY ETHNOGRAPHY?

Ethnographers are well positioned to document how everyday experiences are framed by broader structures. While news media may focus on protests over a 30-peso fare increase, social scientists offer an analysis of the policies, urban growth, wage gaps, and historical context that prompt such movements for reform. Ethnography prioritizes diverse and often overlooked voices, drawing data from the minutia of urban life; this approach adds texture and complexity to academic analyses of inequality. At its best, ethnography brings under-told narratives to the forefront in a way that both "illuminates the unknown" and "interrogates the obvious" (Fassin, 2013, p. 642). Put differently, ethnographic insights often afford a new point of view on an entrenched problem.

Cities have been a significant focus of ethnographic research on inequality for more than sixty years. Foundational works have explored the experiences of people hanging out on street corners, family struggles to make ends meet in racially divided cities, and the foundations of criminalization within structural exclusions (cf. Bourgois, 1996; Liebow, 1967; Stack, 1974; Susser, 1982). More recent research continues to bring together structural analyses and explorations of everyday practices of urban life, incorporating an explicit focusing on the city as a point of analysis (cf. Anderson, 2013; Caldeira, 2000; Holston, 1989; Low, 2000; Roy, 2003; Wacquant, 2008). In this volume, a multidisciplinary group of scholars continue in this tradition to bring the stories, sights, and realities of city living to light, illustrating urban precarity from marginalized perspectives.

As an approach to research, and as a suite of methods, ethnography focuses on the collection of qualitative data about socio-cultural experience. Ethnography is often associated with long-term, in-depth research in which observational and experiential data overlaps with that collected via other methods. The selections in this volume make clear the diverse approaches and methodological tools that are grouped under ethnographic research. Reliably, most authors draw upon the power of participant observation, thick description, and a variety of interview formats. Some contributors use other ethnographic methods to gather and present everyday experiences, including mobile "go-alongs," the analysis of performative texts, archival contextualization, and participatory frameworks. This breadth of empirical data showcases how cities are lived—from the anthropologist's long commute to a hip-hop artist's sung commemoration of his neighborhood park, and from the moment when a caddie walks onto an elite golf course to the decisions of residents from an informal settlement on whether to vote. Each of these perspectives offer a situated view on urban life. While using similar methods and engaged in work around broadly connected topics, the case studies in this volume elucidate the nuance of ethnographic tools when used in thoughtful consideration of everyday lives and spaces. In reading the texts alongside one another, we hope that these ethnographic lenses afford an entry point for discussing and analyzing the dynamics of inequalities that frequently shape the everyday experiences of cities, illustrating ethnography's breadth and depth as an approach to urban inequality.

In the following section, we frame the major topics of this volume, introduce each chapter, and suggest the ways in which ethnographic research contributes to critical understandings of urban inequality within each theme. The case studies included in this volume illustrate how tensions between development and displacement, belonging and contestation, and difference and proximity mobilize diverse stakeholders, often at odds with one another. In these examples, we see actors strategically engage with each other and the policies, structures, and organizations that frame the ways in which inequalities are produced. We also see counter engagements through which individuals and communities reject a precarious reality and set out to creatively address their own needs. These negotiations between engagement and refusal work to shape the axes of urban inequalities. We hope that the volume's diverse case studies will engender further discussion of these critical tensions, of the many ways in which inequalities are reproduced structurally, and of the lasting implications of inequality on everyday urban life. Each chapter demonstrates the power of ethnographic approaches to afford a nuanced consideration of urban inequalities.

## DEVELOPMENT AND DISPLACEMENT

The first set of chapters explores how urban residents experience inequality through the displacements that follow from—or constitute—processes of development and modernization. In these chapters we see examples of cities aspiring to "World Class" status, with plans marked by modern ideals and model urban dwellers. Amid such aspirational global discourses, inequalities become sites in need of intervention, rhetorically framed as absences in development (Escobar, 2011; Ferguson, 1999; Holston, 2008; Roy, 2003). Projects of urban modernization and development are presented not only as attempts to remake cityscapes, but also as plans seeking to forge new kinds of citizens and new relations of sociality. Case studies in this section explore the experiences of individuals and communities as they face disparate processes of development and change in three cities: Casablanca, Morocco; Kuala Lumpur, Malaysia; and Maputo, Mozambique.

The development projects highlighted in these chapters aim to craft more modern cities. Urban development, though, is not a panacea, and the processes involved often obscure and reproduce inequalities—even when successful in rehousing families, eliminating informality, building new infrastructure, or reducing poverty (Pieterse, 2008; Potts, 2007). Indeed, large-scale development projects too often provide homogenous responses to complex challenges. These one-size-fits-all answers—whether in the form of new highways or public housing complexes—discount the myriad ways that individuals build lives for themselves against and within layered exclusions (Escobar, 2011). Chapters highlight how cultural norms and social networks are not always considered in development projects, sometimes relegating tight-knit communities to far-flung edges of resettled areas. Explorations of the lived experiences of development projects also reveal the persistence of hidden informality and the obligatory, quotidian ways used by individuals and communities to circumnavigate the shiny—albeit ill-fitting—solutions imposed upon them (Fischer, McCann, & Auyero, 2014). Marginalized subjects of development often pay a cost in further precarity, as they are distanced from places of employment, schools, or kin networks. Such practices remake routines, often burdening inhabitants with the realities of life in a new place and tearing asunder the cultural and social worlds upon which development inadvertently works.

The striking power of the modern ideal, and of aspirations to development, can be seen in the tensions between formality and informality. Despite their ubiquity, size, and complexity (Smit, 2006), informal settlements are typically seen as the opposite of formal areas—dirty instead of clean, chaotic instead of orderly, illegal instead of legal (Angotti, 2006). Forced evictions are often presented as projects to improve "cleanliness," modernization, or good governance in cities (Berrisford & Kihato, 2006; Potts, 2007). Authors engage the tensions surrounding urban development, often played out on a stage upon which formality and informality are set as opposing poles. Contrary to such rhetoric, informal spaces and processes are inextricably linked to the formal through the movement of people and goods, as well as through the binds of political, social, and economic interconnection (Simone, 2004). Informal spaces and processes are not incomplete, nor undone; they are important urban worlds intimately intertwined with formality. The following three chapters present a complex view of development in which the promises of formality are frequently set at odds with the realities of displacement and invisibility.

In chapter 1, Raffael Beier and Cristiana Strava explore the ways in which housing resettlement can incur significant costs upon resettled families and individuals. The impact of these processes is discussed through the narratives of three individuals displaced from an informal neighborhood in the center of Casablanca, Morocco. Their narratives illustrate how the country's push to eliminate informal housing impressed a singular solution onto a complex lived reality. Here, informal neighborhoods from which residents were displaced from Karyan Central were not short-lived settlements but, rather, spanned a century of development upon land near markets, jobs, and sites of livelihood. The nuanced reflections of individuals in Casablanca show that resettlements incur many costs not taken into account by centralized planners, including the loss of community networks; frequent relocation away from economic, educational, commercial, and social opportunities; life in differently configured and sized housing; and loss of access to services and resources. Through three ethnographic vignettes, Beier and Strava show the social complexity of those living through resettlement and formalizations processes.

In Kuala Lumpur, Malaysia, aspirations to "World Class" city status and "Developed Country" designation have fueled the elimination of informal settlements and the resettlement of residents. As Seng-Guan Yeoh examines in chapter 2, these experiences of movement, resettlement, and remade lives must be understood in the context of Kuala Lumpur's development as a city, beginning with the colonial era and stretching to the current government's expansive modernization plans. Yeoh traces the everyday routine of a woman resettled to a high-rise apartment as she navigates refuse-filled hallways and dark elevator cars in her building, works to run a small food stall and labor within the informal economy, and provides for her children's education. In her story, we see lives that were not entirely made anew by resettlement. Although housed and working, she must linger between informal and formal spaces in order to make ends meet. While her life is the product of modernization plans, she and her family have in many ways been bypassed by the promises of development. From colonial policy to current development goals, Yeoh presents a framework for understanding the necessary relationships between the lives of individuals and the layered context of their local world.

Infrastructure is an increasingly researched site of social experience, and a set of material connections that often make physical inequalities within the distributions of urban resources (Anand, 2017; Larkin, 2013; von Schnitzler, 2016). In chapter 3, Joel Christian Reed considers the informal *my love* transportation network of Maputo, Mozambique, which enable inexpensive transit between urban areas. *My love* consist of transport provided in the back of dump trucks, so-called for the way in which riders must hold on to each other for safety, as if in love. Although new road systems continue to expand in and around Maputo, the incredible suburban growth of recent decades has fueled a need for transit unmet by formal buses or even informal minibus taxis. *My love* transit thus dangerously bumps across the city roads, depicting the necessary making-do of life within an unequal city, the embodied precarity of transit, and the everyday ways in which city dwellers demand to benefit from elusive modernization. Standing along roadways waiting for insufficient minibuses or clinging tightly together in the bumpy backs of trucks, transit becomes a site in which publics cohere—against exclusions and to meet needs—and that works to highlight both economic and infrastructural inequality.

These case studies explore processes of development in a variety of forms. Development is a specter and an elusive promise; it is a way to remake the lives of those excluded from privileged spaces and opportunities, and a means by which communities can make claims upon the city and the state. Considering development from the perspectives of those experiencing displacement—living in a tent on the site of a demolished home, patching together work in the informal economy, riding in the back of *my love* transport—these ethnographic case studies reveal the stories of communities and individuals forging lives while bypassed by modernizing urban dreams.

## BELONGING AND CONTESTATION

A remarkable power of ethnography is its ability to hold contradiction and complexity. Indeed, within the volume's focus on persistent inequality we see a variety of practices that make meaning from, within, and around urban exclusions, forging modes of belonging that counter marginalization. Authors highlight the complexity of power and counter-power by focusing on lived experiences—iterations of social entanglement at the juncture of creation, refusal, and remaking (Abu-Lughod, 1990; Simpson, 2014). Ethnography emphasizes how such actions forge cities as vibrant places, with a cacophony of voices and in never-ending processes of becoming (Simone, 2008). Authors within this section examine the ways in which belonging is crafted, contested, and grounded in three cities: Hermosillo, Mexico; Austin, Texas, United States; and Cape Town, South Africa.

Cities are critical spaces within which to understand tensions of belonging, serving as crucibles created by density, visibility, and postcoloniality (Holston & Appadurai, 1999). Debates around citizenship ground many discussions of inclusion and affiliation, as ideas of inalienable membership in states is stretched by expanding migration, pressures of global capital, and rising internal tensions. What it means to be, or to enact, citizenship is rapidly changing, even as centralized processes of governance seek to contract and limit such definitions (Cabot, 2012; Di Nunzio, 2017; Ong, 2006). Here we think about belonging as a way to focus on collective practices of connection and meaning-making that exist around the constraints and complicity of citizenship as a tool of governance. Belonging is seen as those actions that intersect with centralized processes—voting, land use, development—but are not solely delimited by them. Memory, narrative, and outrage wend around the edges of citizenship, making modes of belonging within the particularity of communities, places, and means.

One limitation of citizenship is found in the contradictions between democracy and neoliberalism (Brown, 2015). Each case study sets localized practices within the context of municipal and state projects which craft abjection through economic, material, and political exclusions. In these cities, neoliberal projects are not isolated temporally or politically; rather, they reiterate and compound specific histories of colonialism, racism, and exclusion. Authors highlight the power of ethnography to draw together global contours and local experiences into powerful conversations of urban politics that show the concrete impact of the widespread adoption of neoliberal ideologies and policies (Ferguson, 1999; Rodgers, 2012; von Schnitzler, 2016). In this section, authors illuminate everyday experiences that push back against forces of socioeconomic and political marginalization, highlighting how lived experience changes the places, processes, and material worlds of cities. Collective power here emerges from practices of creation and refusal as the everyday practices of residents impact the city, engaging with what Bayat has called the "quiet encroachment of the ordinary" (2013, p. 46).

Place-making actions illustrate how urban residents navigate exclusions materially, legally, and culturally. In chapter 4, Lucero Radonic explores how Yaqui communities in Hermosillo, Mexico, claim space through ritual, working not only against the specific exclusions of urban growth and development, but also against wider narratives that symbolically exclude indigenous communities from city spaces. Here, modes of historical and contemporary abjection are met with active reclamations of space, vesting meaning on sites through ritual praxis and everyday actions. The annual production of ephemeral ritual spaces for the Yaqui *cuaresma* festival is enabled through negotiation with private landowners and municipal authorities. Radonic discusses how forces of land development have limited the availability of sites for ritual performances, with access forged against both economic processes of land speculation and symbolic exclusions of indigenous communities from the city. The persistence of Yaqui residents is shown in the vibrancy of the ritual practices, from the minutiae of creating detailed dress to the shared narration of historical land struggles. Radonic shows how the dispossessions of settler-colonialism reach into the present, as does the tenacity and cultural praxis of Yaqui communities to claim urban space.

In Ben Chappell's work in chapter 5, the steamroller of gentrification is set against the power of everyday cultural practice and deeply rooted collective meaning in Austin, Texas. Here, the power of memory and narrative praxis within the Eastside's Mexican American communities are both profound and in immediate risk. Individuals and groups navigate the market-driven interventions of tech start-ups, music festivals, and real estate developers, all of which drive rapid demographic changes. Belonging is forged through creative and collective work set against these socioeconomic changes—as in the lyrics of local rapper Lench Martinez that decry the destruction of local businesses and the decimation of everyday cultural practices while highlighting the ways in which communities persist. The vernacular practices of the Eastside are seen in the landscape and in the actions of long-term residents. Chappell marks the layers of memory and practice through evocative, thick descriptions of place and people that challenge the spatialized power of commodification. At a weekend concert, the arrival of low-riders is met by cheers, neighborhood fast-pitch teams are remembered in murals and stories, and land and space are made meaningful not for finance but for community.

Complex engagements with the material structure of the city provide another way of seeing the layered political and social work of urban life. In chapter 6, Angela Storey explores how exclusions from housing, water, electricity, and sanitation infrastructure in Cape Town, South Africa, fuel widespread discontent with democratic processes. In this context, infrastructure is a powerful potentiality, a sought-after and much-desired coda to the democratic inclusion of 1994's first postapartheid elections. Twenty years later, during the 2014 elections, residents of informal settlements framed their exclusions from citizenship through discussions of absent infrastructure, marking informality as a hyper-politicized urban terrain. Furor with the necessity of using apartheid-era bucket toilets and illegal electricity connections are expressed through anger at a democracy that has bypassed those most excluded, both historically and currently. Through a refusal to docilely engage in a democratic process that has yet to meet their needs, residents highlight how urban inequality becomes the matter of everyday material and political life within the city's periphery. Although wrought through discussions of voting, residents discursively and ideologically push back against elections as a singular pathway for producing meritocratic cities.

Urban belonging is not only a contested terrain, but an uneven playing field. Within these three chapters, residents of each city claim their place within the city through small actions—cleaning land for a ritual site, playing fastpitch at a local park, discussing frustrations with sanitation systems—and through engagement with, or resistance to, centralized processes and those in positions of relative power. Ethnography opens the space within which these tensions may be examined not by seeking resolution, but by noting the power of tenacity, memory, and refusal to be silenced in the face of exclusion.

## DIFFERENCE AND PROXIMITY

The case studies within the third section ground narratives of inequality within the creation and crossing of socio-spatial boundaries. In cities across the world, urban residents orient themselves based on salient social differences such as class, race, or ethnicity—often articulated spatially. The contributors to this section discuss varied urban spaces as sites vested with social and cultural meaning (Low, 2000, 2017), in which the built environment facilitates certain forms of sociality, activities, and engagements (Pellow, 1996; Whyte, 1980). Such meanings are negotiated dialectically, in the myriad ways in which individuals and groups craft sites to meet their needs (Bayat, 2013; Holston, 1989). Such layered processes articulate local power dynamics, illustrating how a subject's position alters access to, and engagement in, urban processes. When a caddy in Mexico City is granted entry by a security guard to an elite golf course, their behavior must shift to that of a docile, helpful, and quiet worker. In this section, authors trace how socioeconomic, racial, ethnic, and national distinctions coalesce at sites over time. In each case study, these processes shape experience, becoming key ways through which groups see and understand their place within the city. Chapters in this section explore the spatialized construction of difference through proximity in three cities: Santiago, Chile; Mexico City, Mexico; and London, England.

Spatialized boundaries, and the inequalities that they throw into high relief, are constructed through language, through materials, and through cultural practices, elaborating notions of who belongs in certain spaces. As Lefebvre argues, perceptions of space are layered upon its material production and uses (1991). Building from this contention, scholars show the many ways through which meaning is inscribed in places (Hayden, 1995; Rodman, 2002). Indeed, the ways that spaces are invested with symbolic and social meaning appear throughout this volume. The works in this section explore how boundaries are maintained, how individuals navigate them, and how perceptions of difference are spatialized in socially meaningful ways. As sites are inscribed with sedimented layers of meaning, they are simultaneously positioned and marked vis-à-vis associated social groups (Ghannam, 2012; Roth-Gordon, 2009). Contributors highlight how perceptions of space are connected with the users of those spaces such that strong associations between specific groups come to be associated with particular urban sites. As inequalities become an orienting feature linked to specific sites, these spatial divisions become normalized, illustrating the ways that boundaries may be self-reinforcing.

The tension between difference and proximity implicitly relies on the crossing of boundaries, and on the mobilities that makes such boundary-crossing possible. In this section, authors explore how movements within and between cities elucidate the boundaries of urban life. In an era of globalization, understanding cities requires attention to multiple scales of mobility and flows of things and people (Amin & Thrift, 2002; Appadurai, 1996). Cities are nodes where increasing speed and traffic of people, capital, materials, and ideas cluster, seen as "spatially open and cross-cut by many different kinds of mobilities" (Amin & Thrift, 2002, p. 3). Growing rural to urban migration, as well as the unprecedented scale of transnational migration (IOM, 2018), attract increasingly diverse populations to metropolitan regions. As flows of people through and into urban centers increase, diverse groups come into contact. Meaningful engagement across social differences is often positioned as emblematic of the urban ethos, adding to the cosmopolitan claim of cities (Çağlar & Glick Schiller, 2018; McCann & Ward, 2011). However, the day-to-day reality of engagement across significant social differences prompts debates, pushback, and contestation. These chapters chart the ways in which diverse groups of individuals interact, cross into each other's spaces, and attempt to negotiate or reinforce socio-spatial boundaries.

In chapter 7, Megan Sheehan explores the experiences of migrants seeking housing in Santiago, Chile, analyzing how migrants become associated with particular city spaces through the intersection of structural exclusions, everyday practices, and popular perceptions. With steady increases of migration to the city, migrants in Santiago face a maze of bureaucratic difficulties in securing housing, even when in possession of documentation and employment. These challenges, and the exploitation of migrants by landlords, result in many migrants being forced to live in expensive, crowded, or poor-quality housing, often within the city's central neighborhoods. Weaving together ethnographic data from both migrants and Chileans, Sheehan discusses how perceptions of migrant use of space are forged not only by the constrained realities of a neoliberal housing market, but also by the spatial perceptions of Chileans, drawn from widespread stereotypes and limited interactions. Popular perceptions of spatial practice mask the actual processes that exclude migrants from better housing, thus compounding the inequalities faced by migrants and reinforcing distinctions made between groups within the urban milieu.

While some socio-spatial divides are porous, others are firmly established. In chapter 8, Hugo Ceron-Anaya discusses elite golf clubs in Mexico City, Mexico, analyzing the social and physical divisions that define spaces and mark users. The boundaries between golf clubs and the surrounding neighborhoods are so entrenched that passersby and local residents do not even know that golf courses sit behind the tree-lined walls. The golf courses are rendered selectively invisible through nondescript walls and unremarkable entryways, illustrating how perceptions of space delineate class relations while obscuring visible class disparities. Ceron-Anaya further examines recursive socio-spatial boundaries by discussing how caddies at these golf clubs are rendered invisible by their sequestration in a separate building on the course. This spatial separation exacerbates social boundaries, as golfers discuss and understand caddies and their skills at a distance, without understanding the time and dedication that caddies bring to their work. As Ceron-Anaya argues, discrete areas of the golf club thus become a way of quietly reproducing multiple modes of social stratification.

In chapter 9, Chiara Minestrelli illustrates how a group of migrant university students in London, England, reflect on the uneven production of space and its lived reality. Arriving in London from many different countries, students exemplify the mobility of a globalized world and the internationalization of higher education. By engaging in creative, participatory workshops in the neighborhood where their university is located, students are able to critically discuss gentrification, development, and displacement. These lessons challenge students to reflect on uneven power dynamics that sit within specific places, and to envision the city from the perspective of marginalized urban voices. Through creative and hands-on actions, urban sites become known as places to students, not merely as invisible backdrops for short-term experiences. As these international students learn about the impacts of gentrification and development, they are challenged to see anew the city and to reframe their own role as urban agents—both during their time in London and when they return to home nations.

Cities bring together diverse populations. But the ways in which people live, work, travel, and socialize are often shaped by boundaries patterned along lines of social distinctions. In these chapters, authors explore how individuals and groups navigate the multiple distinctions and social boundaries assembled in the city either in seeking housing, navigating work spaces, or learning histories of new places. Often overlooked, these social fault lines come into view as ethnographers analyze the ways that people experience and understand key urban sites.

## CONCLUSION

Even amid spatialized inequality and isolation, the case studies in this volume demonstrate how diverse populations craft communities, construct alternatives to meet their basic needs, and—in so doing—remake cities. This collection highlights the importance of everyday experiences and marginalized narratives to shed light on the workings of cities across the globe. Ethnography holds the potential of examining what is often overlooked, providing a "descent into the ordinary" (Das, 2007). Insights from the everyday experiences of marginalized individuals and communities often challenge notions of expertise when addressing inequality. Indeed, who can speak best of the challenges that cities face but those who grapple daily with enduring inequality?

This volume draws together a geographically broad set of cases. The authors examine overlapping social, economic, political, and historical pressures as they frame the way residents navigate daily life in the city. The distinctions between the cities included in this volume—from geography to political structure, economic foundations to colonial histories—are a critical piece for understanding ethnography's scope as a method to navigate hyperlocal experiences and lives. While we seek, as editors, to draw together some of the overlapping experiences found within urban spaces, these connections are not meant to flatten differences but, rather, to heighten them. We hope that reading these case studies alongside each other will show the dynamism of urban lives and the possibilities of ethnographic praxis to make visible everyday narratives within the midst of inequalities.

## NOTE

1. Alvaredo et al. argue that aggressive redistribution via taxes and economic transfers could mitigate income disparities (2018, p. 14).

## BIBLIOGRAPHY


Abu Lughod, L. (1990). The romance of resistance: Tracing transformations of power through Bedouin women. *American Ethnologist, 17*(1), 41–55.

Alvaredo, F., Chancel, L., Piketty, T., Saez, E., & Zucman, G. (Eds.). (2018). *World inequality report 2018*. Cambridge, MA: Belknap Press.

Amin, A., & Thrift, N. (2002). *Cities: Reimagining the urban*. Cambridge, MA: Blackwell.

Anand, N. (2017). *Hydraulic city: Water and the infrastructure of citizenship in Mumbai*. Durham, NC: Duke University Press.

Anderson, E. (2013). *Streetwise: Race, class, and change in an urban community*. Chicago, IL: University of Chicago Press.

Angotti, T. (2006). Apocalyptic anti-urbanism: Mike Davis and his planet of slums. *International Journal of Urban and Regional Research, 30*(4), 961–967.

Appadurai, A. (1996). *Modernity al large: Cultural dimensions of globalization*. Minneapolis, MN: University of Minnesota Press.

Bartlett, J. (2019, October 19). Chile protests: State of emergency declared in Santiago as violence escalates. *The Guardian*. Retrieved from https://www.theguardian.com/world/2019/oct/19/chile-protests-state-of-emergency-declared-in-santiago-as-violence-escalates.

Bayat, A. (2013). *Life as politics: How ordinary people change the middle east*. Palo Alto, CA: Stanford University Press.

Berrisford, S., & Kihato, M. (2006). The role of planning in evictions in sub-Saharan Africa. *South African Review of Sociology, 37*(1), 20–34.

Bourgois, P. (2003). *In search of respect: Selling crack in El Barrio*. Cambridge, England: Cambridge University Press.

Brown, W. (2015). *Undoing the demos: Neoliberalism's stealth revolution*. Cambridge, MA: Zone Books.

Cabot, H. (2012). The governance of things: Documenting limbo in the Greek asylum procedure. *PoLAR: Political and Legal Anthropology Review, 35*(1), 11–29.

Çağlar, A., & Glick Schiller, N. (2018). *Migrants and city-making: Dispossession, displacement, and urban regeneration*. Durham, NC: Duke University Press.

Caldeira, T. (2000). *City of walls: Crime, segregation, and citizenship in São Paolo*. Berkeley, CA: University of California Press.

Das, V. (2007). *Life and words: Violence and the descent into the ordinary*. Berkeley, CA: University of California Press.

De Genova, N. (2005). *Working the boundaries: Race, space, and "illegality" in Mexican Chicago*. Durham, NC: Duke University Press.

Desmond, M. (2016). *Evicted: Poverty and profit in the American city*. New York, NY: Broadway Books.

Di Nunzio, M. (2017). Marginality as a politics of limited entitlements: Street life and the dilemma of inclusion in urban Ethiopia. *American Ethnologist, 44*(1), 91–103.

Escobar, A. (2011). *Encountering development: The making and unmaking of the Third World*. Princeton, NJ: Princeton University Press.

Fassin, D. (2013). Why ethnography matters: On anthropology and its publics. *Cultural Anthropology, 28*(4), 621–646.

Ferguson, J. (1999). *Expectations of modernity: Myths and meanings of urban life on the Zambian Copperbelt*. Berkeley, CA: University of California Press.

Fischer, B., McCann, B., & Auyero, J. (2014). *Cities from scratch: Poverty and informality in urban Latin America*. Durham, NC: Duke University Press.

Ghannam, F. (2012). Meanings and feelings: Local interpretations of the use of violence in the Egyptian revolution. *American Ethnologist, 39*(1), 32–36.

Gootenberg, P. (2010). Latin American inequalities: New perspectives from history, politics, and culture. In P. Gootenberg & L. Reygadas (Eds.), *Indelible inequalities in Latin America: Insights from history, politics, and culture* (pp. 3–22). Durham, NC: Duke University Press.

Grusky, D. (2007). *The inequality reader: Contemporary and foundational readings in race, class, and gender*. New York, NY: Routledge.

Hayden, D. (1995). *The power of place: Urban landscapes as public history*. Cambridge, MA: MIT Press.

Hoffman, K., & Centeno, M.A. (2003). The lopsided continent: Inequality in Latin America. *Annual Review of Sociology, 29*, 363–390.

Holston, J. (1989). *The modernist city: An anthropological critique of Brasilia*. Chicago, IL: University of Chicago Press.

Holston, J. (2008). *Insurgent citizenship: Disjunctions of democracy and modernity in Brazil*. Princeton, NJ: Princeton University Press.

Holston, J., & Appadurai, A. (1996). Cities and citizenship. *Public Culture, 8*, 187–204.

International Organization for Migration (IOM). (2018). World migration report 2018. Retrieved from https://www.iom.int/wmr/.

Larkin, B. (2013). The politics and poetics of infrastructure. *Annual Review of Anthropology, 42*, 327–343.

Lefebvre, H. (1991). *The production of space*. Malden, MA: Blackwell Press.

Liebow, E. (1967). *Tally's corner: A study of Negro streetcorner men*. New York, NY: Little, Brown and Company.

Lin, N. (2000). Inequality in social capital. *Contemporary Sociology, 29*(6), 785–795.

Londoño, E. (2019, October 21). What you need to know about the unrest in Chile. *New York Times*. Retrieved from https://www.nytimes.com/2019/10/21/world/americas/why-chile-protests.html.

Low, S. (2000). *On the plaza: The politics of public space and culture*. Austin, TX: University of Texas Press.

Low, S. (2017). *Spatializing culture: The ethnography of space and place*. New York, NY: Routledge.

McCann, E., & Ward, K. (2011). *Mobile urbanism: Cities and policymaking in the global age*. Minneapolis, MN: University of Minnesota Press.

McGill, K. (2016). *Global inequality: Anthropological insights*. Toronto, Canada: University of Toronto Press.

Mitchell, D. (2003). *The right to the city: Social justice and the fight for public space*. New York, NY: Guilford Press.

Ong, A. (2006). Mutations in citizenship. *Theory, Culture & Society, 23*(2–3), 499–505.

Oxford Poverty and Human Development Initiative (OPHI) & the United Nations (UN). (2019). Global multidimensional poverty index 2019: Illuminating inequalities. Retrieved from http://hdr.undp.org/en/2019-MPI.

Park, R.E., Burgess, E., & McKenzie, R. (1925). *The city*. Chicago, IL: University of Chicago Press.

Pellow, D. (Ed.). (1996). *Setting boundaries: The anthropology of spatial and social organization*. Westport, CT: Bergin & Garvey.

Pieterse, E. (2008). *City futures: Confronting the crisis of urban development*. London, England: Zed Books.

Potts, D. (2007). City life in Zimbabwe at a time of fear and loathing: Urban planning, urban poverty, and operation Murambatsvina. In M.J. Murray & G.A. Myers (Eds.), *Cities in contemporary Africa* (pp. 265–288). New York, NY: Palgrave MacMillan.

Rodgers, D. (2012). Haussmannization in the tropics: Abject urbanism and infrastructural violence in Nicaragua. *Ethnography, 13*(4), 413–438.

Rodman, M.C. (2002). Empowering place: Multilocality and multivocality. *American Anthropologist, 94*(3), 640–656.

Roth-Gordon, J. (2009). The language that came down the hill: Slang, crime, and citizenship in Rio de Janeiro. *American Anthropologist, 111*(1), 57–68.

Roy, A. (2003). *City requiem, Calcutta: Gender and the politics of poverty*. Minneapolis, MN: University of Minnesota Press.

Roy, A., & Ong, A. (2011). *Worlding cities: Asian experiments and the art of being global*. New York, NY: Wiley Blackwell.

von Schnitzler, A. (2016). *Democracy's infrastructure: Techno-politics and protest after apartheid*. Princeton, NJ: Princeton University Press.

Simone, A. (2004). *For the city yet to come: Urban life in four African cities*. Durham, NC: Duke University Press.

Simone, A. (2008). *Johannesburg: The elusive metropolis*. Durham, NC: Duke University Press.

Simpson, A. (2014). *Mohawk interruptus: Political life across the borders of settler states*. Durham, NC: Duke University Press.

Smit, W. (2006). Understanding the complexities of informal settlements: Insights from Cape Town. In M. Huchzermeyer & A. Karam (Eds.), *Informal settlements: A perpetual challenge* (pp. 103–125). Cape Town, South Africa: University of Cape Town Press.

Stack, C. (1974). *All our kin: Strategies for survival in a Black community*. New York, NY: Harper and Row.

Stiglitz, J. (2012). *The price of inequality: How today's divided society endangers our future*. New York, NY: W.W. Norton & Company.

Susser, I. (1982). *Norman street*. New York, NY: Oxford University Press.

United Nations. (2018). 2018 Revision of world urbanization prospects. Retrieved from https://www.un.org/development/desa/publications/2018-revision-of-world-urbanization-prospects.html.

Van Mead, N. (2019). Where are the 15 next megacities? *The Guardian*. Retrieved from https://www.theguardian.com/cities/series/next-15-megacities.

Wacquant, L.J. (2008). Red belt, black belt: Racial division, class inequality and the state in the French urban periphery and the American ghetto. In E. Mingione (Ed.), *Urban poverty and the underclass: A reader* (pp. 234–274). New York, NY: Wiley.

Whyte, W.H. (1980). *The social life of small urban spaces*. Washington, DC: Conservation Foundation.

Wirth, L. (1928). *The ghetto*. Chicago, IL: University of Chicago Press.

World Bank. (n.d.). "Poverty." Retrieved from https://data.worldbank.org/topic/poverty.

*Part I*

# DEVELOPMENT AND DISPLACEMENT

# Chapter 1

# Losing or Gaining Home?

## *Experiences of Resettlement from Casablanca's Slums*

Raffael Beier and Cristiana Strava

In recent decades, unprecedented rates of urbanization on a global level have led to profound changes in existing social, economic, and cultural structures and institutions. No topic has been as exhaustively researched and written about in this context of current hyper-urbanization as the problem of informal housing. Popularized by books like Mike Davis's *Planet of Slums* (2006), the images associated with this global condition are colored by such terms as "poverty," "inequality," "insecurity," and a "lack of basic infrastructures." Locally derived terms have come to be globally understood and circulated, and inhabitants in Morocco—the focus of this chapter—are able to comment that an irregular settlement built near a ravine looks like a *favela*. Indeed, the literature documenting and analyzing this pervasive phenomenon is dominated by case studies from Latin America, with equal space occupied by examples from South Asia and sub-Saharan Africa respectively (Dürr & Jaffe, 2012; Roy, 2011; Simone, 2004). Given the proliferation of such images and their role in constructing a global imaginary of "slums," few would associate a picture of sprawling tin roofs covering squat shanties with the North African Kingdom of Morocco. Nevertheless, urban inequality materialized as informal housing is neither a recent nor a new socio-spatial phenomenon in the region. In recent years, however, the alignment of global agendas and local political and social landscapes have led to an intensification of efforts toward addressing growing inequality.

One such program aiming to tackle the growing problem of informal and unsafe housing was launched in 2004 by Morocco's King Mohammed VI. The countrywide program *Cities without Shantytowns*[1] (in French *Villes Sans Bidonvilles*, henceforth VSB) has the stated aim of eradicating all informal housing in the country and resettling slum dwellers into apartment blocks. In Casablanca's Hay Mohammadi neighborhood, a historically significant and marginalized area on which this chapter will focus, the government evicted close to 30,000 residents from Morocco's oldest shantytown, Karyan Central, and moved them to the newly constructed town of Nouvelle Lahraouiyine, ten kilometers away. Treated with a uniform resettlement solution, affected shantytown dwellers have experienced very individualized notions of displacement.

Drawing on combined fieldwork material gathered by both authors from 2013 to 2019 among several communities targeted with relocation, in this chapter we set out to give an account of the varying experiences of resettlement recounted to us by our research participants. Cristiana Strava's approach consisted of sixteen months (2013–2014) of emplaced participant observation with inhabitants of several quarters of Hay Mohammadi, supplemented by shorter, yearly follow-up visits. This approach is marked by concern with mundane practice and its role in the production of knowledge about space and place (de Certeau, 1984; Feld & Basso, 1996). As such, it places at the center of ethnographic research the everyday, routine, and affect-laden ways (cf. Navaro-Yashin, 2012) in which inhabitants of the urban margins manage to create a sense of home, however precarious and contingent that may be. Complementing this are archival and oral history sources, as well as formal interviews with architects, urban planners, activists, and local officials who in their professional capacity had a direct or indirect involvement with the VSB program. Raffael Beier's field research consisted of 400 structured interviews with resettled former inhabitants of Karyan Central living in Nouvelle Lahraouiyine, as well as nonparticipant observations and in-depth, sometimes repeated conversations and field trips with residents affected by the resettlement project. These conversations took place in Nouvelle Lahraouiyine, Hay Mohammadi, and in the rural province of Doukkala, between December 2016 and April 2017, as well as during shorter visits in March 2015 and November 2018.

By portraying varied pathways to the new town, we argue that different life trajectories, access to or participation in local networks, and socioeconomic positions lead to varying perceptions of and expectations toward resettlement. More specifically, we show that standardized approaches to dealing with informal housing and urban inequality, such as those adopted by the VSB program, are not only ineffective in eradicating these problems but likely produce new forms of marginalization and disenfranchisement. We begin with the historical and political background behind the creation and implementation of the VSB program, focusing on the situation present in Casablanca. We then offer three brief ethnographic accounts that illustrate varying trajectories and experiences of families relocated from Karyan Central, highlighting the very personal notions of inequality within resettlement and practices of home-making. We conclude by arguing that in order to arrive at effective approaches to the issue of informal housing, more attention needs to be paid to the multiple and often entangled factors that affect the communities targeted with resettlement.

## A HISTORY OF INFORMALITY

Informality and housing have long been central concerns of research focusing on developing countries. The pioneering work of Stokes (1962), Turner (1968, 1969), and Frankenhoff (1967) focused mainly on Latin America and conceptualized informal housing as a natural by-product of industrialization, which would likely disappear with further development. However, in recent years, given the proliferation of informal housing, scholars have increasingly questioned whether housing informality is both an outcome of state incapacity and industrialization (Berner, 2016; McFarlane & Waibel, 2016). Largely based on work in India and Egypt, Al Sayyad (2004) and Roy (2005, 2009) have argued that we should see informality as a new mode of urbanization that shapes the production of all kinds of urban space—from slums to exclusive high-end constructions. Accordingly, informality is no longer considered to be outside the control of the state. Instead, informality should be seen as a distinct political planning tool that is used to keep flexibility and planning power in the hands of powerful (state) elites who deal with informality in very different ways (see also Yiftachel, 2009). Whether communities are targeted with formalization, tolerance, or eviction may largely depend on their negotiating power. Acknowledging the active role of the state related to urban informality also helps to understand the recent emergence of new large-scale housing and resettlement programs in many developing countries, from India to Ethiopia and Morocco (cf. Beier, 2019a; Buckley, Kallergis, & Wainer, 2016; Turok, 2016). Building on the logics of booming real estate markets, place-branding, urban competitiveness, and economic regeneration, these programs have come to characterize today's emerging cities. However, before coming back to this, it is worth looking more closely at the Moroccan context.

The history and socio-spatial dynamics of housing informality in Morocco have received very limited attention to date. This is partly owed to the fact that scholarly literature on urban spaces and dynamics in the Middle East and North Africa (MENA) has historically focused on a limited number of themes, such as the trope of the "Islamic city" (Abu-Lughod, 1987), which perpetuates previous Orientalist ideas about the organization and use of urban space in the region (cf. Eickelman, 1974). Emerging social dynamics and urban policies demand a new approach toward city life in the region. Significant work on the techno-politics of colonial urbanism (Abu-Lughod, 1980; Mitchell, 2002; Rabinow, 1989) and the cultural and political ideas embedded in heritage approaches to "traditional" cities (Arrif, 1994) have done much to advance our knowledge of urbanity in these locales. There is, however, a growing literature on the Middle Eastern and North African city which seeks to move beyond these established tropes of exceptionalism, Islamic, and/or "dual city," or the more recent focus on "Dubaization" of urban centers in the region (cf. El-Kazaz & Mazur, 2017). As Belguidoum, Cattedra, and Iraki (2015) have pointed out, North African cities are not homogenous, but instead marked by very diverse and distinct histories of colonial and postcolonial planning (Rabinow, 1989; Wright, 1991), forms of habitation (Navez-Bouchanine, 1990), cultural and economic organization (Singerman, 1996; Zaki, 2010), and locally inflected social-geographies. Our own approach in this chapter is firmly situated within this emerging scholarly landscape, committed toward critically investigating ongoing processes and policies which seek to address the various aspects of existing urban inequality, by documenting and paying attention to the individual experiences of vulnerable and marginalized communities.

Commonly referred to as the country's *poumon economique* (French for "economic lung"), Casablanca grew exponentially from a straggling fishing village at the turn of the twentieth century into a vital node for trade and industry, as well as a "laboratory" for the experimentation with "modern" forms of technocratic urban planning and control (Rabinow, 1989). Currently home to more than 4 million inhabitants, Casablanca is the largest city in Morocco and an important urban hub within the region. The origins of what is often described as informal housing in the city goes back to the 1910s, when the French colonial administration was faced with a dilemma. On the one hand, they were unwilling to share urban space with a growing number of Moroccan rural-to-urban migrants seeking job opportunities in the rapidly growing city. On the other, their cheap labor was crucial for colonial industries. The resulting "compromise" was the tolerance of emerging self-built neighborhoods mostly located on the city's outskirts and in proximity to industries and the harbor, thus providing minimum shelter to workers. Initially built out of recycled materials—in particular tin—these soon became known by the term "bidonville," or tin city (Cattedra, 2006). With time, inhabitants started to invest in their housing environment, replacing most tin with bricks and cement, establishing collectively organized sanitation systems, and claiming their right to basic infrastructure such as water and, later, electricity (Zaki, 2010; figure 1.1). As such, the incremental development and consolidation process of bidonvilles followed typical pathways of auto-constructed neighborhoods as described most prominently by Turner (1977) for the case of Latin America.

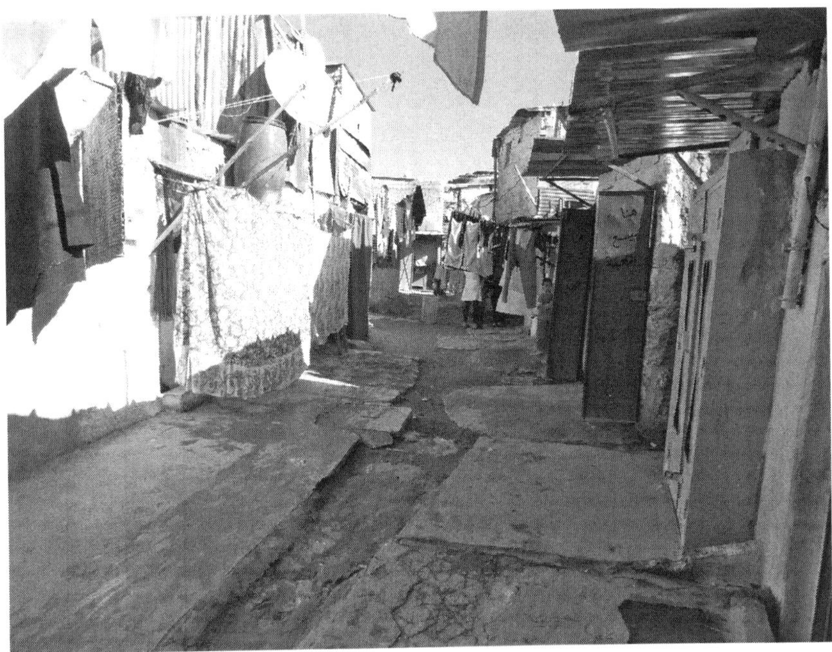

**Figure 1.1 The Bidonville Er-Rhamna in Casablanca's District Sidi Moumen.** *Source*: Author's photograph, December 2016.

While colonial powers initially turned a blind eye to bidonvilles, considering them as a way to evade their own responsibility to build houses for the working class, silent tolerance and neglect were temporarily suspended in reaction to rising tensions that threatened the "formal" parts of the city. Rachik (2002) has called this an urbanism of urgency (*urbanisme de l'urgence*), which began in the mid-1910s with the outbreak of a typhus epidemic in one bidonville. However, the logics of an urbanism of urgency have come to characterize governmental strategies toward marginalized settlements in Morocco and other North African countries until today (Beier, 2018). After the end of colonial rule, governments remained mostly ignorant toward bidonvilles, notwithstanding occasional incidences of social housing and sites-and-services projects. The latter—known in Morocco under the terms *trames sanitaires* and later *recasement*—is the most cost-effective strategy to replace informal neighborhoods and has today become the dominant policy option (Zaki, 2007). In sites-and-services projects, the state offers shantytown dwellers a serviced plot of land at a subsidized price and asks them to build their own house according to formal and predefined building standards.

Following the logic of an urbanism of urgency, the first significant change in the government's approach to bidonvilles took place in the early 1980s, this time as a direct reaction to the "bread riots" that had their origins in Casablanca's bidonvilles (cf. Benlahcen Tlemçani & Missamou, 2000; Rachik, 2002; Zaki, 2007). Soon afterward, the Moroccan government increased repression toward bidonvilles, abandoning policies of on-site upgrading and forcing more and more people to move to resettlement areas, typically located at the urban peripheries. However, these policies have hardly alleviated a growing housing crisis. At the same time, severe droughts in the countryside pushed many people to the cities, where they could not find affordable housing and, hence, contributed to the further expansion of bidonvilles (cf. Benlahcen Tlemçani & Missamou, 2000; Rachik, 2012).

After a short time of reflection under a reformist government at the end of the twentieth century, the 2003 suicide attacks in the city center of Casablanca, committed by several youth coming out of one of the city's most disenfranchised bidonvilles, marked the next turning point of public policy and led to an increase in repression. Soon after this event, Mohammed VI launched the VSB program, seeking to eradicate all bidonvilles across Morocco (cf. Bogaert, 2011). Within the VSB program, a few initial attempts of in situ upgrading were quickly abandoned in favor of mostly sites-and-services but also subsidized housing projects (Zaki, 2013; figure 1.2). However, it would be wrong to understand the VSB program exclusively against the background of a resurgence of state control following political security targets. In fact,

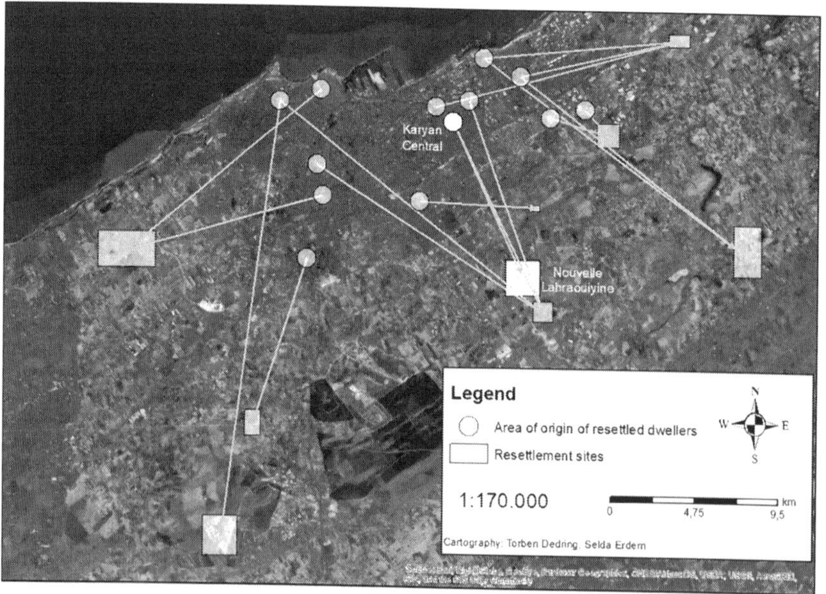


**Figure 1.2 Map of Selected Displacements of Bidonville Dwellers in Casablanca Since 2004.** Cartography: Selda Erdem and Torben Dedring.

the VSB program is also embedded in national modernization strategies seeking to boost the position of Morocco's major cities in global interurban competition. One aim is to develop Casablanca into a modern hub of financial industries, attractive to both international business communities and tourists. According to speeches made by King Mohammed VI, bidonvilles—stigmatized as breeding ground of religious extremism and places of rural backwardness—risk impeding the success of these development strategies (Beier, 2019a; Bogaert, 2013; Zaki, 2013).

Hence, the VSB program is a typical example of the abovementioned global trend back to more quantitative, state-led solutions in affordable housing production (cf. Buckley, Kallergis, & Wainer, 2016; Turok, 2016). Standardized, large-scale, and greenfield housing production promises to be affordable, easy to plan, and rapidly implemented. However, the mere focus on quantity disregards housing functions that go beyond a narrow understanding of housing as shelter. Limited spatial integration, lack of accessible employment, mortgage burdens, loss of access to urban centers, loss of sociability, and inflexible building structures have already been key problems of public housing programs in the 1950s and 1960s (Mangin, 1967; Turner, 1967, 1969). New resettlement sites show similar deficiencies (cf. Beier, 2019a; Patel, Sliuzas, & Mathur, 2015; Spire, Bridonneau, & Philifert, 2017). Hence, it seems necessary to depart from a limited understanding of housing as shelter, toward seeing housing as a crucial aspect within people's individual practices of home-making. This changing conceptualization, which is at the core of this chapter, is necessary for acknowledging inevitable heterogeneity and subjectivity within housing and resettlement. This was also highlighted by Doshi (2013), who focused on gender and ethnicity to describe people's very different forms of agency in several resettlement projects in Mumbai. Thus, by strengthening the notion of home, we aim to underline the subjective experience of housing and show that the abovementioned, rather typical, problems of resettlement often build on very different personal understandings and experiences of inequality.

## FROM KARYAN CENTRAL TO NOUVELLE LAHRAOUIYINE

Karyan Central, the bidonville on which this chapter focuses, was the center of the working-class neighborhood and public marketplace of Hay Mohammadi, near Casablanca's major sites of industrial production. The name Hay Mohammadi refers to King Mohammed V, who visited the mosque of Karyan Central in order to thank the inhabitants for their crucial role in Morocco's Independence movement.[2] Karyan Central was also one of Morocco's oldest bidonvilles, with origins in the late 1910s. Described as a classic "tin city" in the 1930s (Sieburg, 1938), the neighborhood developed incrementally according to residents' financial capacities and changing demands. As the oldest industrial quarter in Morocco, Hay Mohammadi attracted people from various rural areas searching for better economic and life opportunities. Situated in a north-eastern direction from the city's core, demographically the neighborhood continues to be one of Casablanca's most densely inhabited areas. According to the latest official census data from 2014, Hay Mohammadi's population was estimated at approximately 140,000 inhabitants—down from 170,000 recorded in 2010, owing to the relocation of the bidonville inhabitants. The neighborhood occupies a surface of 4.2 square kilometers (Haut Comissariat au Plan, 2014). With a density of 33,300 inhabitants per square kilometer, Hay Mohammadi is almost five times denser than, for example, upper middle-class neighborhoods like Anfa, which boasted a relatively unchanged density of 6,500 inhabitants per square kilometer for the ten preceding years.

At the end of the twentieth century, almost all buildings were built out of bricks and cement and had access to basic services, notwithstanding the inexistence of formal land titles (cf. Navez-Bouchanine, 2012). However, roofs did not always provide shelter from the elements and many people felt vulnerable to fires, heavy rain, as well as discrimination. Historically marked by various experiments of upgrading and resettlement, Karyan Central was home to approximately 35,000 inhabitants in 2009 when plans emerged to resettle its residents to a new town, Nouvelle Lahraouiyine, more than 10 kilometers away and outside Casablanca's municipal boundary (figure 1.2). New, nuclear family-sized apartments were intended to improve people's housing comfort and promised social mobility. The relocation scheme was premised on the fact that each new resettlement plot would house two individual households from the bidonville in what is called an "R+3." This scheme entails a standard 80 square meter home, with a ground floor (*rez-de-chaussée* in French, hence R) and three upper floors. Families then search for a real estate developer who will be charged with the construction of the new building and who keeps, sells, or rents the two lower floors in return. Owing to this specific system's basis on third-party funding, the resettlement was heavily subsidized, if not completely free (cf. Beier, 2019a; Toutain, 2016). However, the following close descriptions of purposefully selected stories of residents affected by resettlement show that experiences and expectations varied in relation to people's own biographies and their degrees of local rootedness. In fact, the prospect of gaining formal titles to a new apartment was in many cases significantly outweighed by a sense of losing home.

## SALIMA: ROOTED IN HAY MOHAMMADI

Salima[3] was born in Hay Mohammadi in 1971 and had spent her entire life in Karyan Central until she was evicted from her home in March 2016. One of the authors met with Salima in February 2017 in a modern, two floor café that she had chosen, close to the hospital of Hay Mohammadi in the middle-class neighborhood Mouahidine. Since losing her family home in Karyan Central, she had been living for free in one of the multistory apartment blocks of the Hassan II housing project in Hay Mohammadi, which offered subsidized apartments to the dwellers of Karyan Central at the end of the 1990s. At that time, one of her sisters was able to purchase her own property and bought the apartment. Salima moved in, along with her mother and the family of her brother. Within the opaque allocation process,[4] Salima's family, although composed of more than one married couple, had only received the right to one plot for Nouvelle Lahraouiyine and was now waiting for a decision after making a request for additional plot rights.

Dressed smartly in trousers, *hijab*, and sunglasses, she started to explain why she could never imagine leaving Hay Mohammadi for Nouvelle Lahraouiyine. She was clear that her home was "Al Hay" (*the* neighborhood) as she called Hay Mohammadi, as if it was Casablanca's only district with "Hay" in its name. Belonging to a *chrifa* family that considers themselves direct descendants of Prophet Mohammed, she made explicit that she enjoyed the respect she and her family received and being part of the neighborhood's local elite—at least in former Karyan Central. She explained further: "They [the VSB authorities] send people from an urban to a rural environment. [Nouvelle Lahraouiyine] is a rural place, I spent four months there because of business, but I could not get used to it, but if I told them [authorities] that I will only sell the apartment I would not get one."

Owing to their location in the proximity of Casablanca's old industrial quarters, Hay Mohammadi and Karyan Central were once considered the border of this industrious city. As Casablanca grew exponentially in the postindependence era and continues to sprawl to this day, the neighborhood has become part of the city's core, with newer peripheries such as Nouvelle Lahraouiyine created on former agricultural land (figure 1.2). Geography alone, however, does not account for the reasons why inhabitants like Salima and our other interlocutors regarded the resettlement site with apprehension. Historical neighborhoods like Hay Mohammadi—though frequently associated in the local public imaginary with decaying infrastructure, crowded housing, occasional criminality, and informality—are celebrated for their rich popular history, colorful and boisterous street life, and entrepreneurial spirit animating every available space. Ambulant sellers walk the narrow alleys at the heart of the neighborhood's dense quarters at all times of day, children improvise games in the sparse open spaces between buildings, and in almost all seasons laundry can be found hanging on public railings lining the car-choked arteries delineating the neighborhood's edges.

It is this particular socio-spatial richness of the neighborhood that Salima hints at in her critique of the resettlement site. Later, during a trip to the market, Salima showed one of the authors around, greeting people on her way and talking vividly to the market traders. If Hay Mohammadi might be characterized by the messy vitality of its street life, then the market at its core represents the climax of that vitality. At various times during the day, and at regular intervals during the week, informal sellers occupy the streets around the formal marketplace and transform the space into a colorful, cacophonous landscape of various edible and nonedible wares. Smells and sounds waft and call across and through the crowds, enticing shoppers.[5] According to Salima, Hay Mohammadi's market was the center of Casablanca, where people from all parts of the city come to buy all kinds of goods from one of the numerous street vendors or from inside the two market halls. Indeed, the market developed in colonial times in response to the demands of the local industrial labor force living in the shacks of Karyan Central and soon grew into one of the most important marketplaces for the city's native population. This did not change in the postindependence era and, although more and more parts of the bidonville were replaced by basic housing estates (for more detail see Strava, 2017), Karyan Central remained the center around which the market flourished. As such, Salima's own, now demolished shop formed part of the market, located at the fringes of the bidonville, where in February 2017 the construction of Casablanca's second tramway was under way.

Salima's family home was located in a different part of the quarter, being one of the most comfortable and established houses of Karyan Central. Before the demolition, it had 120 square meters with six rooms, offering enough space for all the members belonging to Salima's extended family. It took her three days to rescue all the belongings from the house after authorities had announced the forced eviction of the last remaining households. "There were some people crying, because they did not get a notification that they have to leave. The bulldozers demolished their houses with their affairs inside." Because of the lack of space in her current apartment she stored her affairs with several of her friends. In order to protest against the forced eviction of the remaining 500 households of Karyan Central, she continued occupying a tent on the former site of Karyan Central until she was evicted for a second time, in September 2016. Only after this did she move into her sister's apartment. For Salima it was evident that the clearance of Karyan Central has destroyed her home.

## HIND: FROM THE MEDINA TO THE NEW TOWN

Another example of how the specificities of slum dwellers' lives may become erased through the relocation process is offered by Hind and her family. Their biography as bidonville dwellers, and eventually as a resettled household, further speaks to the power of technocratic language to occlude and collapse the variety of experiences of relocation. In Hind's account, there were several homes that her family had been forced to unmake and move out of even before the resettlement. In 2014, Hind had been teaching Arabic literacy classes at a community center in Hay Mohammadi for close to four years. Hind's family moved to Karyan Central in 1994:

> Before then we lived in the *medina qadima* (old town), in a big old house. But there was some trouble, a fight with the extended family over some inheritance so we had to leave. My mother took us—my brother and three sisters, and myself—and moved to Hay Mohammadi, you know, Karyan Central, in a *beraka*.[6] When we moved there from the medina we didn't know anybody. We rented the *beraka* from a man and brought all our things. We had never been to Hay Mohammadi before. We were *welad al medina* (children of the downtown) and we thought everyone was dangerous, and we would have to be very careful. In the medina we had had everything we wanted. It was a shock moving to the Karyan. When we brought our things, furniture, and carpets, and kitchen things, and people in the Karyan saw them, they started calling us *gaour* (foreigner), because they had never seen such things! Back then you couldn't get everything you can now in Hay Mohammadi, so they were behind in a way.

While some of our other interlocutors had been born and raised in the Karyan, Hind's story points to the variety of circumstances through which people come to take up residence in a Moroccan bidonville. It also touches on the social stigma associated with being a bidonville inhabitant, and the ill fame that was associated with the area. Actual risks connected with such precarious living were also all too present in Hind's experience of growing up in Karyan Central. Owing to the improvised nature of the electrical infrastructure, fires were a common occurrence in the bidonvilles. Hind could remember a series of fires, the first of which cost her family all the belongings they had brought from the old home in the medina. She also recalled a fire caused by a woman's cooking stove, which led to the explosion of several gas canisters in the shacks adjacent to it. Eventually, Hind and her family received the eviction notice and were allotted a plot in the resettlement neighborhood. According to the VSB regulations, the households to be relocated are entitled to temporary—usually six months—paid accommodation while the developer completes construction. Hind and her family were placed in such temporary housing, but the developer had not completed construction when the period was up. Hind explained: "These people, they don't just have to build your home and my home. They have contracts for maybe twenty people from the Karyan. So, it took a long time for him to finish. He still has many unfinished homes. After the six months expired, we had to move again and pay for the rent ourselves."

Tired of waiting, Hind and her family moved into the new home, although much work remained to be done. They arranged to be connected to the water and electricity networks and decided to complete the remaining construction on their own. As per the R+3 specifications, Hind, together with her mother, unmarried brother, and her recently married younger sister, took up residence in the second-floor apartment, while her older sister's family lived on the third floor. The second-floor apartment's 48 square meters were visibly insufficient for accommodating five adults and a young child, but, because at the time of the census only one of Hind's sisters had been married, everyone else had been counted as a single household. As a consequence, Hind and her mother slept in the salon by night, while the younger sister, Fatiha, her husband, and their young daughter occupied the room next door. Hind's unmarried brother lived in the remaining room, which also doubled as a storage room for the family. Beyond the limitations of this domestic arrangement, Hind was also aware of pervasive views, as those stated by Salima above, regarding not only the physical but also social distance between the Karyan and Nouvelle Lahraouiyine:

> Some of the people from the Karyan did not like it here. They said they were *haddaryin* (urban) and they thought Lahraouiyine was too isolated and rural for them. So, they rented out their homes and moved back into the city. We stayed though. We are adaptable. It's true that it's very quiet here, not like in the Karyan. There you would leave your door open for the breeze and your neighbors would walk in all the time. Here it's different. No one comes, because no one knows each other.

While the loss of sociality so poignantly evoked by Salima and Hind was overwhelmingly attributed by inhabitants to the breaking up of the bidonville's social fabric, the physical features of the new neighborhood also contributed to the sense of isolation. Set on former agricultural land, adjacent to the former village of what is now referred to as Old Lahraouiyine, the apartment buildings of the resettlement site stick out against the empty fields surrounding them. The grid of streets lining the site have not invited appropriation to date, and in many places are riddled with potholes, still awaiting paving. In the absence of inviting or easily accessible public spaces, households like Hind's tend to eventually retreat to their salons or roof in good weather, leaving them feeling atomized and wistful for the messy communal life of Karyan Central.

## RACHID: DISAPPOINTMENT WITH THE NEW HOME

Rachid, a journalist, political activist, and resident of Karyan Central, is the founder and leader of a neighborhood association that supported residents' claims to adequate housing. Rachid was convinced that the resettlement would help the dwellers to access decent housing and to escape the miserable living conditions in Karyan Central—especially the threat of fires. The association was involved in collective action and lobbying in favor of resettlement solutions. When Rachid heard about the VSB program he was convinced that, after long years of repression, and under the reign of the new, seemingly reformist, King Mohammed VI, public authorities would focus more on people's needs. Rachid trusted Mohammed VI, who stressed in his speeches the role of citizen participation. Rachid also trusted local authorities that ensured him they would develop a just resettlement scheme and would invest in an "exemplary," fully serviced, and well-connected new town. As a result of that promise, in the mid-2000s, his association began to convince inhabitants of Karyan Central of the advantages of the new town. They later helped residents through administrative processes and supported them in cases of perceived injustices concerning the attribution of plots.

However, in March 2017, when one of the authors met with Rachid in Nouvelle Lahraouiyine, his enthusiasm about resettlement had disappeared: "Authorities have been lying since the beginning!" The promises about participation and the new town turned out to be rather a form of authorities' co-optation of local leaders, with the intention to facilitate and speed up the clearance of the bidonville. Rachid not only criticized a lack of transparency within the resettlement process but was also concerned about corruption and the actual state of the new town—underserviced, insecure, and largely disconnected from the city core (figure 1.3; figure 1.4).

Reflecting on the process of implementation, Rachid explained that his association had already started in 2007 to request more detailed information concerning resettlement from local authorities in Hay Mohammadi (e.g., dates, attribution criteria, and location of the new town): "It was always the same reply. They said I should not worry; the file would be in the hands of the king." Only by the end of 2009 had authorities convened a roundtable in order to inform selected citizen representatives about the resettlement conditions. Rachid took part: "When I asked them whether the project was made by the king, a fight erupted, and my question was not heard. They paid some people to start fighting in case of critical questions. Later, one of the persons involved

**Figure 1.3 An Unfinished Street in Nouvelle Lahraouiyine.** *Source*: Author's picture, January 2017.

**Figure 1.4 Open Waste Incineration in Nouvelle Lahraouiyine.** *Source*: Author's picture, November 2018.

confirmed that." In addition, authorities also tried to directly bribe Rachid to prevent his association from slowing down the implementation when helping people to claim their rights within the resettlement process: "They [local authorities] said, tell us what you want. You can get the best plot in Nouvelle Lahraouiyine and with a shop in the ground floor!" Normally people had no choice and had to take part in a lottery of plots. To avoid attempts at corruption and to prevent the loss of his credibility among residents of Karyan Central, Rachid decided to make his right to a plot over to his mother.

In 2013, Rachid left Karyan Central and moved into temporary accommodation, before moving into the new apartment in 2015. In the meantime, Rachid and his association had already started to denounce serious deficiencies of Nouvelle Lahraouiyine: "In 2010 [after the first residents had moved to Nouvelle Lahraouiyine], there were no services, nothing at all: no taxis, no security, no light, but lots of dogs and waste." It was the association that convinced the taxi syndicate to operate a shared taxi service connecting Nouvelle Lahraouiyine with Hay Mohammadi. Thus, in March 2017, notwithstanding some improvements concerning transport, security, and electricity in Nouvelle Lahraouiyine, Rachid's hope for a better, less marginalized, and less vulnerable life that had marked the time after the announcement of the VSB, had transformed into deep disappointment with the state of the new town: "It is only the external image after the attacks in 2003 that motivated the state to intervene in the bidonvilles, it is not because the state or the king likes us. In fact, the responsible persons do not care at all about citizens' wellbeing!"

By the end of 2018, Rachid had left Nouvelle Lahraouiyine, mentally ill and with severe despair, and he had found refuge in his parents' house in the rural province of Doukkala. From a distance he was occasionally engaged in the writing of protest letters and Facebook posts, denouncing the deteriorating conditions in the new town, especially the catastrophic waste management (figure 1.4) and the insufficient supply and maintenance of other public services and infrastructure. Only his children have remained in his semifinished house in Nouvelle Lahraouiyine, visiting him occasionally in the countryside.

## CONCLUSION

The brief biographic accounts of Salima, Hind, and Rachid, and their varying experiences of and expectations toward resettlement, put into question uniform resettlement schemes as a solution to the "challenge of slums" (United Nations Human Settlements Programme, 2003). The problems of standardized resettlement projects and the displacement of thousands of urban citizens to the margins of urban agglomerations become even more disturbing against the background of re-increasing preferences toward these solutions among many governments in the global South (cf. Beier, 2019a; Buckley, Kallergis, & Wainer, 2016; Turok, 2016). Besides typical deficiencies—such as a single focus on standardized housing; a loss of social networks; insufficient access to transport, jobs, and education; inadequate provision of public services; and a general impression of neglect, all problems that have been known for long (cf. Berner, 2016; Cernea, 1993; Plessis, 2005; Turner, 1968, 1969)—the different pathways from Karyan Central to Nouvelle Lahraouiyine make obvious that resettlement outcomes are largely shaped at a personal level for resettled citizens. The question of losing or gaining home not only depends on the individual pathway to the new town—or in other words, the personal experiences with the process of resettlement, as the case of Rachid shows—but also in the trajectories that brought people to the shantytown. As such, Hind, who moved to Karyan Central only because of family conflicts, is much more open toward the new settlement than Salima, who is deeply rooted in Hay Mohammadi and who could not imagine moving to Nouvelle Lahraouiyine.

Finally, the very personal notions of inequality that are entangled with the experiences of resettlement show that it is necessary to go beyond one-size-fits-all solutions. Too often, in official discourses and policy agendas, as well as in scholarly literature, issues related to urban inequality and informal housing appear in abstracted forms, treated as numerical, standardized data that renders such issues amenable to technical problem-solving. While there are certain, often historical, patterns and structures that can be distinguished among the conditions that produce and reinforce urban inequality in places like Casablanca, the occluding of heterogeneity—both at the level of lived inequality, and of individual positionalities and perceptions among those inhabiting informal housing—can lead to counterproductive practices of urban governance. Significantly, as the stories of our interlocutors emphatically demonstrate, such standardized solution risks robbing inhabitants of their agency, not only in terms of erasing the complex histories of their belonging and home-making but also at the level of acknowledging their right to choose where to make a home in the city. To a certain extent, living in Karyan Central has been the result of individual choices of residency, always implying an individual's need to balance advantages and disadvantages under given restrictions. Therefore, it is inappropriate to ignore these choices of residency, to disregard heterogeneous attachments to the neighborhood, and to impose the same solution to all, based on assumed demands. Instead, choice should be an inevitable aspect of all affordable housing policies. Moreover, the drafting of suitable approaches requires openness toward creative, needs-based, and citizen-led solutions that may prioritize the upgrading of existent structures as an alternative to resettlement. However, as long as governments continue to prioritize large-scale solutions, fast implementation, and the clearance of land, resettlement solutions will hardly result in sustainable solutions.

## NOTES

1. The translation "Cities Without Slums" is also common, but we prefer to translate *bidonville* into "shantytown," because in the Moroccan context the term "slum" refers to different types of settlements besides *bidonvilles*.

2. Because of its significant role in the independence movement, Hay Mohammadi and its origin, Karyan Central, have become famous even beyond Casablanca. However, during the Years of Lead, a period known for human rights abuses of the former king Hassan II, the neighborhood also became known as a place of political repression, and it was the site of an infamous detention center (cf. Strava, 2017).

3. Names have been changed by the authors to preserve anonymity.

4. In fact, the conditions of the allocation of plots were based on outdated census data and remained inaccessible to the population. To the residents it remained unclear who exactly is eligible to a plot in the new town—all married couples or only entire households?

5. However, with the construction of the second tramway line, the local government has also aimed at establishing a formalized order at the market of Hay Mohammadi, trying to move informal street vendors toward formalized stalls in renovated and newly built market halls (*qissariat*) (Beier, 2019b).

6. A shanty-home is commonly referred to in Moroccan dialect as a *beraka*, or "barrack," which is speculated to be derived from the French term "baraque."

## BIBLIOGRAPHY

Abu-Lughod, J. (1980). *Rabat: Urban apartheid in Morocco*. Princeton, NJ: Princeton University Press.

Abu-Lughod, J. (1987). The Islamic city—Historic myth, Islamic essence, and contemporary relevance. *International Journal of Middle East Studies, 19*(2), 155–176.

Al Sayyad, N. (2004). Urban informality as a 'new' way of life. In A. Roy & N. Al Sayyad (Eds.), *Urban informality: Transnational perspectives from the Middle East, Latin America and South Asia* (pp. 7–30). Lanham, MA: Lexington Books.

Arrif, A. (1994). Le paradoxe de la construction du fait patrimonial en situation coloniale. Le cas du Maroc. *Revue du monde musulman et de la Méditerranée, 73*(1), 153–166.

Beier, R. (2018). Social movements as drivers of urban policy: The case of the Arab uprisings in North Africa. In A. Schoch & R. Bürgin (Eds.), *Urbane Widerstände—Urban resistance* (pp. 63–78). Bern, Switzerland: Peter Lang.

Beier, R. (2019a). *From the city to the desert. Analysing Shantytown resettlement in Casablanca, Morocco, from residents' perspectives*. Berlin, Germany: Logos.

Beier, R. (2019b). The world-class city comes by tramway: Reframing Casablanca's urban peripheries through public transport. *Urban Studies*, online first. https://doi.org/10.1177%2F0042098019853475.

Belguidoum, S., Cattedra, R., & Iraki, A. (2015). Villes et urbanités au Maghreb. *L'Année du Maghreb, 12*, 11–32.

Benlahcen Tlemçani, M., & Missamou, R. (2000). Habitat clandestin et insalubre au Maroc: vers une stratégie d'intervention plurielle. *Les Annales de la Recherche Urbaine*, *86*, 111–118.

Berner, E. (2016). Housing disablement: Market failures, haphazard policies and the global proliferation of slums. In G.M. Gomez & P. Knorringa (Eds.), *EADI global development series. Local governance, economic development and institutions* (pp. 98–117). Basingstoke, England: Palgrave MacMillan.

Bogaert, K. (2011). The problem of slums: Shifting methods of neoliberal urban government in Morocco. *Development and Change*, *42*(3), 709–731.

Bogaert, K. (2013). Cities without slums in Morocco? New modalities of urban government and the Bidonville as a neoliberal assemblage. In T.R. Samara, S. He, & G. Chen (Eds.), *Routledge studies in human geography: Vol. 43. Locating right to the city in the global south* (pp. 41–59). New York: Routledge.

Buckley, R.M., Kallergis, A., & Wainer, L. (2016). Addressing the housing challenge: Avoiding the Ozymandias syndrome. *Environment and Urbanization*, *28*(1), 119–138.

Cattedra, R. (2006). Bidonville: paradigme et réalité refoulée de la ville du XXe siècle. In J.-C. Depaule (Ed.), *Collection Les mots de la ville: Vol. 4. Les mots de la stigmatisation urbaine* (pp. 123–163). Paris, France: Éditions UNESCO; Éditions de la Maison des sciences de l'homme.

Cernea, M.M. (1993). Anthropological and sociological research for policy development on population resettlement. In M.M. Cernea & S.E. Guggenheim (Eds.), *Anthropological approaches to resettlement: Policy, practice, and theory* (pp. 13–38). Boulder, CO: Westview Press.

de Certeau, M. (1984). *The practice of everyday life* (Trans. Steven Rendall). Berkeley, CA: University of California Press.

Davis, M. (2006). *Planet of slums*. London, England: Verso.

Doshi, S. (2013). The politics of the evicted: Redevelopment, subjectivity, and difference in Mumbai's slum frontier. *Antipode, 45*(4), 844–865.

Dürr, E., & Jaffe, R. (2012). Theorizing slum tourism: Performing, negotiating and transforming inequality. *European Review of Latin American and Caribbean Studies/Revista Europea de Estudios Latinoamericanos y del Caribe, 95*, 113–123.

Eickelman, D. (1974). Is there an Islamic city? The making of a quarter in a Moroccan town. *International Journal of Middle East Studies, 5*(3), 274–294.

El-Kazaz, S., & Mazur, K. (2017). Introduction to special section: The un-exceptional Middle Eastern city. *City & Society, 29*(1), 148–161.

Feld, S., & Basso, K. (Eds.). (1996). *Senses of place*. School of American Research Press.

Frankenhoff, C.A. (1967). Elements of an economic model for slums in a developing economy. *Economic Development and Cultural Change, 16*(1), 27–36.

Haut Commissariat au Plan. (2014). *Annuaire Statistique de la Région du Grand Casablanca*. Casablanca, Maroc. Retrieved from https://www.hcp.ma/reg-casablanca/attachment/640385/.

Mangin, W. (1967). Latin American squatter settlements: A problem and a solution. *Latin American Research Review*, *2*(3), 65–98.

McFarlane, C., & Waibel, M. (2016). Introduction: The informal-formal divide in context. In C. McFarlane & M. Waibel (Eds.), *Urban informalities: Reflection on the formal and informal* (pp. 1–12). New York, NY: Routledge.

Mitchell, T. (2002). *Rule of experts: Egypt, techno-politics, modernity*. Berkeley, CA: University of California Press.

Navaro-Yashin, Y. (2012). *The make-believe space: Affective geography in a postwar polity*. Durham, NC: Duke University Press.

Navez-Bouchanine, F. (1990). L'enjeu limitrophe: entre le privé et le public, un no man's land? La pratique urbaine au Maroc. *Espaces et sociétés, 62,* 135–160.

Navez-Bouchanine, F. (2012). Les nouvelles voies de la négociation dans les politiques de résorption des bidonvilles au Maroc: Entre recasement et accompagnement social. In F. Navez-Bouchanine & A. Deboulet (Eds.), *Effets sociaux des politiques urbaines: L'entre-deux des politiques institutionnelles et des dynamiques sociales: Algérie, Maroc, Liban, Mauritanie* (pp. 166–218). Paris, France: Éditions Karthala; Centre Jacques Berque; Emam-CITERES.

Patel, S., Sliuzas, R., & Navdeep M. (2015). The risk of impoverishment in urban development-induced displacement and resettlement in Ahmedabad. *Environment & Urbanization, 27*(1), 231–256.

Plessis, J. du. (2005). The growing problem of forced evictions and the crucial importance of community-based, locally appropriate alternatives. *Environment and Urbanization, 17*(1), 123–134.

Rabinow, P. (1989). *French modern. Norms and forms of the social environment.* Cambridge, MA: MIT Press.

Rachik, A. (2002). *Casablanca: L'urbanisme de l'urgence.* Casablanca, Morocco: Najah El-Jadida.

Rachik, A. (2012). Casablanca: Ein ländliches Zuwanderungsgebiet? In J. Gertel & I. Breuer (Eds.), *Kultur und soziale Praxis. Alltagsmobilitäten: Aufbruch marokkanischer Lebenswelten* (pp. 317–326). Bielefeld, Germany: Transcript.

Roy, A. (2005). Urban informality: Towards an epistemology of planning. *Journal of the American Planning Association, 71*(2), 147–158.

Roy, A. (2009). The 21st-century metropolis: New geographies of theory. *Regional Studies, 43*(6), 819–830.

Roy, A. (2011). Slumdog cities: Rethinking subaltern urbanism. *International Journal of Urban and Regional Research, 35*(2), 223–238.

Sieburg, F. (1938). Le role économique de Casablanca vu par un écrivain allemand. *Bulletin Economique du Maroc, 5*(21), 205–207.

Simone, A. (2004). *For the city yet to come: Changing African life in four cities.* Durham, NC: Duke University Press.

Singerman, D. (1996). The family and community as politics. In D. Singerman & H. Hoodfar (Eds.), *Development, change, and gender in Cairo* (pp. 145–189). Bloomington, IN: Indiana University Press.

Spire, A., Bridonneau, M., & Pascale, P. (2017). Droit à la ville et replacement dans les contexts autoritaires d'Addis Abeba (Éthiopie) et de Lomé (Togo). *Métropoles* [en ligne] 21.

Stokes, C.J. (1962). A theory of slums. *Land Economics, 38*(3), 187–197.

Strava, C. (2017). At home on the margins: Care giving and the 'un-homely' among Casablanca's working poor. *City & Society, 29*(2), 329–348.

Toutain, O. (2016). The experience of private investment and funding: The relocation of the Karyan Thomas and Douar Skouila households: The Essalam operation in Casablanca. In J.-C. Bolay, J. Chenal, & Y. Pedrazzini (Eds.), *GeoJournal library: Vol. 119. Learning from the slums for the development of emerging cities* (pp. 137–147). Cham, Switzerland: Springer International Publishing Switzerland.

Turner, J.F.C. (1968). Housing priorities, settlement patterns, and urban development in modernizing countries. *Journal of the American Institute of Planners, 34*(6), 354–363.

Turner, J.F.C. (1969). Uncontrolled urban settlement: Problems and policies. In G.W. Breese (Ed.), *The city in newly developing countries: Readings on urbanism and urbanization* (pp. 507–534). Englewood Cliffs, NJ: Prentice-Hall.

Turner, J.F.C. (1977). *Housing by people: Towards autonomy in building environments.* New York, NY: Pantheon Books.

Turok, I. (2016). Housing and the urban premium. *Habitat International, 54*(3), 234–240.

United Nations Human Settlements Programme (UN-Habitat). (2003). *The challenge of slums: Global report on human settlements 2003.* Sterling, VA: Earthscan.

Wright, G. (1991). *The politics of design in French colonial urbanism.* Chicago, IL: University of Chicago Press.

Yiftachel, O. (2009). Theoretical notes on 'gray cities': The coming of urban apartheid? *Planning Theory, 8*(1), 88–100.

Zaki, L. (2007). L'action publique au bidonville: l'État entre gestion par le manque, "éradication" des kariens et accompagnement social des habitants. *L'Année du Maghreb, 2*, 303–320.

Zaki, L. (2010). L'électrification temporaire des bidonvilles Casablancais: Aspects et limites d'une transformation. *Politique africaine, 120*, 45–66.

Zaki, L. (2013). Montée en puissance des mobilisations dans les bidonvilles et transformation de l'action publique au Maroc: de l'ouverture des années 1990 au printemps arabe. In P.-A. Barthel & S. Jaglin (Eds.), *Vol. 7. Conférences & Séminaires, Quartiers informels d'un monde arabe en transition: Réflexions et perspectives pour l'action urbaine* (pp. 37–52). Paris, France: Agence Française de Développement.

# Chapter 2

# Kuala Lumpur

## World Class City Formation and Urban (In)Equities

Seng-Guan Yeoh

For the ruling elites of the Global South, the developmental pathway of the Southeast Asian country of Malaysia is often perceived as an enviable success, worthy of emulation. At a cursory level, the kinetic "progress" of Malaysia is aesthetically indexed by the array of gleaming high-rise office complexes, luxury condominiums, expansive shopping malls, and elevated city highways that are redefining the skyline and landscape of the capital city of Kuala Lumpur. Despite being surpassed as the tallest building structure in the world more than a decade ago, the iconic Petronas Twin Towers continue to be a hyper-nationalist statement of global intent, in addition to a popular tourism destination in Kuala Lumpur's central business district.[1]

Conventional official statistics support the perception of Malaysia's successful development. The World Bank ranks this country of 30 million as an upper middle income and newly industrialized country, generating a per capita gross national income (GNI) of US$11,000 (Eleventh Malaysian Plan, 2015). By 2020, the country's visionaries expect GNI per capita to reach US$15,000, reaching the coveted status of a high-income country. Since 1970, the local economy has been achieving a real GDP growth of 6.2 percent per year (Eleventh Malaysian Plan, 2015). The country transformed from a predominantly extractive agriculture-based economy in the 1970s to a manufacturing-focused economy in the mid-1980s to a service economy in the 1990s. Moreover, between 1970 and 2014, the incidence of poverty has been substantially reduced from 49.3 percent to 0.6 percent, while hard-core poverty has been eradicated (Eleventh Malaysian Plan, 2015). State attention has now shifted to addressing the poorest 40 percent of the population,

2.7 million "B40 households," by providing more capacity and opportunities for them to increase their income levels. In terms of settlement patterns, at least 75 percent of all Malaysians now reside in urban centers throughout the country (Eleventh Malaysian Plan, 2015). The federal territories of Kuala Lumpur and Putrajaya—a recently planned city where the federal administrative enclave is situated—are considered "fully urbanized" and the national capital of Kuala Lumpur generates close to 15 percent of the country's GDP (Eleventh Malaysian Plan, 2015). Under the 11th Malaysian Plan (2016–2020), the government plans to continue investing in selected competitive cities in order to transform them into "talent hubs" for strong economic agglomeration and improve their urban livability (Eleventh Malaysian Plan, 2015).

This chapter examines the spectacular transformation of Kuala Lumpur into a World Class City and the concurrent nationalist project of eliding an array of racialized inequalities constituted during the British colonial period. Notwithstanding the substantive gains achieved over the last few decades, I devote attention to trends that push back upon perceived development gains in Kuala Lumpur. This chapter tracks the changing faces of urban inequities as refracted through colonial and postcolonial governance strategies in the Malaysian context.

My chapter combines historical analyses and ethnographic data. I begin with an ethnographic vignette of Letchumi before providing an abbreviated recounting of historical forces which have structured the lives of individuals like her. Letchumi's story directly connects with many of the historical urban trends and state policies seeking to address poverty in Malaysia. While this particular vignette is based on fieldwork conducted for several weeks in 2014, my mother and I have frequented the morning wet market where Letchumi conducts her business for many years, and where we got to know each other. Other ethnographic and archival details for this chapter are derived from intermittent fieldwork conducted in Kuala Lumpur since the mid-1990s.

## LABORING FIGURES

By 4:30 a.m. every morning Letchumi, a woman in her late 40s, is already awake. The night before she stayed up late to prepare the ingredients for her Indian food stall in the nearby morning wet market. She peels, slices, and grinds several large bowls of onions and chilies. Next, she dices a small basket of potatoes that will be used as the filling for curry puffs. The rest of the time she spends preparing a large pot of *dhal* (lentil) curry and a bucket of watery rice flour paste that will be converted into fresh *tosai* pancakes at the market. She seldom seeks the help of her two teenaged children, as she wants her daughter to concentrate on her studies and her son is often away doing late night shift work. She is a single parent. Years ago, she chose to leave her husband because of domestic abuse. Before she retires for the night, she loads the fully laden pots and pans onto a shopping trolley in readiness for the next morning.

In the morning, after a cold bath, she departs from her compact two-room apartment unit situated on the thirteenth floor. She was permitted to rent this unit cheaply when the entire squatter *kampung* (village) where she was staying was demolished to make way for the construction of low-cost public housing flats. As the *kampung* was situated on state land, most of the residents could remain in the locality and were not compelled to be relocated elsewhere in Kuala Lumpur. If private land was involved or if the local authorities had decided to enter into a joint business venture with private developers to convert state land for the construction of medium range or luxury condominiums, Letchumi and her family likely would have been resettled at a greater distance from their former house.

Letchumi wheels the trolley along a narrow, lit corridor leading to the elevators. The walls of the elevator lobby, as with the other common areas and staircases, are grimy and covered with children's scrawls and graffiti. While some of the graffiti are invectives not to throw garbage anywhere, others are sexual taunts or expressions of youthful lust. The movement of the trolley is hampered, as some residents use the corridor as an extended storage space for bulky items like bicycles. Although frustrated, Letchumi does not complain. She wants to avoid creating ill feelings with her non-Indian neighbors, especially Malay-Muslims who make up a sizeable proportion of the building residents. She opines that, unlike in the squatter *kampung* before, a palpable sense of cross-ethnic community feeling is lacking in the high-rise flats as residents tend to confine themselves to their own family members and interact only with members of similar ethno-religious groups.

Inside the elevator, several of the buttons are missing, and the ceiling lights do not often work. Residents must endure the darkness while in the elevators and must get off at the level closest to their floor. Moreover, several times each year, the lifts serving the seventeen-story building break down and it takes a while before they get repaired.

From the flats it takes about 15 minutes walking along the main road to arrive at the wet market where Letchumi sells her goods. Throughout the journey, the pots and pans rattle nosily as the trolley traverses tarmac roads, and Letchumi is careful not to let their contents spill. Just before she enters the market proper, Letchumi stops at a Chinese roadside shrine to leave a small offering of food, light three joss-sticks, and ask for daily blessings from the local guardian deity. The wet market is situated within a sprawling area known as a "New Village." Nearly 600 of these "New Villages" were developed across Malaysia in the 1950s. This particular "New Village" consists largely of ethnic Chinese residents. Although it was considered a place of incarceration and deprivation a few decades earlier, living conditions in the area have improved. Early residents were farmers and laborers, but their descendants have ventured into a range of self-employed businesses, incrementally bettering their household's economic prospects. In more recent years, due to its strategic location close to the city center and entry/exit points of the network of elevated toll highways, the material infrastructure of the area is undergoing rapid changes. A visible sign of this transformation is the construction of luxury condominiums near to the wet market.

At this early hour only the pork sellers are in the market, chopping up pig carcasses into smaller, manageable pieces. Nevertheless, by 6:00 a.m., the market is buzzing with activity as truckloads of supplies like chicken, fish, and vegetables arrive from the wholesale markets and distant farms. Many of these stalls employ migrant workers primarily from neighboring Indonesia. As not all of them are legally documented, stall owners are alert to the possibility of occasional crackdowns by officials from City Hall. During this time, their workers are told to become "invisible," and to confine themselves indoors to escape easy detection.

Because Letchumi's food business is rather modest in size, she works alone. Indeed, she rarely takes time off from work—only two days for the Hindu celebration of Deepavali in November and when she is not feeling well or has urgent matters to attend. Her net earnings fluctuate according to the days of the week. The best days are on the weekends, while the other days are comparatively slow. To supplement her income, Letchumi works afternoons as a cook for a Chinese household in another part of Kuala Lumpur. Her regular customers at the market are mainly Chinese and Indians; very few Malays patronize her stall. Besides her native Tamil and the national language of Malay, Letchumi has learned to speak the Chinese Cantonese dialect fluently because of frequent social interactions with Chinese friends and acquaintances since her youth. In particular, because of Letchumi's past difficulties carving out a living as a single parent, she regards highly the work ethic of the Chinese in comparison to Indians and Malays. She generalizes that the latter tend either to be petty or to lack business acumen and entrepreneurship. Moreover, she feels that the Malaysian government gives preferential access to financial aid, scholarships, and quotas in businesses and education to Malay-Muslims rather than extending them equally to all ethnic groups in need of support. For her, socioeconomic disparity is keenly felt by the urban poor of Kuala Lumpur.

## COLONIAL URBAN FORMATIONS AND POSTCOLONIAL URBAN MODERNITY

Letchumi's modern-day Kuala Lumpur is not a spatiotemporal *tabula rasa*. Like the trajectories of other former colonial outposts in Southeast Asia, the settlement was created because of a convergence of disparate circumstances, paramount of which was its strategic commercial location vis-à-vis native Malay settlements. In 1880, the British administrators decided to move their state capital 35 kilometers upstream, from the preexisting royal port settlement of Klang to a small thriving tin mining trading post started by Sumatran and Chinese pioneers at the confluence of two rivers. Within two decades, the foundational spatial form and urban aesthetics of Kuala Lumpur had been laid out, informed by modern Western spatial imaginaries and innovations, including the shape of "Garden City" urban planning aspirations, building construction technologies, and urban hygiene (Gullick, 2000).

In the precolonial milieu, Malay settlements were predominantly coastal, riverine, or port hubs, of which the most prominent was the Islamic Melaka Sultanate during the Age of Commerce (Reid, 1988). The creation of large human settlements in the interior was avoided because of the formidable barriers of swamps, dense tropical forests, and the corporeal dangers of wild animals and diseases, like malaria and dengue fever. The inhospitable interior was inhabited by a diverse array of tribal indigenous peoples—today collectively known as the "Orang Asli"—who had learned to adapt to these conditions over millennia.

From around the mid-nineteenth century onward, British rulers began to expand their territorial control into the hinterland from the Straits Settlement littoral enclaves of Penang, Singapore, and Melaka. To attract speculators and investors to set up cash-crop plantations and large-scale mining activities, colonial governors rejected indigenous land tenure practices as unsuitable for a monetized economy. Instead, they imposed the Torrens Land System, first developed in Australia. This system afforded property owners security in land tenure, eliminated rival claims and encumbrances, and was enforceable through a centralized administrative machinery (Wong, 1975). Prior experiences of colonial rule in British India, the frequency of Muslim-led rebellions in neighboring Dutch Indies (Indonesia), and local political conditions informed the decision to adopt the overt posture of nonintervention in "Malay religion and customs," which later became legislative fiat. This also translated into Malays continuing to work as farmers and fishermen rather than as urban laborers and merchants (Kratoska, 1985). A liberal migration policy was also crafted to attract foreign migrant labor, as well as an array of entrepreneurs and petty capitalists to facilitate wealth extraction in British Malaya. A significant proportion of migrants originated from impoverished regions of present-day China, India, and Indonesia, subsequently laying the tripartite template for administrating and managing the pluralistic ethno-religious politics (and poetics) of modern-day polyglot Malaysia (Leow, 2016). For migrant workers of these milieu, including Letchumi's ancestors, the difficult—if not exploitative and substandard work and living conditions—have become the subject of several historical studies (Rimmer & Allen, 1990), and the stuff of family narratives and fictional postcolonial retellings.

To facilitate the efficient and predictable movement of goods and people, the British incrementally built an infrastructural network of transportation links, both rail and roads, that were skewed along the western coast of Peninsular/West Malaysia (Kaur, 1985; Lim, 1978). The "plural society" (coined by colonial administrator John Furnivall) was most salient in the new towns birthed along the transportation links where various material, social, and cultural imprints of Western modernity took root. In most cases, these urban centers were demographically and commercially dominated by Chinese, Indians, and British merchants, while most native Malays as well as indigenous Orang Asli ("original peoples") resided in rural smallholdings and forested areas (cf. Kahn, 2006). Before the start of World War II, many of these towns were already thriving because of a buoyant trade in tin, rubber, and other agricultural commodities.[2] However, the ravages of war saw a significant, albeit temporary, depopulation of many towns, as residents fled to the jungle, plantations, and the countryside for refuge, and to escape Japanese atrocities.

Before political independence was granted in 1957, the largest urban population growth rate occurred in the preceding decade when the British forcibly resettled around 600,000 people—mostly Chinese farmers—into hastily built, perimeter-fenced settlements, situated close to existing towns in order to cut off the supply chain to an insurgent Communist Party intent on wresting control through armed guerrilla conflict. Euphemistically called "New Villages," these settlements, initiated under the Briggs Plan, resulted in a significant increase in urban population, with each having a population of 1,000 persons or more.[3] A corollary effect was the migration of thousands of individuals to small towns in order to escape these securitized hamlets. Finding insufficient or unsuitable lodgings for their families, many turned to residing in existing squatter settlements, or starting up new ones on vacant private and public lands in and around towns. Not surprisingly, Kuala Lumpur was a powerful magnet for this flow and the subsequent phenomenal growth of squatter settlements in the capital city.

On a broader level, the colonial legacy of a socio-spatial duality between Malay and non-Malay citizens has been mobilized as a master narrative for postcolonial corrective social engineering. Two watershed policies

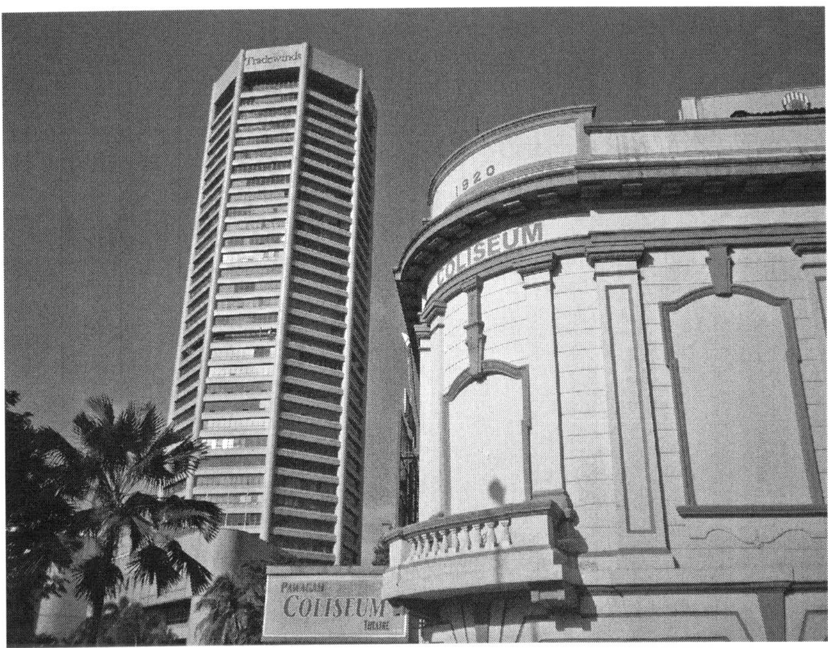


**Figure 2.1 Old Business Precinct.** *Source*: Photo by author.

laid the groundwork for the transformation of the demographic and social fabric of urban centers in Malaysia. The first arose in the aftermath of the traumatic events of the "race riots" of May 13, 1969, which erupted mainly in Kuala Lumpur after general election results that were unfavorable to the ruling ethnic-based coalition. In line with the interventionist "growth with distribution" thrust of the New Economy Policy (NEP, 1971–90), the government exponentially stepped up its involvement in restructuring the country's economy by increasing Malay economic and corporate interests through quotas, especially in the areas of private sector employment, business, mining, and manufacturing in order to address glaring rural Malay poverty (Ishak, 2000; Ragayah, 2004). Moreover, rural Malays were encouraged to "modernize" by seeking out better education, employment, and business opportunities offered in towns and cities, especially in Kuala Lumpur. In sum, the NEP emphasis on addressing economic inequality in horizontal communal—rather than vertical non-communal—terms has led to the significant decrease of rural Malay poverty and the creation of an urban Malay middle class (Embong, 2001). However, detractors contend that the NEP has also generated a host of inequities like rent seeking, institutional decline, the marginalization of working-class Tamils and Orang Asli peoples, and has contributed to seriously undermining social cohesion between Malay and non-Malay citizens of the country (cf. Gomez, Saravanamuttu, & Mohamad, 2013; Willford, 2014; Yeoh, 2005b). For individuals like Letchumi, their personal experiences of disenfranchisement and lack of opportunities are attributed to the outworking of the NEP and its subsequent incarnations.

The second watershed policy was promulgated after the formal end of the NEP in 1991. Affirmative action for Malays and other *bumiputeras* (a broader communal category encompassing the Orang Asli in West Malaysia and natives of Sabah and Sarawak in East Malaysia) was not discarded, as it was contended that the NEP targets had not yet been realized. With the catchphrase of Wawasan 2020 ("Vision 2020: The Way Forward"), Prime Minister Mahathir Mohamad outlined in the National Development Policy (1991–2000) a grand narrative for arriving at the status of a "fully developed" and self-sufficient industrialized nation by the year 2020 through an intensification of key economic and social activities. The NDP also recognized that unintended regional disparities had worsened during the NEP (Gomez et al., 2013) and a package of spatially attuned policies was introduced to promote a more balanced development of major sectors of the economy and in various regions of the country.

After the lapse of the NDP, the National Vision Policy (NVP, 2000–2010) and the subsequent National Transformation Policy (NTP, 2011–2020) were formulated. Although the discursive tone shifted, the affirmative action priorities of the NEP has been kept intact. For instance, the NTP launched by then prime minister Najib Razak embodies more cogently the ideology of neoliberalism, promoting private sector-led initiatives, meritocracy, and the plea for Malaysians to acquire flexible mind-sets and knowledge-based skills in order to be more productive in the face of a competitive and mobile global marketplace. In tandem with this shift, the government imposed a Goods and Sales Tax (GST) and the removal of broad-based subsidies in favor of targeted subsidies like the BR1M (Bantuan Rakyat 1 Malaysia [Peoples Aid 1 Malaysia]) program, which supports low-income groups in line with rationalizing public expenditure.[4] Moreover, capitalizing on the strategic gains made during the NEP implementation in building up Malay share of corporate wealth, the ownership and control of this sector shifted to publicly listed government linked investment companies (GLICs) under the jurisdiction of the minister of Finance (Gomez, Padmanabhan, Kamaruddin, Bhalla, & Fisal, 2018). In sum, despite countervailing cosmopolitan trends among younger generations of Malaysians, the legacy of a racialized calculus has remained deeply ingrained and hegemonic in the Malaysian social imaginary and political landscape. From the perspective of working-class individuals like Letchumi, the imprints of racialization in their everyday lives are as palpable as ever despite recent populist initiatives like BR1M.

## THE WORLD CLASS CITY, SPATIAL CLEANSING, AND LOW-COST HOUSING

As described in the ethnographic vignette, Lecthumi lived in a squatter settlement before she was given the opportunity to rent a high-rise public housing unit as part of the People Housing Project (PPR). Her shift in residential fortunes closely mirrors Kuala Lumpur's spectacular morphing over the last three decades. In the early 1990s, then prime minister Mahathir Mohamad announced Vision 2020. Henceforth, government policies underscored privatization and corporate entrepreneurialism as the key engines for transformation. Included in this grand vision was the rebranding and remaking of Kuala Lumpur in the mold of a "World Class City." Conversely, a "zero squatter policy" was pursued, legitimizing the erasure of the anti-utopian other—urban squatter settlements—and promoting representations of space and urban assemblages associated with city visionaries, urban planners, and real-estate developers in line with global markers of capitalism (Lefebvre, 1991; Sassen, 1994). Since this period, the country also began to recruit and attract new supply lines of cheap and flexible migrant labor from Southeast and South Asia for the construction, manufacturing, and plantation sectors (Chin, 1998; Parthiban, 2015). Today, Malaysia is the largest importer of migrant labor in Southeast Asia, hosting between two and four million documented and undocumented workers, constituting about 30 percent of the total Malaysian workforce.[5]

Prior to the 1990s, squatter settlements had faced periodic intervention from local authorities. For instance, surveys conducted in the 1950s indicated that a third of Kuala Lumpur's population was made up of squatters, and that 70 percent were ethnic Chinese. Since these settlements were believed to be "deeply infested with Communists" and their labyrinthine layouts made police surveillance difficult, the clearing of these settlements was deemed necessary (Johnstone, 1983, p. 257). More than a decade later, following a similar spatial disciplinary logic, a subcommittee was set up under the National Operations Council, as it was alleged that squatters played a catalytic role in the May 13 disturbances. Subsequently, *The Squatter Clearance Regulations 1969* was enacted, providing extensive powers for eviction and demolition. Between 1969 and 1975, about 18,000 squatters—60 percent of whom were identified as ethnic Chinese—were forcibly evicted from the city center. However, only 34 percent of those evicted were subsequently provided with public housing in the form of high-rise rental flats elsewhere in the city (Yeoh, 2010, p. 132).

Throughout the late 1970s and 1980s, squatter evictions were periodically carried out for redevelopment purposes, but they were not done on a large scale. Despite these punitive actions, the combination of in-migration, the lack of affordable public housing, and the resilience of the urban poor resulted in a sizeable proportion of vacant land in Kuala Lumpur being quickly and opportunistically reoccupied by squatters. In comparison to past migratory patterns, the new waves now comprised significant numbers of Malay-Muslims drawn to the capital city by the affirmative action opportunities opened up by the NEP. Forming an important group of voters for the Malay-based United Malay National Organization (UMNO), the specter of negative political repercussions tied to forcible evictions was part of the political calculus encouraging inaction (Yeoh, 2001). Indeed, several high-ranking Malay politicians were known to cultivate patronage relationships with these settlements through the provision of basic infrastructure services in exchange for political loyalty.

Compared to the previous milieu, however, the 1990s ushered in a radically different evaluation of these settlements. Demolitions were systematic, large-scale, unrelenting, and, in many cases, hastily executed in the name of producing a "World Class City" within a specified time frame. The litany of human suffering that ensued provoked local civil society groups to rally to the cause. Activists asserted that many of these settlements had been in existence for decades and were indirectly acknowledged by state authorities in the form of the provision of basic amenities periodically renewed just before the general elections. The civil society groups contended that these factors transformed slums into thriving urban villages, arguing that a more consultative process in keeping with international human rights standards should have been followed (Yeoh, 2001).[6] When bulldozers, accompanied by City Hall officials, came to demolish these settlements, they frequently faced vociferous and defiant civil society groups together with affected squatters. Altercations often led to arrests before the demolitions were carried out. Many of these standoffs, successful or otherwise, were copiously documented via photos and videos and, combined with poignant narratives from affected residents, deployed to inspire other settlements facing imminent eviction to collective action, regardless of their ethno-religious origins.

Following the Second United Nations International Conference on Human Settlements (Habitat II) in 1996, the Malaysian government substantially increased the budget allocation for the construction of public high-rise housing for rent or sale. Called the People's Housing Project (PPR), the project aligned with Habitat II's slogan of "adequate, affordable and quality housing for all," and squatter evictions and relocation were seen as necessary to free up valuable urban land for redevelopment. The government required private developers building on land where squatter settlements had been to construct high-rise, subsidized, low-cost housing as part of the compensation package. The Asian financial crisis of the late 1990s provided a brief reprieve, as numerous construction projects in the public and private sectors were put

**Figure 2.2 Part of the Central Business District of the City.** *Source*: Photo by author.

on hold or abandoned. In the 2000s, as the Malaysian economy recovered enough for selected projects to be revived, the government announced that the "zero squatter" target was met, and that Kuala Lumpur was now officially rid of squatter settlements once and for all.

Nevertheless, detractors contend that while the provision of public and low-cost high-rise housing has definitively resolved the housing woes of the urban poor and low-income groups, a litany of other kinds of disruptions and inequities have arisen in its wake. Letchumi was fortunate as her PPR flat was situated near her former residence and her market stall. Many other former squatters, however, found that their flats were often not located near where they had lived for decades, and in proximity to their places of work, businesses, and schools. Moreover, in many cases, basic amenities like schools, shops, and markets were not available when residents moved into these flats. This translated into further burdens in the form of additional travelling time and costs. Another point of contention was that long-standing social networks of kin and friendships were often broken up, as the authorities preferred to fragment and recombine residents from different ethno-religious backgrounds and disparate squatter settlements into these units. The compact size and modular design of these units provided yet another source of alienation. In the mid-1990s, during my fieldwork in a squatter settlement situated on the outskirts of the business district of Kuala Lumpur, it was not uncommon to come across two or even three generations of family members living together. In many cases, it was possible that these modest wooden structures could be modified, or even expanded, when needed and when circumstances allowed. In contrast, despite having a secure roof over their heads, the two-bedroom concrete public or low-cost flats (550–600 square feet) has made this an impossible option for residents. In response to criticisms of oppressive housing over the years, the newer generation of PPR flats now have slightly larger floor plans of 800 square feet with the choice of three bedrooms and one bathroom, or two bedrooms and two bathrooms.[7]

In addition to cramped residential spaces, an array of other everyday woes appears from time to time in local newspapers. These stories highlight concerns such as high levels of criminality and personal insecurity, low collection rates of maintenance fees, vandalism, and the poor upkeep of elevators, garbage disposal, and children's playgrounds.[8] My own observations in a number of these flats over the years corroborate these claims. Within a few short years of their occupation, the buildings often rapidly deteriorate in appearance and utility, given the high density of residents using them. Moreover, the design and layout of these structures heighten rather than disperse the potential for interpersonal frustration and frictions. This can range from intrusive sounds, like loud music and family quarrels, to strong smells from cooking, laundry, and garbage emanating from individual units and wafting into shared areas.[9] Compared to the organic morphology of squatter

**Figure 2.3 High-Rise Low-Cost Flats Built in the Late 1980s to Accommodate Squatters.** *Source*: Photo by author.

settlements, where residents from similar ethnic or religious backgrounds—if not kin—had tended to bunch together for security, and "buffer zones" were created when necessary (Yeoh, 2005a), the socio-spatial regime in PPR apartments has generated new challenges for everyday social cohesion, not least in the area of religious soundscapes. Because of the concentrated presence of Malay-Muslim residents in these ethno-religiously mixed apartments, nearby *suraus* and mosques have proliferated to facilitate the fulfilment of religious obligations. For disgruntled non-Muslim residents with whom I have spoken, the predawn call to worship (*azan*) announced through loud powerful speakers are often cited as intrusive "religious noise" and not of the same scale as prayers and worship rituals performed within and in front of their own units. But because of their perceived minority status and wishing to avoid altercations, they have largely suppressed outward displays of displeasure. More generally, however, most residents have learned to adapt to each other's presence through an array of everyday risk avoidance strategies.

In sum, the recent impressive development of Kuala Lumpur can be envisaged as a tale of two cities (King, 2008; Yeoh, 2014). Prior to the push to transform the Kuala Lumpur cityscape, the spectacle of urban poverty could be said to be embodied in the expansive squatter settlements it accommodated. These "unsightly" and "eyesore" structures have now been relegated to history, and significant strides have been made in providing affordable permanent housing for those displaced by the evictions. Nevertheless, the plight of the urban poor has merely shifted from public view to within the walls of modern-looking, low-cost housing.

## THE URBAN PRECARIAT

For decades, indicators of poverty in Malaysia have been determined through the Poverty Line Income (PLI) framework despite criticism that this approach underestimates poverty. Recently, a competing measure was adopted in the 11th Malaysian Plan (2016–2020). The Multidimensional Poverty Index (MPI) focuses on relative deprivation in the areas of health, education, and living standard. Notwithstanding this belated shift, inflationary pressures, rising costs in goods and services, and the removal of broad-based subsidies have translated into greater financial challenges for a significant portion of Kuala Lumpur's city dwellers, particularly the low-income laborers and the urban poor. Many of the latter have sought ways to supplement their incomes by taking on additional part-time jobs or setting up small food-vending businesses in their local neighborhoods and bazaars. In many cases, they face competition from foreign migrant workers willing to work for lower wages and longer hours, an attitude appreciated by cost-conscious Malaysia employers.

One manifestation of these interconnected trends has been the rising visibility of homelessness in downtown Kuala Lumpur (Yeoh, 2017). Recent estimates indicate a floating population of around 1,000–1,500 individuals cutting across ethno-religious and migrant groups. A sizeable proportion are elderly and single female parents. Not long after the tragic death of a two-year homeless Malay child in 2014, city authorities decided to forcibly remove and detain large numbers of the homeless population through increased legislative powers. Mobile soup kitchens servicing the homeless community were banned within a commercial shopping zone popular with foreign tourists, and the authorities noted that individuals caught giving alms would be fined. Municipal authorities rationalized their drastic actions in terms of maintaining hygiene and keeping the precinct clean of unsightly "eyesores." In response, civil society groups, together with concerned denizens, took to social media to rally support for the soup kitchens and to decry the actions of the city authorities. Many individuals also flocked to the streets at night to take turns standing vigil with homeless individuals and the mobile soup kitchens, and to face-off with the raiding officials. Others decided to buy and distribute packed food in defiance of the ban. During this period, mobile soup kitchens reported a substantial increase in food and cash donations, and in volunteers. The stand-off ended only when then prime minister Najib Abdul Razak unexpectedly turned up at one of the feeding stops of a long-established multiethnic mobile soup kitchen. Photos of his chit-chats went viral in social media. Thereafter, the authorities announced a "more consultative" approach with the soup kitchen providers.

Within the walls of high-rise low-cost flats, the issue of hunger and nutrition is not necessarily any better. In late 2017, UNICEF Malaysia released the findings from fieldwork conducted the prior year among 966 household heads and 2,142 children living in 17 low-cost flats and working-class neighborhoods in Kuala Lumpur (UNICEF, 2018). The report revealed that underweight (22%), stunting (23%), and wasting (32%) among children under the age of five living in Kuala Lumpur's PPR apartments are double the city's average (UNICEF, 2018). Moreover, the number of obese children is six times higher (23%), reflecting high consumption of low-cost, high calorie, nonnutritious foods among these same residents (UNICEF, 2018). The prevalence of malnutrition was also higher among four-year-olds than two-year-olds, reflecting the transition from breast milk to solid food (UNICEF, 2018). One in ten children eat fewer than three meals a day, and 97 percent of households cite high food prices as the key issue preventing parents from preparing healthy meals for their children (UNICEF, 2018). Additionally, while almost all the children between ages seven and seventeen are in school,

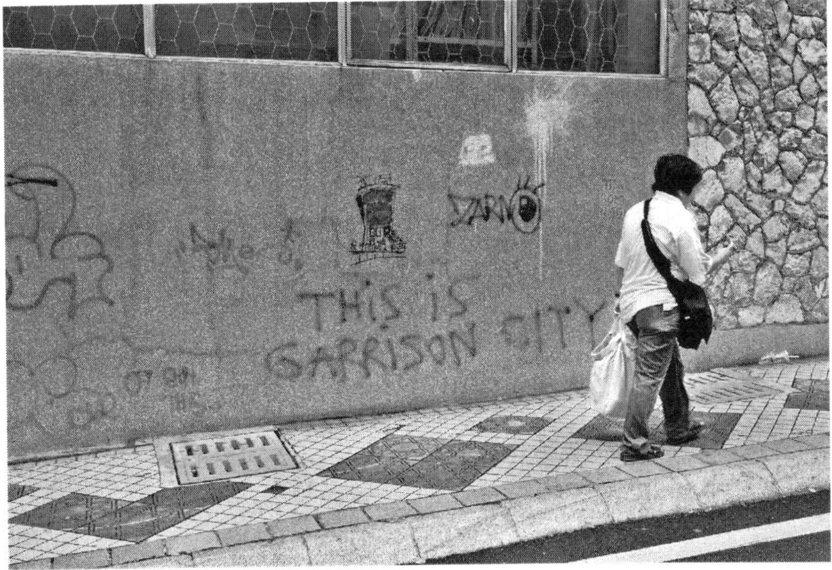


**Figure 2.4 Located Near to an Established Soup Kitchen in Downtown Kuala Lumpur.** *Source*: Photo by author.

only 50 percent of five- and six-year-olds attend preschool, compared with a 92 percent national enrollment (UNICEF, 2018). One in three of the households surveyed had no reading materials for children under eighteen, while four in ten households had no toys for children under five (UNICEF, 2018). Following the MPI format, 99.7 percent of children living in low-cost PPR flats in Kuala Lumpur are categorized as living in relative poverty, and 7 percent in absolute poverty (UNICEF, 2018).

A high-ranking government official disputed the claims of UNICEF Malaysia, contending that the situation is not as dire as depicted. He took offence to the report comparing Malaysia to Ghana, given the contrasting development status of the two countries. Moreover, he touted governmental subsidy programs like the BR1M which can provide immediate monetary relief for the urban poor and low-income groups, in addition to other projects that aim to economically uplift those in need (New Straits Times, 2018b).

## CONCLUSION

Following conventional indicators and barring any major economic hiccups, Malaysia is set to approach—if not reach—the holy grail of "developed country" status by 2020, three decades after this goal was first announced. The manifestations of this exponential transformation are most impressive in the capital city. Concurrent with national development, Kuala Lumpur is being recreated in line with the attributes of "World Class" city, and with the aspiration of admittance into the pantheon of Global Cities. However, as I have suggested in this chapter, this great leap forward has also been marked by narratives of violence, repression, and human suffering, largely shouldered by the urban poor and foreign migrant workers. Moreover, notwithstanding significant strides in the reduction of rural and urban poverty over the last three or four decades, the overall complexion of this transformative project continues to be hampered by racialized perspectives inherited from the British colonial era and mobilized by the postcolonial government's pragmatic politicking. Viewing socioeconomic inequities primarily in horizontal communal terms has informed the various policies implemented to remedy this malady. Notwithstanding the numerous criticisms of and serious flaws within this approach, a significant development has been the production of a large urban Malay middle class, primarily concentrated in Kuala Lumpur. They are also joined by a growing precariat class produced by the vagaries of a globally open national economy.

In May 2018, the landmark elections resulted in Barisan Nasional Party being ousted from power by the opposition coalition, Pakatan Harapan. This marked the first time since independence (in 1957) that the government changed hands. A few of the unpopular policies, like GST, were quickly abolished in keeping with preelection promises. Expectations were high that more systemic and deep-seated problems like corruption and racialized politics would be addressed, and Pakatan Harapan's bold election slogan of a New Malaysia will emerge and take root. Because of the "bad policies" of former prime minister Najib Abdul Razak hindering the fulfilment of Vision 2020, Pakatan Harapan launched a "Shared Prosperity Vision 2030" in its place.

Not long after the May 2018 general elections, I caught up with Letchumi at the morning wet market. She was perplexed about Barisan Nasional's defeat—given their aura of political invincibility over the decades. At the same time, she was also drawn to the new possibilities embodied in the election promises of Pakatan Harapan. Most pertinent were those of ridding the country of the legacy of racialized politics and uplifting economically underprivileged Malaysians like her regardless of their ethno-religious origins. A year later, her initial euphoria was tempered by the lack of concrete progress. Despite corruption prosecutions for many high-ranking political leaders, little tangible progress in decreasing the costs of everyday living seemed to have been made by Pakatan Harapan. Equally worrying, grassroots-based Malay-Muslim associations and political parties have been building alliances in preparation for the next elections. Their characteristic rallying cry is the need to fortify and defend Malay-Muslim interests against the perceived disenfranchisement of their "special status" in the milieu of cosmopolitan New Malaysia.

Not surprisingly, these dialectical forces and trends are felt most agonistically in the capital city of Kuala Lumpur, the premier site of World City formation and perpetual configuration of urban (in)equities in the country.

## NOTES

1. Prime Minister Mahathir Mohamad expressively wanted the Twin Towers to have "an identifiably Malaysian shape and incorporate some Islamic features . . . [and] . . . it would also become a Malaysian landmark, proof of what we have achieved, and a symbol of what we hoped to accomplish in the future" (Mahathir, 2011, p. 642).

2. It was observed that British Malaya had an "unusual degree of urbanization for a country where half the working population is engaged in agriculture and with very minor industrial development" (Cooper, 1951, p. 118). Between 1911 and 1970, urban growth in the peninsula outstripped the growth rate for the total population (Aiken & Leigh, 1975, p. 546).

3. This definition was adjusted with the 1970 census to 10,000 persons and above, then again with the 1991 census to reflect a more realistic level of urbanization. Inter alia, "urban areas" are delineated areas and their adjoining developments have urban characteristics and a combined population of 10,000 persons or more.

4. Between 2012 and 2017, around RM25.62 billion have been distributed. The number of recipients has ranged from 4.18 million (in 2012) to 7.2 million (in 2017) (New Straits Times, 2018a).

5. https://www.iom.int/countries/malaysia

6. To buttress their claims, these civil society groups coined the phrase, *peneroka bandar* (urban pioneers), in place of *setinggan*, in order to harken back to precolonial indigenous practices of land tenure (Ali, 1998; Hashim, 1994).

7. Currently, there are about 75,000 PPR units and low-cost apartments in Kuala Lumpur (The Star, 2018).

8. This situation is not confined to public housing. In 2016, a government survey of 7,325 high-rise residential properties in Peninsular Malaysia revealed that 69 percent of condominiums and apartments were managed at a standard ranked "below par" (Meikeng, 2016).

9. In early 2018, the dire living conditions of these high-rise low-cost flats once again come to public attention with the death of a teenager boy killed by a chair thrown out from the upper floors of a twenty-first-story flat (Ramlan, 2018).

## BIBLIOGRAPHY

Aiken, R.S., & Leigh, C.H. (1975). Malaysia's emerging conurbation. *Annals of the Association of American Geographers*, *65*(4), 546–563.

Ali, S.H. (1998). Squatters and forced evictions in Malaysia. In K. Fernandes (Ed.), *Forced evictions and housing rights abuses in Asia* (pp. 91–102). Karachi: City Press.

Chin, C.B.N. (1998). *In service and servitude: Foreign domestic workers and the Malaysian "modernity" project.* New York: Columbia University Press.

Cooper, E. (1951). Urbanisation in Malaya. *Population Studies, 5*(2), 117–131.

*Eleventh Malaysian plan 2016–2020: Anchoring growth on people.* (2015). Putrajaya, Malaysia: Economic Planning Unit, Prime Minister's Department.

Embong, A.R. (2001). *State-led modernisation and the new middle class in Malaysia.* Basingstoke, England: Palgrave.

Gomez, E.T., Padmanabhan, T., Kamaruddin, N., Bhalla, S., & Fisal, F. (2018). *Minister of finance incorporated: Ownership and control of corporate Malaysia.* Petaling Jaya, Malaysia: SIRD.

Gomez, E.T., Saravanamuttu, J., & Mohamad, M. (2013). Malaysia's new economic policy: Resolving horizontal inequalities, creating inequities? In E.T. Gomez & J. Saravanamuttu (Eds.), *The new economic policy in Malaysia: Affirmative action, ethnic inequalities and social justice* (pp. 1–30). Singapore: SIRD/NUS Press/ISEAS Publishing.

Gullick, J.M. (2000). *A history of Kuala Lumpur, 1857–1939.* Kuala Lumpur, Malaysia: Malaysian Branch of the Royal Asiatic Society.

Hashim, M.N. (1994). *Peneroka bandar menuntut keadilan* [Urban settlers seeking justice]. Kuala Lumpur, Malaysia: Daya Komunikasi.

Ishak, S. (2000). Economic growth and income inequality in Malaysia, 1971–95. *Journal of the Asia Pacific Economy, 5*(1/2), 112–124.

Johnstone, M. (1983). Housing policy and the urban poor in Peninsular Malaysia. *Third World Planning Review, 5*(3), 249–271.

Kahn, J. (2006). *Other Malays: Nationalism and cosmopolitanism in the modern Malay world.* Singapore: NUS Press.

Kaur, A. (1985). *Bridge and barrier: Transport and communications in colonial Malaya, 1870–1957.* Singapore: Oxford University Press.

King, R. (2008). *Kuala Lumpur and Putrajaya: Negotiating urban space in Malaysia.* Singapore: NUS Press.

Kratoska, P. (1985). The peripatetic peasant and land tenure in British Malaya. *Journal of Southeast Asian Studies, 16*(1), 16–45.

Lefebvre, H. (1991). *The production of space.* Oxford, England: Blackwell.

Leow, R. (2016). *Taming Babel: Language in the making of Malaysia.* Cambridge, England: Cambridge University Press.

Lim, H. (1978). *The evolution of the urban system in Malaya.* Kuala Lumpur, Malaysia: Penerbit Universiti Malaya.

Mahathir, M. (2011). *A doctor in the house: The memoirs of Tun Dr Mahathir Mohamad.* Petaling Jaya: MPH.

Meikeng, Y. (2016, September 25). Lower levels in high rise living. *The Sunday Star.* Retrieved from https://www.thestar.com.my/news/nation/2016/09/25/lower-levels-in-high-rise-living/.

New Straits Times. (2018a, March 7). Govt prepared to consider higher BR1M for urban poor. Retrieved from https://www.nst.com.my/news/government-public-policy/2018/03/342420/govt-prepared-consider-higher-br1m-urban-poor.

New Straits Times. (2018b, March 13). Malaysia's education Minister Mahdzir Khalid questions UNICEF report on malnourished kids among urban poor. Retrieved from https://www.straitstimes.com/asia/se-asia/malaysias-education-minister-mahdzir-khalid-questions-unicef-report-on-malnourished.

Parthiban, M. (2015). *Politics of the temporary: An ethnography of migrant life in urban Malaysia*. Petaling Jaya: SIRD.

Ragayah, H.M.Z. (2004). Income distribution and poverty eradication in Malaysia: Where do we go from here? In A.R. Embong (Ed.), *Globalisation, culture and inequalities: Essays in honour of the late Ishak Shari* (pp. 172–203). Bangi, Malaysia: Penerbit Universiti Kebangsaan Malaysia.

Ramlan, Y. (2018, January 17). Boy's death a glimpse into frustrations of low-cost flat dwellers. *The Malaysian Insight*. Retrieved from https://www.themalaysianinsight.com/s/32896/.

Reid, A. (1988). *Southeast Asia in the age of commerce, 1450–1680, Vol. 1*. New Haven, CT: Yale University Press.

Rimmer, P.J., & Allen, L.M. (Eds.). (1990). *The underside of Malaysian history: Pullers, prostitutes, plantation workers*. Singapore: Singapore University Press.

Sassen, S. (1994). *Cities in a world economy*. Thousand Oaks, CA: Pine Forge.

The Star. (2018, April 29). Making home ownership a reality. Retrieved from https://www.thestar.com.my/news/nation/2018/04/29/making-home-ownership-a-reality/.

UNICEF. (2018). *Children without: A study of urban children poverty and deprivation in low cost flats in Kuala Lumpur*. Putrajaya: UNICEF Malaysia.

Willford, A.C. (2014). *Tamils and the haunting of justice*. Honolulu, HI: University of Hawai'I Press.

Wong, D. (1975). *Tenure and land dealings in the Malay states*. Singapore: Singapore University Press.

Yeoh, Seng-Guan. (2001). Creolized utopias: Squatter colonies and the postcolonial city in Malaysia. *Sojourn: Journal of Social Issues in Southeast Asia, 16*(1), 102–24.

Yeoh, Seng-Guan. (2005a). House, kampung and taman: Spatial hegemony and the politic (and poetics) of space. *Crossroads: Interdisciplinary Studies for Southeast Asian Studies, 17*(2), 71–103.

Yeoh, Seng-Guan. (2005b). Managing sensitivities: Religious pluralism, civil society and interfaith relations in Malaysia. *The Round Table: Commonwealth Journal of International Affairs, 94*(382), 629–640.

Yeoh, Seng-Guan. (2010). Quotidian peace (and violence) in a squatter colony. In K.W. Francis Loh (Ed.), *Building bridges, crossing boundaries: Everyday forms of inter-ethnic peace in Malaysia* (pp. 117–146). Jakarta and Petaling Jaya: The Ford Foundation and Malaysian Social Science Association.

Yeoh, Seng-Guan (Ed.). (2014). *The other Kuala Lumpur: Living in the shadows of a globalising Southeast Asian city*. London and New York: Routledge.

Yeoh, Seng-Guan. (2017). The World Class city, the homeless and soup kitchens in Kuala Lumpur. *Current Sociology*. Special issue on Spatial Sociology edited by Martin Fuller and Martina Low, *65*(5), 571–586.

## Chapter 3

# Full of *My Love*

## *Notoriously Dangerous Informal Mass Transit in Maputo*

Joel Christian Reed

The first minibus did not have time to stop.[1] The second was able to zigzag but bounced off a car in the next lane and smashed into a light pole, blocking the road behind it entirely. A third minibus collided with the second, sustaining the most damage. After the pile-up, onlookers described the vehicles involved as heaps of scrap metal, barely recognizable. This took place on Maputo's *Circular*, a highway unlike most in Mozambique—newly built and pristine, but then littered with gas, oil, blood, and glass. Forty-two people went to the hospital that morning, fifteen in critical condition. Three were immediately admitted to surgery. Nine had multiple fractures, four of them compound. Five obtained internal abdominal injuries. Still others suffered facial wounds. Nobody died, but medical professionals described the outcome as a living nightmare for the survivors.[2] The cause of the crash was a carelessly executed lane change by an open bed truck carrying dozens of people, some seated and some standing up, all packed in the back—a common site in Maputo. Known colloquially as "my love" transport, these industrial vehicles stop and go throughout the city, picking people up, dropping them off, offering rides for pocket change.

*My love* are notoriously dangerous, not just for passengers but also for surrounding traffic. It is hard for drivers to see around the sides or use the mirrors, so it is up to everyone else to be careful. Mozambicans think it both a menace and necessity but are accustomed to *my love* transport on the streets of their capital city. There are not enough minibuses and taxis are too expensive, so this option emerged, occupying an unregulated market niche and a legal grey zone. Analyzing *my love* in the tradition of thick description[3] helps attend not only to such economic realities but also to messages relayed via these trucks and what they say about the social code. Like Ryle's wink

(Geertz & Darnton, 2017, p. 6), if done on purpose it was a conspiratorial gesture; if done involuntarily it was simply a twitch of the eye. To be able to debate the difference is one goal of ethnography, and whether *my love* are merely trucks or of significantly more cultural significance is up for interpretation. Here I will examine the risks and benefits Mozambicans see in *my love* in a time of rapid infrastructural modernization.

The objective of this chapter is to illustrate the importance of transport and road conditions to social experiences of inequality. One can become more aware of inequality through mobility; confronting others with different opportunity can refine a relative sense of vulnerability and access to resources. Mozambique has achieved nothing close to the "modern infrastructure ideal" (Graham & Marvin, 2001), the uniform vision underpinning normative concepts of safe and reliable transit. While the consequences are at times tragic, the persistence of *my love* transport carries strong implications and multiple meanings, serving as a public referendum. It is at once an index of failed government, economic progress, local innovation, and transformative potential. Occurring alongside large-scale state and market investment, *my love* is more than just informal transit: it is social mobilization for infrastructure, a grassroots means to access services, and (perhaps more subtly) a platform for engaging the government and making visible collective demands.

As an anthropologist employed by the Demographic and Health Surveys (DHS) Program, my visit in 2018 to Maputo is to train the next group of local fieldworkers for an upcoming malaria survey.[4] In collaboration with employees from Mozambique's Ministry of Health and National Statistics Institute, our routine requires long, daily travel back and forth to the training site, and excursions to peripheral areas to carry out fieldwork practicums. I have seen what awaits those who leave behind the comfortable confines of central Maputo—terrible road conditions, poor quality transport, and weak connections to underserved areas. As a former Fulbright Scholar in Mozambique, I rode *my love* many times. However, in my current professional role, I ride a government bus. Primary data are, therefore, based on observations, comments from colleagues and trainees, and events which occurred between March and May 2018. A round trip from central Maputo to an outlying suburb is described here to expose the subtle features of inequality in this beloved, cosmopolitan city. The suburb, a growing city called Matola, is less expensive and so close to Maputo that it absorbs the population overflow and consequences of gentrification discussed later in more detail.

The two cities trend closely together on several demographic characteristics. According to the last census, Maputo is the most populous city (INE, 2019), at 1.08 million persons, but Matola is catching up, at 1.03 million. As of 2018, the nation's entire population reached 28 million persons, 49 percent of whom are under fifteen years old (INS & ICF, 2019). A young nation,

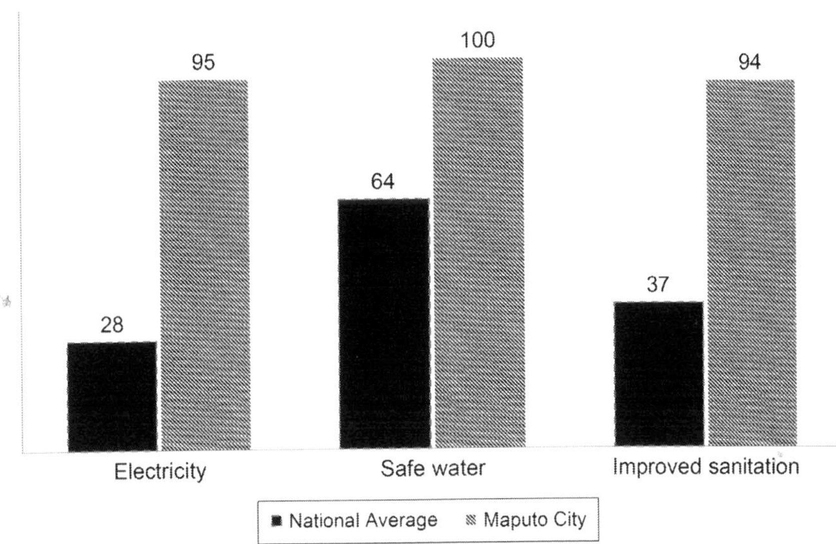


**Figure 3.1 Percentage of Households with Electricity, Safe Water, and Improved Sanitation.** Figure by author, data from (INS & ICF, 2019).

financially struggling and in search of opportunity, is unlikely to reject fast, cheap transport. Moreover, urban areas like these are more financially attractive than rural ones, containing 54 percent of the wealthiest class (INE, 2019). Cities are seven times more likely to have electricity in Mozambique (95 percent of Maputo residents have electricity, compared to just 28 percent of the nation, see figure 3.1) (INE, 2019). Other shortcuts to lifestyle upgrades include Mozambique's safest piped water (100 percent drink from improved water sources in Maputo, compared to 64 percent in the rest of the country), and adequate sewage and toilet facilities (94% of Maputo residents have improved sanitation, compared to 37% overall) (INES & ICF, 2019). A country free to choose these beneficial aspects of modernization sees roads and transport not as invasive or dangerous, but as desirable, unifying, and pregnant with dreams of success—altering perceptions of life's potential achievements.

## *MY LOVE*: INFRASTRUCTURE, POWER, AND VULNERABILITY

If roads affect the social and material landscape, so too do the people and vehicles who use them. The road network alone does not directly integrate a nation, and what people creatively do with roads does not follow automatically from state policy (Campbell, 2012; Thevenot, 2002). Roads are rightly critiqued for opening up territory to exploitation (Fahrig & Rytwinski, 2009), even facilitating kidnapping and war (Shepler, 2016). An increasing number of development scholars and social justice activists, however, are pro-road, noting their necessity in delivering the basic conditions of modern living, permitting the flow of goods and services, and in hardening the presence of the state—what Mann (2012) calls "infrastructural power." The continuing construction and usage of roads thrives not just as an economic tool but as a major political and ideological apparatus of state sovereignty, and, more importantly, also as a powerful element of an entirely new sociocultural condition (Dalakoglou, 2012).

The growing urban studies literature, moreover, has moved away from explaining why cities in the developing world fail to achieve the same infrastructural standards of cities in the more developed North (Lawhon, Nilsson, Silver, Ernstson, & Lwasa, 2018), shifting to an analysis of "what is there" and how people use it. Current accounts reframe infrastructure as hybrid (Furlong, 2014), as progressing ad-hoc or incrementally (Silver, 2014), as well as imperfect, peopled, and lived (Graham & McFarlane, 2014). The concept of "heterogeneous infrastructure configurations" (HICs), as pursued by Lawhon et al. (2018, p. 7), views infrastructures as geographically unique socio-technological artifacts. The idea of HICs moves beyond the framework of formal or informal, as well as debates over state, local, or private ownership and responsibility. This prevents overvaluing any one particular technology or intervention and permits considering how progress moves over time and in smaller steps. Despite the risks and drawbacks, *my love* complies with the idea of HICs as an integral component of Maputo's infrastructure, available for study and worthy of speculation.

The situation, on one hand, is a mildly rebellious one. The nonconformist nature of an innovation like *my love*, driven as it is by its own internal logic and practicality, places it outside the frame of much established debate on roads and road usage. The flouting of the rules suggests the mobilization of what Harvey and Knox call "impossible publics" (2015, p. 179), whose participation qualifies as an awkward form of engagement with the forces that govern their lives. Though these forces have determined, for example, which roads are the best, where taxis are to be stationed, or the maps and routes of legally approved public transit, the presence of *my love* suggests that more or different people demand some tangible benefit from Maputo's modernizing infrastructure than previously imagined. Using the same roads that other vehicles use, *my love* are not irreconcilable with preexisting infrastructural logic. However, this method of gaining attention qualifies as an alternative mode of publicity that is on many levels blunt, effective, and charged with the hope of reform.

On the other hand, the situation is one of some injustice. The dynamics that allow and contribute to *my love* have brutal consequences. Impaired or absent access to needed resources, such as mass transit, result from the materiality of the city and from people's placement within it. This changes the question of *why* people ride *my love*, to who *must* ride in the back of these trucks—namely, poor urbanites. Trucks and roads then become productive sites for exploring questions about the political economy of social suffering in cities. Given histories of planning and design decisions (Rabinow, 2003), spatial relations between city centers, suburbs, and squatter settlements (Caldeira, 2001), and how prejudice materializes in urban architecture to serve preexisting social hierarchies and distinctions (Mbembe, 2008), the harm done to already vulnerable groups of people exposes the social machinery of oppression discussed by scholars of structural violence (Farmer, 2004). Building upon this, the concept of "infrastructural violence" (Rodgers & O'Neill, 2012) reminds us that social suffering is often experienced in material terms (Miller, 2005). Though not attributable to any one actor or group of actors, the conditions under which infrastructure becomes violent, and for whom, becomes ethnographically graspable through looking at *my love* in and around Maputo City.

## WHY *MY LOVE*?

That *my love* circulate at all in Maputo is a symptom of an underlying crisis, primarily one of equity and disparity. With improving infrastructure comes increased congestion and accidents, 90 percent of which occur in developing nations (Banza et al., 2018; Gosselin, Spiegel, Coughlin, & Zirkle, 2009). Africa has the highest rate of road injuries compared to other world regions (WHO, 2015). Moreover, among the world's Portuguese-speaking countries, Mozambique is the leader in road deaths, at 31.6 per 10,000 people, about triple that of the United States (Lutxeque, 2015). The urban population in the country overall has risen from 22 percent in 1997, reaching 36 percent in 2011 and 46 percent in 2015 (INE, 1998; INE & MISAU, 2013; INS, 2015). Populations in towns and suburban centers closest to Maputo have tripled in the past ten years (INE, 2017), increasing demand for public transit in the capital more so than anywhere else.

This southeast African nation has the third worst roads in the world (WEF, 2014). While 64 percent of roads in Mozambique are considered to be in good condition, only 20 percent are paved, and these are restricted mostly to main trade and transit routes. Relatively reliable *terra batida* (or packed earth) dirt roads account for the other 80 percent, and are frequently traveled upon but usually uncomfortable. Of the 36 percent of roads in bad condition, about 6 percent are considered totally unpassable. The first attempt to classify Mozambique's roads was undertaken in 1931 by the Portuguese colonial government, which divided them into first, second, and third tiers (Neto, 2017).

The current government, led by the Frelimo Party, elaborated upon this system but continues to use these categories. There are now *estradas primárias, secundárias*, and *terciárias* (primary, secondary, and tertiary roads), each level less developed than the last, reflecting a pronounced asymmetry, and presenting mangled roadways for large industrial trucks used by *my love* to transverse.

There are hopes and means for improvement. In Maputo, several mega road projects have been undertaken in recent years, intended to unify the greater metropolitan area (Klopp & Cavoli, 2017). Investment in infrastructure is high but limited. The Maputo-Catembe Bridge, scheduled for completion in 2018, will be the largest suspension bridge in Africa, part of a US$700 million dollar project. The *Estrada Circular*, made up of six independent road sections intended to alleviate traffic in Maputo City, is a US$315 million dollar project. Upgrades to the *estradas nacionais* (national roads, or ENs) connecting Maputo with nearby Matola is a US$40 million dollar project. Such improvements are held up as evidence of the nation's progress and promoted as a public good (Andersen, Jenkins, & Nielsen, 2015).

Notably, however, for a nation that has constructed so many new roads, and enjoyed enormous economic and development gains recently (Mazzolini, 2017), the travel experience—especially for the urban underclass—remains stressful, burdensome, and dangerous. Seasonal downpours, flooding, and poor drainage leave streets prone to crumbling and degradation (Gascon, Rojas-Rueda, & Torrico, 2016). Increased traffic and haphazard driving lead to road rage and fiery crashes (Sambo, 2017). None of this deters commuters as they move back and forth between neighborhoods, crafting and consolidating networks to meet their needs. Indeed, reliance on *my love* confirms what prior scholars have noted, that the people have a collective voice in such developments through their everyday actions within and against existing systems, thus helping to construct the city (Gato & Salazar, 2018) and produce the urban landscape (Buckley, 2014).

*My love* are just as ubiquitous in Maputo as the standard minibus is in many other African cities. They are not licensed, but they do not have to hide; drivers often pay bribes if they get stopped. *My love* charge just as much to get from point A to point B as the minibuses (or *chapas)*, only without the added bonus of seats, roofs, windows, or doors. *My love* are notoriously uncomfortable and unsafe. Other than available space, there is no clear limit on the number of passengers who might climb aboard. Aside from luck, there is no protection from rain or shade from the sun. People regularly fall out of *my love*, and this is related to *my love*'s presence in neglected villages and neighborhoods with the bumpiest, muddiest, most degraded, and potholed roads.

Though Mozambique is a Portuguese-speaking country, it is *my love* and not *minha amor*—the term remains in English. As one of my colleagues remarked, it sounds less offensive and more elegant that way. The reason for this fond nickname—*my love* transport—is not because it is a preferred travel option. It is because people must hang on for dear life. Riding in *my love*, the best chance a person has for arriving safely to their destination is to wrap their arms around their neighbor, tightly, like lovers. As people do this, it gives the appearance of groups of happy couples shooting down the road in a glowing, caring embrace. The name *my love* is counterintuitive, because nobody really loves it. Defying what the urban ought to be, it is the sort of transport one would expect to see in an isolated rural area with no other options. Yet, Maputo, the capital city, is full of *my love*, which points to a burgeoning urban population, an increasing reliance on road transport, and the state's incapacity to get a handle on either.

## MAPUTO: FULL OF *MY LOVE*

At the continental scale, the narrative of "Africa rising" has dominated ideas of development success, particularly in the first decade of the twenty-first century (Brooks, 2017). Mozambique, war ravaged and impoverished in the 1980s, has experienced one of the highest GDP growth rates in sub-Saharan Africa in recent years.[5] Much of this has to do with the country's openness to foreign direct investment, which has fostered large-scale projects in aluminum, coal, and natural gas, as well as other extractive industries like emeralds, fishing, and timber. Mozambique has followed the policy prescriptions of major donors like the World Bank and IMF, receiving substantial amounts of overseas development assistance (Pérez Niño & Le Billon, 2014).

Partnerships with BRICS[6] countries have accelerated the nation's development (Carmody, 2013). Chief among these is China, which in addition to sponsoring several shopping malls, also rebuilt the Bank of Mozambique, extended the *marginal* avenue 20 miles along the beach to Marracuene, and undertook construction of a gigantic bridge to connect downtown Maputo to Catembe across the bay. These projects all range in the hundreds of millions of dollars, but the benefits were concentrated in already prosperous zones, illustrating how some sites in Maputo are favored more than others. The result is a stark, intense difference between the best and the worst of the city. Upon leaving the main thoroughfares—from which many visitors do not venture, but most locals must—the façade of progress crumbles and the veneer of improvement is not quite so glossy.

Maputo has a reputation as one of southern Africa's most charming cities (Da Silva, 2018). Known in colonial times as Lourenço Marques, it inherited many Portuguese architectural influences. Ambulatory plazas, acacia and jacaranda-lined streets, and larger-than-life monuments greet pedestrians at every turn. Freshly built modern high rises take their place alongside ornate traditional homes with red-tile roofs that could easily occupy Lisbon. Spiraling columns, vaulted arches, medieval turrets, and richly decorated verandas are commonplace features, even for buildings which house humble businesses. Traditional *azulejo* tiles,[7] with their interlocking geometric and floral motifs, can be found lining the walls both of expensive cafes and the more affordable local bars. Much of life is lived outside, whether dining, sipping espresso, dancing, or watching soccer on wide screen television.

This is what the city offers, but there are gradations to it and levels of access (Arndt, Jones, & Salvucci, 2015). Goods and services are grouped in cascading price points, and people self-sort according to class. Like many buzzing, popular cities, value gets more reasonable at a distance from the city center. A soda at a café on Julius Nyerere Avenue will cost ten times more than on Vladimir Lenin, just a few blocks away. This does not matter, though, to the right people. The Mozambican upper crust enjoys an exaggeratedly high standard of living. Though slightly more spacious, rent for the luxury condominiums in Maputo is on par with those in Manhattan, and such buildings include 24-hour doormen. Out of the elevators, nannies with strollers, and dog walkers with leashes descend to provide fresh air and relief to their respective charges. For other elites, expensive SUVs with tinted windows wait to whisk them away to any of the secure gated communities that have sprung up over the past few years. The economy is booming and life is getting better in Maputo, but not for everybody. There are uglier elements to the city that many try to ignore.

Outside the hotels and cafes, street sellers haunt the sidewalks, hawking everything from potato chips to cigarettes, cell phone credit, intricate wood carvings, and colorful local art. Standing just beyond the property line of the more upscale establishments, hawkers hold at eye level batiks of women carrying water on their heads, traditional cookware and table cloths, maps of the nation divided by ethnic group, and toy trucks made from Coke cans, plastic straws, and chicken wire. Beggars, some of them children, follow tourists for blocks, calling out in English "my friend," and asking for money, food, or other help. Not far from the sites that most interest visitors, the sidewalks are cracked, broken, or incomplete. Cars park there and along the medians, blocking walkways and forcing people into the streets, where drivers honk, weave, and try their best to avoid striking pedestrians. There are traffic bottlenecks, even on foot. Corners with bus stops are unpassable during rush hours, clogged with people waiting to board the next *chapa*. When it arrives, fights sometimes break out over who gets to cram inside. The losers wait for the next one, or for *my love* if they are willing, as most are.

Maputo has undergone changes over the years due to both formal and informal planning (Roque, Mucavele, & Noronha, 2016). Prior to independence, the center of town was known as *Cidade de Cimento*, the city of cement or concrete. This area was the more organized colonial section, designed with straight roads and city blocks, and where Portuguese administrators and immigrants dwelled. It was surrounded by informal settlements known as *Cidade de Caniço*, the city of reeds, where black Mozambicans lived in shacks made from cheaper materials. Today these colonial distinctions are less obvious. *Cidade de Caniço* is fully incorporated in the city's fabric as neighborhoods, *bairros*, with relatively well-developed roads, piped water, and electricity.

However, the colonial legacy is still felt, especially spatially. Luxury hotels, expensive restaurants, shopping malls, and an upscale housing market dominate what was *Cidade de Cimento*. The more crowded *bairros* suffer from flooding, infrastructural decay, and more frequent interruptions to power and other basic services. Gentrification has forced some residents to relocate to the periphery, more distant *subúrbios* (suburbs) where land is cheaper and more available, but still appealing as an investment. People now occupy the *subúrbios* in the same way they claimed the *Cidade de Caniço* during colonial times, in the hopes that the city will absorb them, and that proximity to wealth and centers of accumulation will translate into the promise of a better future for them, their families, and their children.

Residents in and around Maputo live lives that depend on movement, traveling frequently across the different zones of the city (Piscitelli, 2018). Circulation between the periphery (the *subúrbios)* and central Maputo (*Cidade de Cimento* and the *bairros*) is costly in terms of time, patience, stress, and even lives. Maputo depends on this connectedness, and thrives on the constant relay of commodities for sale and people for cheap labor. The city is building up as well as building out (CNN, 2015)—construction cranes dot the landscape of central Maputo, constantly erecting new high rises and office parks. But it is the building out aspect that is most worrisome for climate scientists and for those with concerns about urban quality of life. As in colonial times, Maputo's "urban metabolism" (Zhang, Yang, & Yu, 2015) is much healthier at the core than at the periphery. Highly segregated poorer residents bear the brunt of modernization and progress. This hidden debt includes traffic fatalities and congestion, social dysfunction, environmental degradation, and harmful effects on personal and community health (Capps, Bentsen, & Ramírez, 2015; Rakodi, 2005).

## THE EN2 AND EN4 TO MATOLA

A single trip to Matola shows its economic vitality; the city has a densely populated and still expanding industrial and commercial zone. It is home to chemical plants, Coca-Cola, a brewery, aluminum and concrete factories, cereal processors and grain silos, gas distributors, pharmaceutical and glass manufacturers, and corporate offices for multinationals like Shell. Countless warehouses and businesses dot the road to Matola. There are plenty of strip malls, gas stations, and mega supermarkets. It is the very definition of urban sprawl, although the scenery is not entirely concrete.

Leaving central Maputo in our government bus on the EN2 (see figure 3.2), we cross marshland at sea level, where the highway cuts through a field of tall green grass. On the left in the distance is the ocean, the Maputo Bay cityscape with its high-rise office buildings, and the half-built bridge to Catembe. On the right, a lone shack emerges with a woman sweeping her backyard. Closer

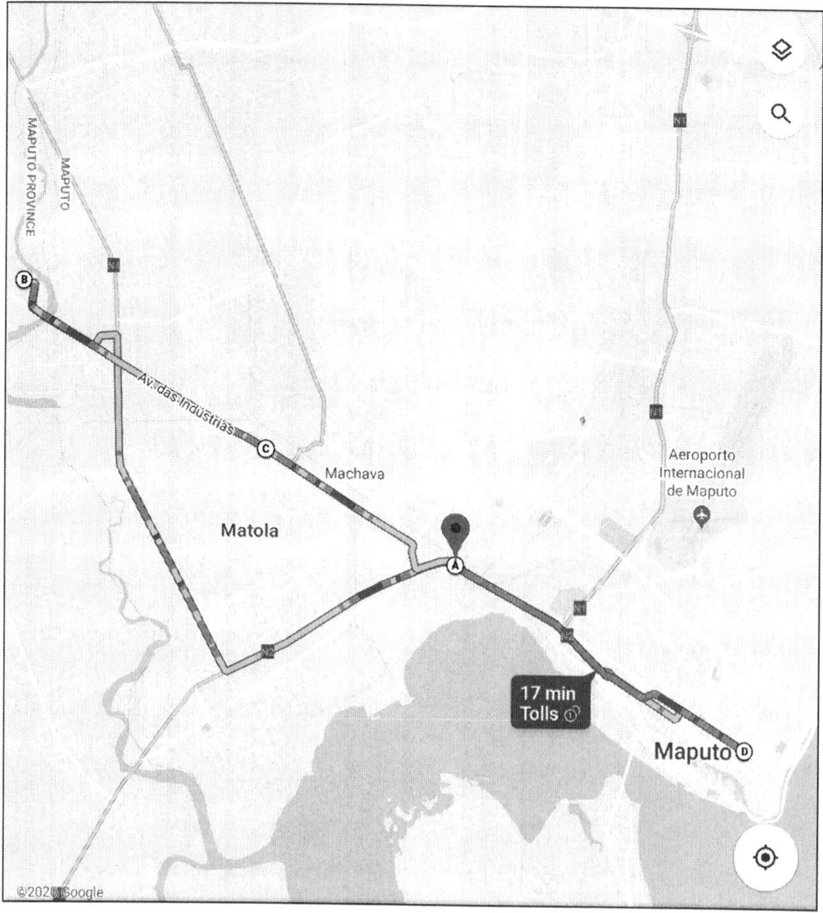


**Figure 3.2 Maputo to Matola Map.** *Source*: (Google Maps).

to the road, some chickens peck the ground for food, oblivious to the parade of cars and their noxious emissions. Just before the toll booth (or *portagem* in Portuguese, and on the map), I spot a sign stating "Slow Down Please Don't Kill Us" in English, but, because nobody dares to walk, it is not clear who put it there or whom exactly benefits.

It is a visual shock when the toll booth appears, like a giant, uncaring, but very efficient fortress, all metal, and clearly South African built. The paint isn't peeling. The roof is angled to optimize shade and let the rain runoff. It costs about 50 cents per car, more for larger vehicles. To pay, twelve stalls serving both directions should be sufficient, but it is always backed up, especially if going with traffic. The effects of toll roads have been debated by academics (Glaister & Graham, 2006; Inturri & Ignaccolo, 2011). The idea that they may harm equity by pricing poor people off the roads is countered by the likely increase of informal transport. There are enough *my love* around, hauling people in the back like sacks of charcoal, suggesting that is the case. There are concerns, too, that drivers will divert to alternative routes, with unintended consequences (Van Dijk, Krygsman, & de Jong, 2015). Nobody gets around the toll booth, unless by cutting through neighborhoods, which avoids the fee but creates other, potentially worse, complications.

As we stop to pay the toll, I become aware of our privilege. In the thirty-passenger government bus with my local counterparts, we have many empty seats. People in the *chapas* and big city buses coming from the other direction are packed inside like sardines, their arms, hands, and faces smashed against the glass almost comically, as if in a cartoon. When I catch their eyes, I do not laugh. They look checked-out and vacant, hundreds of people with each lost in their own dizzying array of thoughts.

About 44,000 vehicles pass through the Maputo-Matola toll every day, chiefly commuters (Voice of America, 2017). Vehicles paying with cash are at a disadvantage. Our bus, however, has a prepaid transponder. We aim toward the prepaid line, which moves a bit faster due to the automatic gate. Lines are long, and cars can get stuck here if people are not creative. Our driver seizes a moment to zip around a group of dump trucks, creating his own lane where there was none before, securing us an earlier place in line. Everyone is trying to get somewhere at the same time—students, workers, and women selling peanuts.

Just before we reach downtown Matola, two things rise above the palm trees—cell phone towers and electrical lines. We pass two pedestrian bridges interspersed among the houses, bars, and patches of corn and cassava. It is easy to accelerate in these open stretches, trying to squeak through yellow lights, and make up for lost time. We turn right on the EN4, a road infamous for the number and severity of car crashes, despite being newly repaired and perfectly paved. In the first two months of 2018 alone, seventy-six accidents occurred on the EN4 resulting in deaths or injuries (Sambo, 2018a). In one of the worst ever accidents, a single vehicle killed twenty-seven youngsters, mostly kids under thirty years old, as they celebrated *carnaval*[8] (Lusa, 2018). The driver, probably drunk, ignored police orders to stop, lost control, and jumped the curb, where the party was occurring. The vehicle tumbled into its victims, killing twenty-seven and sending another thirty-one people to the hospital.

Local news sources are awash with such tragedies, blaming drivers for negligence and public institutions for poor law enforcement (Verdade, 2014). Between the National Transit Police, the Ministry of Transport and Communication, and the National Institute of Road Transport, all of which claim some jurisdiction over traffic and infrastructure, regulation appears to have little positive effect. Mozambique is the only southern African nation that requires all drivers to attend driving school, but on average thirty people die weekly, even on the *estradas primárias* and *secundárias*, which the government brands as successful symbols of modern development. The contract for repairs to the EN4 alone was valued at about US$40 million (Verdade, 2014). Due to landmine removal—a relic of the wars fought by Mozambique's communist government before and after independence—the private company[9] which took on the EN4 contract called it one of the most dangerous roads in the world when they first began work on the project. Despite the excellent asphalt, bridges, markings, and signage that make travel seem safer now, the EN4 remains haunted by unseen traps and potential death.

## AVENIDA DA INDÚSTRIAS

We turn left from the EN4 onto *Avenida da Indústrias* (Avenue of Industry), a secondary road that starts in Maputo but turns tertiary as it traverses Matola. This change is first marked by the transition from asphalt to *terra batida*, an unpaved road. Due to frequent use, it is bumpy and unwelcoming, marred by countless holes and ditches. Alongside the road, there is a bustling outdoor market that serves the rapid growth of housing construction of housing in this area. Ten years ago, the area consisted of rural villages and unoccupied bush, but now gated communities and two- to three-story homes dominate. Laid out on the side of the road for quick and easy purchase are piles of sand, crushed rock, and bags of cement, all ingredients for mixing concrete. Sitting on the shelves of makeshift market stalls, beside tomatoes, onions, and mounds of dried fish, are PVC pipes, coiled-up water hoses, and car parts such as gas caps, rubber belts, and mufflers. Scenery on the *Avenida da Indústrias* is more diverse than on the EN4. Women market vendors mingle with construction workers, school teachers, and white-collar government employees living one hour's drive from their jobs in Maputo City.

There is gridlock even on this side street. The stop light governing the main entrance and intersection is out—and has been for weeks—causing backups, angst, and loss of patience. It is the rainy season, so in some places the road has disappeared under massive puddles of water, forcing vehicles to a crawl as they seek the surest path, swerving at almost 90-degree angles which, at higher speeds, would cause them to tip and roll over. Some of the water-logged sections are the size of swimming pools and take up the entirety of what should be the road. Not by law, but by unspoken contract, the bigger vehicles have the right of way. Smaller cars follow them gingerly through the puddles after gauging the depth and whether or not they will be able to make it through. Given the state of the road, no minibuses or other public transport pass by here. The only option, for those without private vehicles, are the open bed *my love* trucks which circulate at high frequency. Predictably, one or two arrive every ten minutes, quickly filling with passengers.

Some *my love* are full-sized dump trucks—Canter, Toyota Dyna, Tata, and Townace brands—carrying sand and gravel back and forth to construction sites. Owners of companies and project supervisors cannot control it, but drivers take advantage of return trips. On one leg of their journey, after dropping off a regular load, they carry people in the back instead of their initial product. In these cases, the truck beds are so deep and the walls are so high that they completely obscure the occupants. People cannot climb out on their own. The driver must exit the cab, fasten a ladder to the back, and open the large metal gate, which serves as a door. Many people are packed inside, perhaps one to two hundred. When the gate is lowered, some exit the dump truck, coughing with handkerchiefs or shirts covering their mouths. To avoid police stops and fines, the dump trucks take the dirt roads whenever possible. They are found outside schools when classes adjourn, ready to serve as informal school buses.

Completing our work day in Matola, we discover that the EN4 is horribly backed up. The congestion is, first, related to an overabundance of semitrailer trucks coming from the South African border. But there is another reason—an intense downpour of rain recently started. Mozambique is well known for periodic flooding and 2018 was one of the worst years in recent memory: an estimated 80,000 people in the northern provinces were either displaced or made homeless (Domingos, 2018). Rains caused an avalanche of trash at the Hulene garbage dump in Maputo, killing seventeen people as it collapsed on their houses (Davies, 2018). In Matola this day, downpours were causing severe disruption, felling electric poles and trees, flooding streets and homes, and opening up craters that delayed traffic for hours (Noticias, 2018). Instead of the EN4, our driver decides to return to Maputo via *Avenida da*

*Indústrias*, taking what should have been a shortcut through the neighborhood of Machava.

We quickly discover why this road is less traveled. It is mixed residential and industrial, with just two lanes closely flanked on either side by homes, bars, medium-sized factory lots, warehouses, gas stations, and small shops. There is no room for trailblazing, no space to swerve and avoid potholes, which must be met head on. The pavement in places is terribly broken, forcing the smaller cars in front of us come to an almost complete stop to prevent damaging the undercarriage. Visibility is bad. The rain is falling so hard that the street looks more like a river, cars more like boats, and sidewalks more like muddy banks. The choicest tracks for cars to take are few, and jealously fought over. As one vehicle after another follows the leader, long, impenetrable lines form, encroaching onto the wrong side of the street and blocking the intersections. Like soldier ants, the trail of cars becomes thick and difficult to interrupt. Even a large bus like ours finds itself stuck, boxed in, and unable to advance. The only available strategy is to inch forward, making near bumper-to-body contact with the car blocking our path, threatening to proceed and strike. It is an effort at intimidation that the next driver takes seriously. He stops and lets us by. Staring out from inside the bus, I see similar scenes playing out for other cars around us.

Pedestrians returning home are wading in water up to their ankles, covering their heads with newspapers, sacks, and backpacks. Riders in the back of *my love* have umbrellas open, hunkered closely together, protected not by glass or seatbelts but only by the colorful nylon with Scotch Guard sealant that most Americans carry with them in their purse, backpack, or car. Our trip back to Maputo takes two and a half hours when it should have taken one. We ride past homes with critical flood damage, on poorly lit streets where the electricity is out. Another stretch of highway, the "ring road" (AllAfrica, 2018), should have been open by now, connecting Matola to Maputo and providing relief from such chaos. An unsubstantiated rumor suggests the contracted company is holding out, waiting for the EN2 toll road to recoup more funds before opening the new detour. True or not, the rumor reveals people's dissatisfaction, registered each day in the congestion, delays, damage to vehicles, wasted fuel, and crashes.

## CONCLUSION: INTERPRETING *MY LOVE*

Associated ambiguously with both opportunity and death, *my love* are more than mere trucks. They are fueled not just by gasoline, but by forces ranging from desperation, entrepreneurship, (in)efficiency, exploitation, and the pursuit of private gain. Symbolically, they represent freedom, the best chance to get to work, school, or business. Practically, they function as cheap and accessible mass transit in a place of immense shortage. *My love* are exceedingly important in the *subúrbios*. With just a 13 percent rise in population in the last twenty years, compared with a 210 percent rise in the periphery (INE, 2017), Maputo City is effectively emptying out. *My love* serve these commuters, absorbed and ejected at fixed times by their places of study or work, who can or must make difficult trips like the one described in this chapter on a regular basis. Attached to the hope of reform and economic advancement, these so-called peripheral areas share the same high levels of potential as did the colonial core of the city (Viana, 2015). The unstated preference is that they be fully integrated and made accessible by any means.

The advantages of this arrangement include the maintenance of the charm of central Maputo at little cost to visitors or the upper class. The disadvantages are born in the periphery by the majority, climbing aboard *my love*, arriving each day to school or work inscribed in a world order that points to road travel as an irreversible, nonnegotiable necessity. *Cidade de Caniço* and *Cidade de Cimento* combined long ago, giving rise to a city center with unified *bairros*. Likewise, the *subúrbios* can no longer be separated from greater Maputo. Linked by transportation, the city has become a metropolitan area.

"To live with dignity, our population growth must be accompanied by adequate infrastructure," Mozambique's president Nyusi said during a recent visit to Matola: "Where good infrastructure doesn't yet exist, it is your right to demand it" (Office of the president of Mozambique, 2018, my translation). This statement affirms the state's approach to infrastructure as a public good, at the same time acknowledging the people's role in spurring its progress. All the stakeholders agree that urban mobility must be expanded. *My love*, by this logic, fulfills a vital mission, as the answer to the minibus shortage, and as the supply for the demand to which Nyusi alludes—but without official government approval.

Economic pressures of everyday life for the poor foster reliance on *my love* to fill vital transit needs. Riots in 2008 and 2010 (Casciani, 2010) highlighted economic discontent with inflation and food and gas prices and were effective, forcing the government to back down. That recent history may explain why no official administrative measures are taken against *my love* (Folha de Maputo, 2016). This exceptionality, however, leaves the nation free to develop its fantastic new bridges, toll booths, and even new transport options like the recently introduced light rail Metrobus which prices poor people out of the market without fear of retribution from poor urbanites (see AllAfrica, 2017).

Maputo thrives on high tolerance of the informal (Rogerson, 2017). Remaking the front stage of the nation in the form of multimillion-dollar road and bridge projects signals emancipation, liberation, and hope for collective improvement.

Yet, it is impossible to eliminate the everyday self-organizational strategies of its citizens (Salazar, Broto, & Adams, 2017). In all likelihood, *my love* will continue to be a popular transport option and an important part of everyday life in the city. More work could be done on this topic. Anthropologists do not study roads and trucks; we study *on* the roads and *in* the trucks. This effort at a thick description of the context of *my love* points to the need for more systematic research with riders, owners, families, government officials, and traffic authorities managing the impacts of this reality on a long-term basis.

Are riders of *my love* "impossible publics" or victims of infrastructural violence? Are they "winking" at the state, or "twitching" involuntarily just to get the ride? The action of climbing aboard *my love* remains the same regardless of intent, making these distinctions dependent upon context, the nature or urgency of the voyage, and the attitudes and identities of specific participants. Exploring such questions in detail could be the aim of future ethnography, along with whether *my love* qualify as civil protest or state malfeasance. For now, the radical heterogeneity of *my love*, while risky and irresponsible, represents incremental progress, granting mobility without creating enough friction to be banned. Mobility may increasingly become an indicator of successful equality, requiring more insight into the qualities of mobility itself and making the safety and reliability of transport one of the least understood social justice and global health issues today.

Regarding *my love*, there is unspoken mutual agreement that the risks are worth the rewards. Whether viewed as a problem or answer, *my love* is evidence of the ways in which roads are accessed by a collective majority. The trucks and their riders represent economic dynamics of how change occurs, suggesting people will find ways of integrating and working toward a future vision.

## NOTES

1. The author would like to acknowledge colleagues at the Instituto Nacional de Saúde (INS) and Instituto Nacional de Estastícas (INE) for the company on these long daily rides and the conversation that led to the chapter topic.

2. Emildo Sambo (2018b), correspondent at *Verdade Online*, captured these unfortunate moments in print from this accident that occurred on April 22, 2018.

3. For Clifford Geertz (2017) and other interpretive anthropologists, the task of "reading" the culture is paramount. The approach permits the accurate reporting of data while encouraging subjective contextual conclusions in a creative prose style to make the researcher's findings more valuable and accessible to others.

4. My professional work involves extended travel to Mozambique to support and implement surveys conducted by the Demographic and Health Surveys (DHS) Program, in partnership with host country governments and funded by USAID.

5. Mozambique's gross domestic product rose 675 percent from 1990 to 2014, from US$2.5 to US$16.9 billion (World Bank, 2018). Still, the country ranks 181 out of 187 on the United Nations Human Development Index (UNDP, 2016), a low position shared with South Sudan.

6. BRICS stands for Brazil, Russia, India, China, and South Africa.

7. For a fascinating overview of *azulejo* tiles including their importance to the culture of the Iberian Peninsula, see Coentro et al. (2017).

8. A celebration that typically occurs just prior to Ash Wednesday and the beginning of Lent in predominately Christian nations. Inexplicably, it is often celebrated *during* Lent in Mozambique, as was the case here.

9. Toll roads along the EN2 and EN4 are controlled by Trans Africa Concessions, a private company responsible for highways all the way to Witbank in neighboring South Africa (www.tracn4.co.za).

## BIBLIOGRAPHY

AllAfrica. (2017, December 20). Mozambique: Test run for metrobus. *Agencia de Informacao de Mocambique (Maputo)*. Retrieved from http://allafrica.com/stories/201712200118.html.

AllAfrica. (2018, March 15). Mozambique: Maputo ring road still not complete. *Agencia de Informacao de Mocambique (Maputo)*. Retrieved from http://allafrica.com/stories/201803150467.html.

Andersen, J.E., Jenkins, P., & Nielsen, M. (2015). Who plans the African city? A case study of Maputo: Part 1—the structural context. *International Development Planning Review*, *37*(3), 329–350. https://doi.org/10.3828/idpr.2015.20.

Arndt, C., Jones, S., & Salvucci, V. (2015). When do relative prices matter for measuring income inequality? The case of food prices in Mozambique. *The Journal of Economic Inequality*, *13*(3), 449–464. https://doi.org/10.1007/s10888-015-9303-5.

Banza, L.N., Gallaher, J., Dybvik, E., Charles, A., Hallan, G., Gjertsen, J.-E., … Young, S. (2018). The rise in road traffic injuries in Lilongwe, Malawi: A snapshot of the growing epidemic of trauma in low income countries. *International Journal of Surgery Open*, *10*, 55–60. https://doi.org/10.1016/j.ijso.2017.11.004.

Brooks, A. (2017). Was Africa rising? Narratives of development success and failure among the Mozambican middle class. *Territory, Politics, Governance*, 1–21. https://doi.org/10.1080/21622671.2017.1318714.

Buckley, M. (2014). On the work of urbanization: Migration, construction labor, and the commodity moment. *Annals of the Association of American Geographers*, *104*(2), 338–347. https://doi.org/10.1080/00045608.2013.858572.

Caldeira, T.P.R. (2001). *City of walls: Crime, segregation, and citizenship in São Paulo*. Berkeley, CA: University of California Press.

Campbell, J.M. (2012). Between the material and the figural road: The incompleteness of colonial geographies in Amazonia. *Mobilities*, *7*(4), 481–500. https://doi.org/10.1080/17450101.2012.718429.

Capps, K.A., Bentsen, C.N., & Ramírez, A. (2015). Poverty, urbanization, and environmental degradation: Urban streams in the developing world. *Freshwater Science*, *35*(1), 429–435. https://doi.org/10.1086/684945.

Carmody, P. (2013). *The rise of the BRICS in Africa: The geopolitics of south-south relations*. New York: Zed Books.

Casciani, D. (2010, September 1). Deadly Maputo clash over prices. *BBC*. Retrieved from https://www.bbc.com/news/world-africa-11150063.

CNN. (2015, March 16). Maputo, capital of Mozambique, is on the rise. *CNN Travel*. Retrieved from https://www.cnn.com/travel/article/mozambique-maputo-boomtown/index.html.

Coentro, S., Alves, L.C., Relvas, C., Ferreira, T., Mirão, J., Molera, J., … Muralha, V.S.F. (2017). The glaze technology of Hispano-Moresque ceramic tiles: A comparison between Portuguese and Spanish collections. *Archaeometry*, *59*(4), 667–684. https://doi.org/10.1111/arcm.12280.

Dalakoglou, D. (2012). 'The road from capitalism to capitalism': Infrastructures of (post)socialism in Albania. *Mobilities*, *7*(4), 571–586. https://doi.org/10.1080/17450101.2012.718939.

Da Silva, J.J. (2018). Espaço público, lazer e qualidade de vida em Maputo, Moçambique. *Boletim Campineiro de Geografia*, *7*(2), 343–359.

Davies, R. (2018, February 20). Mozambique – 17 dead in Maputo as garbage dump collapses. *Floodlist*. Retrieved from http://floodlist.com/africa/mozambique-maputo-garbage-collapse-february-2018.

Domingos, A. (2018, February 20). Mozambique: Floods displace thousands in Mozambique. *CAJ News Agency (Johannesburg)*. Retrieved from http://allafrica.com/stories/201802200635.html.

Fahrig, L., & Rytwinski, T. (2009). Effects of roads on animal abundance: An empirical review and synthesis. *Ecology and Society*, *14*(1). Retrieved from https://www.jstor.org/stable/26268057.

Farmer, P. (2004). An anthropology of structural violence. *Current Anthropology*, *45*(3), 305–325. https://doi.org/10.1086/382250.

Folha de Maputo. (2016, February 8). Anunciada a Morte do My Love. *Folha de Maputo*. Retrieved from http://www.folhademaputo.co.mz/pt/noticias/nacional/anunciada-a-morte-do-my-love/.

Furlong, K. (2014). STS beyond the "modern infrastructure ideal": Extending theory by engaging with infrastructure challenges in the South. *Technology in Society*, *38*, 139–147. https://doi.org/10.1016/j.techsoc.2014.04.001.

Gascon, M., Rojas-Rueda, D., & Torrico, S. (2016). Urban policies and health in developing countries: The case of Maputo (Mozambique) and Cochabamba (Bolivia). *Public Health Open J*, *1*(2), 24–31. https://doi.org/10.17140/PHOJ-1-106.

Gato, L.G., & Salazar, N.B. (2018). Constructing a city, building a life: Brazilian construction workers' continuous mobility as a permanent life strategy. *Mobilities*, 1–13. https://doi.org/10.1080/17450101.2018.1466504.

Geertz, C., & Darnton, R. (2017). *The Interpretation of Cultures* (3rd ed.). New York, NY: Basic Books.

Glaister, S., & Graham, D.J. (2006). Proper pricing for transport infrastructure and the case of urban road congestion. *Urban Studies*, *43*(8), 1395–1418. https://doi.org/10.1080/00420980600776475.

Gosselin, R.A., Spiegel, D.A., Coughlin, R., & Zirkle, L.G. (2009). Injuries: The neglected burden in developing countries. *Bulletin of the World Health Organization*, *87*(4), 246–246a.

Graham, S., & Marvin, S. (2001). *Splintering urbanism: Networked infrastructures, technological mobilities and the urban condition*. New York: Routledge.

Graham, S., & McFarlane, C. (Eds.). (2014). *Infrastructural lives: Urban infrastructure in context*. New York, NY: Routledge.

Harvey, P., & Knox, H. (2015). *Roads: An anthropology of infrastructure and expertise*. Ithaca, New York: Cornell University Press.

INE & MISAU. (2013). *Inquérito Demográfico e de Saúde 2011*. Maputo, MZ: INE and Macro International.

Instituto Nacional de Estastícas (INE). (1998). *Inquérito Demográfico e de Saúde 1997* (p. 283) [Demographic and health studies report]. Maputo, MZ: INE and Macro International.

Instituto Nacional de Estastícas (INE). (2017). *Divulgação dos Resultados Preliminares IV* (p. 4) [Recenseamento Geral da População e Habitação]. Maputo, MZ: Instituto Nacional de Estatísticas.

Instituto Nacional de Estastícas (INE). (2019). *Resultados Definitivos, Censo 2017* [IV Recenseamento Geral da População e Habitação]. Maputo, MZ: Instituto Nacional de Estatísticas.

Instituto Nacional de Saúde (INS). (2015). *Inquérito de Indicadores de Imunização, Malária e HIV/SIDA em Moçambique 2015 (IMASIDA)* (p. 507). Maputo, MZ e Rockville, MD, EUA: ICF Internacional.

Instituto Nacional de Saúde (INS) & ICF. (2019). *Inquérito Nacional sobre Indicadores de Malária em Moçambique 2018*. Maputo, Moçambique; Rockville, Maryland, EUA: INS e ICF.

Inturri, G., & Ignaccolo, M. (2011). Modelling the impact of alternative pricing policies on an urban multimodal traffic corridor. *Transport Policy*, *18*(6), 777–785. https://doi.org/10.1016/j.tranpol.2011.04.002.

Klopp, J.M., & Cavoli, C.M. (2017). The paratransit puzzle: Mapping and master planning for transportation in Maputo and Nairobi. In T.P. Uteng & K. Lucas (Eds.), *Urban mobilities in the global south* (pp. 95–110). New York: Routledge.

Lawhon, M., Nilsson, D., Silver, J., Ernstson, H., & Lwasa, S. (2018). Thinking through heterogeneous infrastructure configurations. *Urban Studies*, *55*(4), 720–732. https://doi.org/10.1177/0042098017720149.

Lusa, A. (2018). Despiste de veículo ligeiro mata 23 pessoas em Maputo. *Observador*. Retrieved from https://observador.pt/2018/03/25/despiste-de-veiculo-ligeiro-mata-23-pessoas-em-maputo/.

Lutxeque, S. (2015). Moçambique lidera índice de mortes por acidentes de viação na CPLP. *DW.Org*. Retrieved from http://www.dw.com/pt-002/mo%C3%A7ambique

-lidera-%C3%ADndice-de-mortes-por-acidentes-de-via%C3%A7%C3%A3o-na-cplp/a-18877018.

Mann, M. (2012). *The sources of social power: Volume 4, globalizations, 1945–2011*. New York: Cambridge University Press.

Mazzolini, A. (2017). An urban middle class and the vacillation of "informal" boundaries—insights from Maputo, Mozambique. *Geography Research Forum, 36*, 68–85.

Mbembe, A. (2008). Aesthetics of superfluity. In S. Nuttall & A. Mbembe (Eds.), *Johannesburg, the elusive metropolis* (pp. 37–67). Durham, NC: Duke University Press.

Miller, D. (Ed.). (2005). *Materiality*. Durham, NC: Duke University Press.

Neto, A.G. de J. (2017). A circulação interna de mercadorias no território moçambicano: um país sobre rodas. *GeoTextos, 13*(2). https://doi.org/10.9771/1984-5537geo.v13i2.23319.

Noticias. (2018). Chuvas transtornam em Maputo e Matola. *Jornal Notícias*. Retrieved from http://www.jornalnoticias.co.mz/index.php/capital/76214-chuvas-transtornam-em-maputo-e-matola.

Office of the president of Mozambique. (2018, April 27). "Exigir instalação de infraestruturas é um direito"—Presidente Nyusi/Actualidade/Início—Portal da Presidência da República de Moçambique. Retrieved from http://www.presidencia.gov.mz/por/Actualidade/Exigir-instalacao-de-infraestruturas-e-um-direito-Presidente-Nyusi.

Pérez Niño, H., & Le Billon, P. (2014). Foreign aid, resource rents, and state fragility in Mozambique and Angola. *The ANNALS of the American Academy of Political and Social Science, 656*(1), 79–96. https://doi.org/10.1177/0002716214544458.

Piscitelli, P. (2018). Mobile urbanity in Southern Africa. The socio-spatial practices of informal cross-border traders between Johannesburg and Maputo. In A. Petrillo & P. Bellaviti (Eds.), *Research for Development. Sustainable Urban Development and Globalization* (pp. 33–47). https://doi.org/10.1007/978-3-319-61988-0_3.

Rabinow, P. (2003). Ordonnance, discipline, regulation: Some reflections on urbanism. In S.M. Low & D. Lawrence-Zúñiga (Eds.), *The anthropology of space and place: Locating culture* (pp. 353–362). Malden, MA: Blackwell.

Rakodi, C. (2005). The urban challenge in Africa. In M. Keiner, M. Koll-Schretzenmayr, & W.A. Schmid (Eds.), *Managing urban futures: Sustainability and urban growth in developing countries* (pp. 47–72). Burlington, VT: Routledge.

Rodgers, D., & O'Neill, B. (2012). Infrastructural violence: Introduction to the special issue. *Ethnography, 13*(4), 401–412. https://doi.org/10.1177/1466138111435738.

Rogerson, C.M. (2017). Policy responses to informality in urban Africa: The example of Maputo, Mozambique. *GeoJournal, 82*(6), 1179–1194. https://doi.org/10.1007/s10708-016-9735-x.

Roque, S., Mucavele, M., & Noronha, N. (2016). Subúrbios and cityness: Exploring imbrications and urbanity in Maputo, Mozambique. *Journal of Southern African Studies, 42*(4), 643–658. https://doi.org/10.1080/03057070.2016.1189273.

Salazar, D., Broto, V.C., & Adams, K. (2017). Urban infrastructure and energy poverty in Maputo, Mozambique. In A. Allen, L. Griffin, & C. Johnson (Eds.), *Environmental Justice and Urban Resilience in the Global South* (pp. 259–276). https://doi.org/10.1057/978-1-137-47354-7_14.

Sambo, E. (2017). Insegurança rodoviária impera nas estradas moçambicanas. @ *Verdade Online*. Retrieved from http://www.verdade.co.mz/motores/62116.

Sambo, E. (2018a). Condutores seguem matando no país e MTC manifesta vontade de rever diploma sobre inspecção de veículos. @*Verdade Online*. Retrieved from http://www.verdade.co.mz/motores/65141.

Sambo, E. (2018b). Por pouco imprudência de condutores acabava em tragédia na Estrada Circular de Maputo. @*Verdade Online*. Retrieved from http://www.verdade.co.mz/motores/65560.

Shepler, S. (2016). Sierra Leone, child soldiers and global flows of child protection expertise. In J. Knörr & C. Kohl (Eds.), *The upper guinea coast in global perspective* (pp. 241–252). New York: Berghahn Books.

Silver, J. (2014). Incremental infrastructures: Material improvisation and social collaboration across post-colonial Accra. *Urban Geography*, *35*(6), 788–804. https://doi.org/10.1080/02723638.2014.933605.

Thevenot, L. (2002). Which road to follow? The moral complexity of an "equipped" humanity. In J. Law, A. Mol, B.H. Smith, & E.R. Weintraub (Eds.), *Complexities: Social studies of knowledge practices* (pp. 53–87). Durham, NC: Duke University Press.

UNDP. (2016). *Human development report—Mozambique* (p. 9). Geneva, Switzerland: United Nations Development Program.

Van Dijk, J., Krygsman, S., & de Jong, T. (2015). Toward spatial justice: The spatial equity effects of a toll road in Cape Town, South Africa. *Journal of Transport and Land Use*, *8*(3), 95–114.

Verdade. (2014). Acidentes de viação continuam a matar por incompetência e desleixo... @*Verdade Online*. Retrieved from http://www.verdade.co.mz/tema-de-fundo/35/51037.

Viana, D.L. (2015). Postcolonial transformation of the city of Maputo: Its urban form as the result of physical planning and urban self-organization. In C.N. Silva (Ed.), *Urban planning in Lusophone African countries* (1 ed., pp. 171–182). Burlington, VT: Routledge.

Voice of America. (2017). Custo de portagens aumentou em Maputo. *VOA*. Retrieved from https://www.voaportugues.com/a/portagens-maputo/4145434.html.

WEF. (2014). *The global competitiveness report 2014–2015: Full data edition*. The Global Competitiveness and Benchmarking Network. Geneva, Switzerland: World Economic Forum.

WHO. (2015). *Global status report on road safety 2015*. Geneva, Switzerland: World Health Organization.

World Bank. (2018). Mozambique | Data. Retrieved June 2, 2018, from https://data.worldbank.org/country/mozambique.

Zhang, Y., Yang, Z., & Yu, X. (2015). Urban metabolism: A review of current knowledge and directions for future study. *Environmental Science & Technology*, *49*(19), 11247–11263. https://doi.org/10.1021/acs.est.5b03060.

*Part II*

# BELONGING AND CONTESTATION

# Chapter 4

# Part and Parcel of Urbanization

## *Contested Claims to Land Access and Urban Indigenous Spaces in Hermosillo*

Lucero Radonic

Sitting on the dusty ground, a young man sews aluminum cocoons onto a string.[1] Shaped into very small pyramids, these cocoons are made of recycled cans and have small beads inside. He has already finished one string, which is wrapped around his left lower calf, and he is now rushing to finish the one for his right calf before the afternoon procession starts. Beto is one of the many men who participate in the indigenous Yaqui (*Yoeme*) Lenten and Easter observances in the *barrio* of El Coloso, one of two historically indigenous Yaqui neighborhoods in Hermosillo, the capital city of Sonora, Mexico. As a boy, Beto became involved under the tutelage of his grandfather who arrived in Hermosillo from the Yaqui ancestral homeland, 200 miles to the south, in the 1920s. Without slowing the rhythm of his needle, he explains that someone stole his *tenabaris*—from the word *teneboim* in the Cahita language—the night before. "Probably some pot-head took them, just to hassle with me," he adds in a resigned tone that betrays that this is not a rare occurrence. And precisely because he knows that *tenabaris* often go missing, Beto had made extra cocoons when preparing during the preceding months. He notes that to replace *tenabaris* made from butterfly cocoons would have been a different story because they are harder to come by and significantly more expensive. Traditional ankle rattles are made of butterfly cocoons, however, the areas where they used to grow have been overtaken by industrial and housing developments. Upon finishing what turns out to be a much shorter string, he wraps it around his right ankle, stands up, and stamps his feet. "Anyway, I like this type better," he remarks referring to the aluminum pyramids. "They sound harsher, plus they are cool," he adds while walking away to join a group of about eighty men who are about to walk in procession across their inner-city neighborhood (figure 4.1).

**Figure 4.1 Tenabaris on the Feet of Yaqui *Chapayekas*.** *Source*: Photo by author.

Scholars working on urban indigeneity have documented how public opinion and institutional frameworks still hold a pervasive belief that authentic indigenous people belong to and in the countryside, and that indigenous urban presence is associated with cultural rupture (Fixico, 2001; Lobo & Peters, 2001; Peters & Andersen, 2013; Watson, 2010, 2014). Mexico is one place where indigenous urban presence has largely been overlooked or scorned as a social problem. In the few cases in which indigenous connections to the city are considered, they are usually framed as a relic of the past through an institutionally sanctioned fetishism of pre-Columbian architecture or a sanitized revaluation of cultural practices turned into folkloric performances. To paraphrase Wainwright, this acknowledgment of indigenous "presence" in cities is a way of speaking *of* and *for* the indigenous populations, but without them (2008, p. 103). This reproduces a systematic omission of indigenous peoples' contribution toward the production of urban spaces and of their right to the city—the right to inhabit the city and produce urban spaces that reflect their experiences, needs, and desires (Lefebvre, 1996). In fact, in Hermosillo's urban history, the Yaqui people are relegated to less than a footnote. To counter this omission, it is necessary to document the challenges and constrains that many urban indigenous people face in everyday life, as well as the creative and mundane practices through which they counter urban inequality.

In the city of Hermosillo, the enduring Yaqui struggles for secure tenure over land upon which to carry out the religious celebrations inherited from their ancestors highlight Yaqui political invisibility and ongoing marginalization. Paradoxically, the figure of the Yaqui deer dancer (*saila maso)* adorns the state's code of arms as an appropriated symbol of strength and independence, and, over the last two decades, Yaqui rituals dances have grown to become a celebrated part of Hermosillo's cultural repertoire. Featured in promotional materials issued by the city, as well as by other public and private institutions, Yaqui rituality is portrayed as an asset in a city trying to become cosmopolitan through the rhetorical embrace of multiculturalism. However, urban Yaqui men and women, and their descendants, have to confront a series of structural barriers when claiming the right to carry out their cultural practices as urban indigenous people. Drawing on ethnographic fieldwork, this case study illustrates the often-invisible geographies of settler colonialism, understood here as the historical structures of dispossession that persist in the present (Safransky, 2014). Yaqui accounts of their prolonged search for inalienable land parcels elucidate their long-term urban presence and persistent inequality in terms of access to land and representation. As was articulated by an elderly Yaqui man from Hermosillo, "You could say that urbanization encroached upon us. The contradiction," he added, "is that we are an urban tribe and we are part and parcel of that same urbanization."

This chapter draws from long-term ethnographic research in Hermosillo, Mexico. In 2011–2012, I conducted ten months of ethnographic fieldwork. This long stretch was preceded and followed by shorter annual visits during which I first developed and then maintained relationships with research participants, regularly updating my data through 2016. The core of my ethnographic fieldwork took place in the city of Hermosillo, specifically in the two Yaqui barrios. My fieldwork organically developed around religious observances as they are closely articulated with the politics of urbanization, including real estate development and access to natural resources. The analysis I present in this chapter integrates qualitative data obtained through participant-observation, semi-structured and informal interviewing, and community mapping exercises. As a participant observer, I was routinely involved in the planning and celebration of religious ceremonies by helping prepare food, giving rides to religious officials and attendees, going around town to fetch materials needed for the celebrations, and attending the all-night vigils, where I usually sat with the women drinking coffee and chatting in low voices in between dances and songs. I conducted 70 semi-structured interviews with people associated with the Yaqui barrios, as well as with individuals knowledgeable about urban planning and real estate development in

Hermosillo. Interviews focused on Yaqui struggles over lands for residential and ritual purposes, and on Hermosillo's recent urban expansion. Outside of formal interview settings, I conducted informal interviews with barrio residents and staff from local government institutions whom I met at diverse events. Finally, I worked with several community leaders to create maps identifying the changing locations of their ritual grounds. As we traveled the city by foot and by car to identify the lots where Yaqui ceremonies were once held, research participants articulated a history of urban development from their position as Yaqui residents.

## STUDY CONTEXT: URBAN AND INDIGENOUS IN MEXICO

Over the last three decades, Latin America has witnessed indigenous mobilizations demanding recognition of indigenous rights to self-determination and denouncing state-sanctioned practices facilitating the dispossession of indigenous lands and destruction of indigenous livelihoods. In Mexico, the modern indigenous movement was catalyzed by the 1994 uprising led by the *Ejército Zapatista de Liberación Nacional.* As Hernandez (2002) notes, the struggles of the Zapatistas, and the wider indigenous push for autonomy that they engendered, are not only struggles against state politics but also for the construction of new collective imaginaries regarding the national and ethnic identities of the movement's participants and Mexican society as a whole. In other words, these struggles are tied to enduring ethnic inequality and demands by indigenous peoples for full participation as citizens in the making of the modern state.

These mobilizations prompted constitutional reforms in 2001, broadening the scope of who could legally identify as indigenous (de la Peña, 2006; Espinoza Sauceda, Escalante Betancourt, Gallegos Toussaint, López Bárcenas, & Zúñiga Balderas, 2001; González Galván, 2002; López Bárcenas, 2001; Pérez Portilla, 2002). Prior to 2001, only individuals who spoke an indigenous language were recognized as indigenous by the Constitution. The reforms enabled individuals to self-ascribe as indigenous, even if they do not speak a native language. This important change highlights the lack of access that indigenous individuals had—even to be acknowledged as members of a native community. After these reforms, the registered indigenous population in Mexico increased from 10.2 million to 16.1 million. About 30 percent of the indigenous population, mainly non-native speakers, live in cities with over 100,000 inhabitants (Instituto Nacional de Estadísticas y Geografía [INEGI], 2010). Among them are the Yaquis of Hermosillo, Sonora.

## THE YAQUI DIASPORA IN HERMOSILLO

The Yaqui homeland is located in southeastern Sonora, about 200 kilometers south of the capital city of Hermosillo (figure 4.2). After independence from Spain in 1821, the Mexican government sought to promote foreign

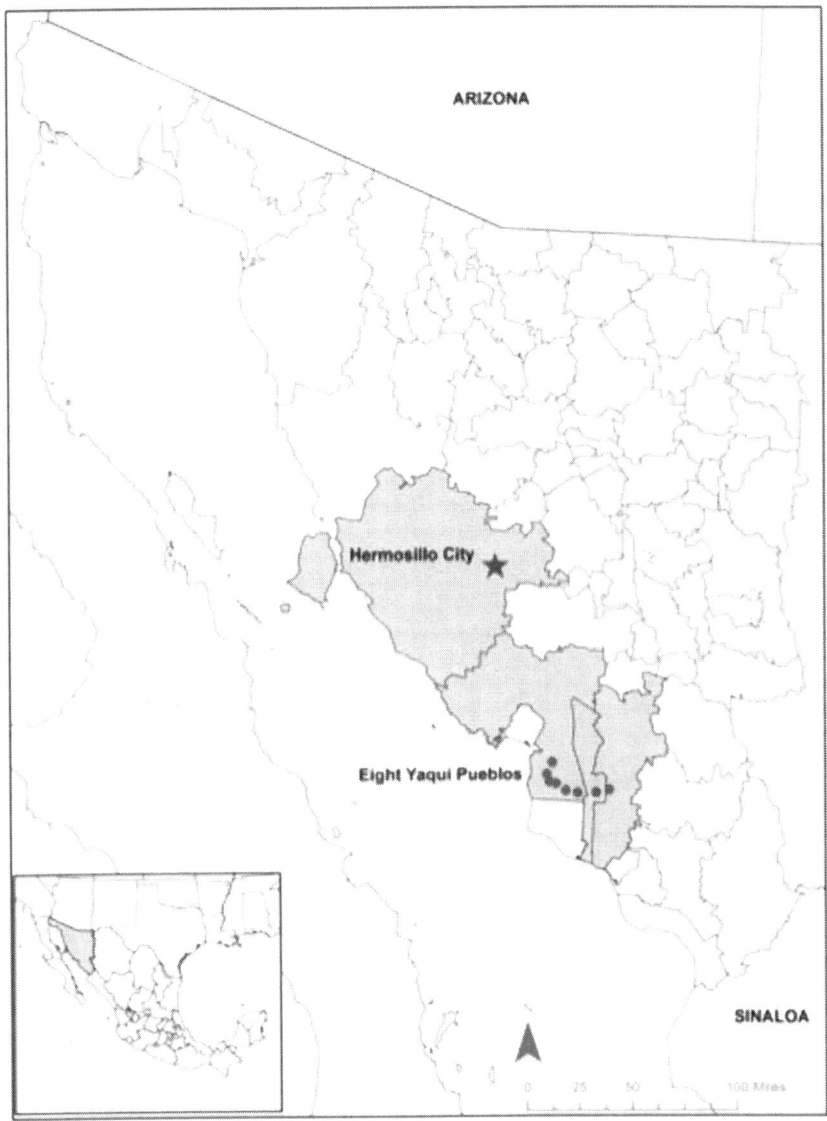


**Figure 4.2 Map Showing the City of Hermosillo and the Eight Yaqui Pueblos in the State of Sonora, Mexico.** *Source*: (Radonic, 2014).

investment in the fertile Yaqui valley—the heart of the Yaqui homeland—and sanctioned land expropriation for the benefit of Mexican and American settlers (Aboites, 1987; Dabdoub, 1980; Hu-DeHart, 1984). In this context, the state established legal guidelines for the demarcation, measurement, subdivision, appraisal, and sale of what it deemed as vacant lands. Consequently, lands belonging to indigenous communities were declared vacant and subsequently privatized because they lacked property titles, and customary land use practices were not legible to developers and lawmakers. Through this system, the Yaqui people were dispossessed from much of their traditional territory in the late nineteenth century, giving rise to the violent conflicts that resulted in the Yaqui diaspora and the eventual formation of the Yaqui barrios of Hermosillo (Padilla Ramos, 1995; Spicer, 1980). Current precarity of Yaqui access to land for ritual purposes in Hermosillo is a new strand of colonial dispossession, one applied to capital expansion in this urban frontier. In this case, urban spaces seasonally used for Yaqui ceremonies continue to be seen as vacant, which highlights the perpetuation of a colonial ideology of property in the modern city, where indigenous place making goes largely unrecognized.

The two traditional Yaqui barrios were established in the early 1900s on rough terrain atop the hills on the then-periphery of town. When the barrios were first established, Hermosillo had just over 10,000 residents and covered 107 hectares (Instituto Municipal de Planeamiento [IMPLAN], 2006). By the late 1980s, elected representatives and real estate developers elaborated a master plan to turn Hermosillo into the financial capital of northwestern Mexico. From 1980 to 2015, Hermosillo underwent a construction boom and tripled in size, reaching a population of roughly 812,000 people and covering a surface area of over 16,500 hectares (Instituto Municipal de Planeamiento [IMPLAN], 2006). With urban expansion, the barrios were engulfed by the city. Today, they lie at the center of town—less than 2 kilometers from the downtown area and the new commercial and administrative districts. Despite their central location, they remain at the margins of urban infrastructure, with households having limited access to basic urban services like potable water and solid waste collection.

The barrio of El Coloso[2] is bisected by one paved street; this sole artery provides vehicular access. From there, networks of pedestrian alleyways expand toward two hills where homes have been built over the years. As was the case with the barrio itself, the network of alleyways grew informally as lots were claimed, subdivided, inherited, and sold. Although the alleyways constitute the only transit network within the neighborhood, they are in a state of disrepair that physically marks the neglect of municipal authorities. The ground is uneven, and the paved segments are few and far between (figure 4.3). Because of the rocky substrate, water and sewage pipes mainly

**Figure 4.3 Alleyway in the Barrio of El Coloso, Hermosillo.** *Source*: Photo by author.

run above ground, which makes them vulnerable to damage from foot traffic, gravel-slides, and vandalism, as well as amenable to pirated connections, when necessary. At one point or another, all pipes spout leakages and can rapidly turn the alleys into ephemeral streams. Neighbors are continually tending to the leaks, but it is hard to keep up with their maintenance. The rough condition of the terrain is an accepted inconvenience for most residents, who have to avoid holes, rocks, and puddles of uncertain water. But, for the elderly and people with limited mobility, it constitutes a health risk. Elderly people often report twisted ankles, bruised knees, and broken bones resulting from falls along their way. A more extreme, but not unique, case is that of a pregnant woman who gave birth in the alley when she could not walk the remaining 200 meters to reach a taxi at the bottom of the hill. The newborn was named *Lluvia* in honor of the troublesome rains that had turned the alley into unsurpassable terrain. As these examples illustrate, the neighborhood's uneven and unsupported development impacts everyday experiences of barrio residents, highlighting the lived reality of inequality.

Despite the material and legal precarity of the neighborhoods, their central location in this growing city has increased the market value of the land, especially for the few remaining large, flat, and undeveloped lots that are used for ritual celebrations. Seasonal access to land and the population's right to be in the city as indigenous people is ever more precarious as pressure by state entities and land speculators increases. These outside authorities conceptualize such sites as valuable vacant land with future potential for construction projects conducive to capital accumulation—a new strand of settler colonialism.

Today, not all Yaquis from Hermosillo live in these barrios and not everyone living there is Yaqui or a Yaqui descendant. However, almost every Hermosillo resident who claims a Yaqui cultural identity traces their roots back to one of these barrios before tracing their lineage to one of the pueblos in the ancestral homeland. For example, a second-generation Hermosillo resident, Beto, the young man profiled at the beginning of this chapter, describes himself as first and foremost "Puro Coloso." Upon conversation, he will explain that he gets his "Yaqui side" from his grandfather's natal pueblo of Vicam. While diaspora is part of the collective memory of Yaquis from Hermosillo, it is not part of most autobiographical renderings. From an emic perspective, the Yaquis of Hermosillo do not consider their relationship to the city through the primary lens of their mass displacement and relocation away from the ancestral homeland. For second- and third-generation Hermosillo Yaquis, the ancestral homeland is decentered in favor of the urban realm. Hermosillo is their primary site of emplacement. As a Yaqui elder explained:

> We will hang on to our land, to our barrio. This is what is traditional for us. This is a tradition that comes from the barrio [. . .] . Back in the day our ancestors fought for their territory down in the Yaqui River, but due to different reasons, like the Yaqui wars and the removal to the South, they had to come to Hermosillo and make their territory here. Hence, this is the territory we have got to defend. They established themselves here, and people need to understand that, we need to defend that which the elders left us as inheritance.

## INTERSECTIONAL MARGINALIZATIONS: EVERYDAY LIFE IN THE BARRIOS

A significant portion of the urban Yaqui population in Hermosillo is part of the marginal proletariat sector that finds employment—often irregularly—in low-paying, labor-intensive, and nontechnical activities. Most men have experience in a range of skilled and manual labor positions associated with the construction sector. They are employed by private companies as construction workers, or by the municipality as plumbers, electricians, sweepers, gardeners, and general maintenance personnel to keep the city running. They are among the laboring hands that build and maintain the new Hermosillo, the "clean, tidy, and modern city" outlined in the municipal urban development programs. Women usually work extended hours as laborers in assembly lines, as cleaning personnel in homes, businesses, and city buildings, or as clerks and cashiers in stores in the nearby commercial area. Among the younger generation, some have attended high school, and a few are studying at the public university or technical college. Those cast-off by the formal labor market due to criminal records or drug-related problems take part in the informal economy, illustrating the perseverance and broad skill set of this marginalized population. Yet, some are involved in the illegal sector of the informal economy, specifically in the pervasive drug trade that has permeated everyday life across many regions of Mexico.

These barrios and their residents are stigmatized throughout the city of Hermosillo. Residents of other neighborhoods hastily label them as dirty, dangerous areas, and breeding grounds for criminals. This blanket statement overshadows the many biographies characterized by hard work and achievement or fall and redemption. Stigmatization also has on-the-ground implications, as seen by the rerouting of the bus in order to skip the neighborhood, the systematic neglect of municipal workers to the neighbors' requests for service maintenance and expansion, or the refusal of retail companies to deliver in the area. Reflecting on the underlying source behind her neighborhood's ill reputation, a woman who was born and raised in the barrio explains that in the old days the gangs were extremely territorial and would throw stones at police patrols and any other vehicles that would dare enter. She then adds, "but this is a thing of the past. Most of those gangsters are now reformed grandpas, or they have died or become imprisoned." Her husband, who wears around his wrist the indelible mark of the iconic rosary of an extinct gang, agrees with her. He then adds, "and maybe they fear us because the Yaquis are here."

The struggles that barrio residents face daily are shared by many other working-class people across this sprawling industrial city. However, the way they experience the city and urban inequality is shaped by the intersectionality of socioeconomic class and ethnicity. As originally articulated by Crenshaw (1989), intersectionality recognizes that there are mutually constitutive forms of social oppression rather than a single axis of difference. For the urban Yaqui, their contemporary experience of urban marginalization is inseparable from a history of conflictive relationships between the Mexican state and the Yaqui people. Moreover, their struggles over urban citizenship today are mediated by a culturally distinct system of beliefs and practices shared with their kin in the ancestral homeland along the lower Yaqui River and grounded in the socio-environmental reality of Hermosillo. Paradoxically, while men from the barrios are sought after to perform ritual dances in state ceremonies, their demands over lands for ritual purposes in the city are described by government officials as "out of place," challenging the continuance of Yaqui tradition. In this way, the urban Yaquis are rendered abject residents of the city. As Anand explains, extending on the work of Murphy (2006) and Ferguson (1999), "abjection is a social and political process through which particular populations are pushed beyond the bio-political care of the state or other institutions, even as they remain central to the constitution of social (or political) collectives" (2012, p. 489). In Hermosillo, the iterative process of abjection is made through complex and contentious struggles over limited access to land and resources for religious celebrations.

Thus, what sets the urban Yaquis and their descendants apart from other working poor residents in Hermosillo is marked by the religious system that permeates everyday life. The ways in which people deal with misfortune, grief, remorse, gratitude, and hope are mediated by ritual ceremonies, which integrate Catholic and pre-Columbian indigenous beliefs and practices. Diverse diasporic Yaqui communities have created and recreated ritual spaces everywhere they have settled for any length of time, leading scholars to argue that the Lent and Easter observances, like those celebrated in Hermosillo, are central to Yaqui ethnic identity (Painter, 1971; Spicer, 1940, 1980). As other scholars have described for diverse Native American populations in the United States and Canadian cities, seasonal gatherings and ritual celebrations serve to reinforce a sense of social belonging *both* to the native community *and* to the city (Peters & Andersen, 2013; Ramirez, 2007). While very few Yaqui born in Hermosillo speak the native language of their ancestors, many are familiar with and able to use the expressions that correspond to religious ceremonies. As sixty-year-old Roberto explains, "Our parents did not teach us the dialect because they wanted us to mingle with the *yoris* [the non-indigenous Mexicans] but they did transmit their traditions to us." For four generations, the Yaquis of Hermosillo have continued to practice their religious traditions—the most salient of which is the Lent and Easter observances (from now on referred together as the *cuaresma*). Despite the seasonality to the cuaresma practices, Yaqui rituality is part of everyday life, even when no specific ceremony is approaching. In the barrios, there is a running commentary concerning ritual activity: Who is going to takeover so-and-so's position as ritual officer now that he is in jail? Is so-and-so's daughter learning to sing hymns like her mother did? Have the elders arranged for a bus to take people to the traditional homeland for the patron saint's feast day? What type of *chapayeka* mask is so-and-so planning to make? Does anyone have leather available to make a belt for the *pascola* dance? And more pressing than all other questions: will there be a space where to conduct the celebrations this year?

## THE YAQUI CUARESMA: CONTESTING AND CLAIMING THE RIGHT TO THE CITY

The cuaresma is a cultural practice through which participants engage with each other and with Yaqui tradition, claiming a right to urban space and contesting the way property is understood and managed in the capitalist city. To be celebrated, the cuaresma requires an open space large enough to accommodate processions, all-night vigils, and dance gatherings that may bring together more than 100 people. The primary ritual space is established by placing fourteen small wooden crosses along the external periphery of an open field. The crosses delineate the *conti vo'o* or way of the cross. In this way, participants simultaneously claim, prepare, and transform this urban space, marking the site in connection with Yaqui tradition and claiming their right to the city as indigenous residents.

At the beginning of the cuaresma, two temporary buildings are erected to host the church and the ritual dances respectively.[3] Because they are built from branches (*ramas* in Spanish), these structures are known as *ramadas*. Traditionally, these ramadas were made with mesquite posts and branches of mesquite, cottonwood, or reed, depending on availability. As recently as the mid-1990s, mesquite and cottonwood were still used for construction, but these species have become hard to find as trees dried out when the river that crosses Hermosillo was channeled and desert areas were cleared for urban development. Thus, ramadas in contemporary Hermosillo are at times built from a combination of palm leaves and branches from non-native ornamental trees, metal poles, wooden beams, cardboard boxes, and tarpaulin.

Increased attendance by the broader Hermosillo community has brought tighter regulations on the observance of the cuaresma. Classified now by the city as a massive public event, ceremonial groups are required to get a municipal permit. To be granted permission to use a site and celebrate, they must jump through a series of bureaucratic hoops. They need to prove their rightful access to the land and to the Yaqui tradition. At odds with Mexico's constitutional acknowledgment of self-ascription, applications must include an endorsement letter from the municipal agency responsible for promoting culture and art to certify that the petitioners are indeed Yaqui. To fulfill this request, leaders must travel to the *pueblos* to get a letter from Yaqui civil authorities documenting that they are part of the Yaqui tribe. Since most groups do not have land tenure, they also need to get another letter from the property owner—either the city's land trust or a private real estate company—confirming they can use the land for the duration of the cuaresma. Every year, Yaqui communities face uncertainty in gaining permission to temporarily occupy these sites. Their precarious access to land, and to natural resources such as mesquite and cottonwood, illustrates how city decisions and urban development—over which barrio residents have no control—shape the ability to continue celebrating their traditions in this urban environment.

Once they have access to land, and authorization from the city, group leaders must work the land to make it adequate for the celebrations. Yearly they improve and clean these parcels. The spaces where men and women offer their sweat and sleepless nights while marching, dancing, praying, and cooking are left unattended after their seasonal permit expires. Throughout the year, these unoccupied lots are overtaken by piles of construction refuse and trash, while the summer and winter rains run their course across the land, often opening gullies and sprouting high weeds. Consequently, group leaders have to borrow or rent machinery to clear the vegetation, remove rubbish, and even level the ground. When the ground is finally even and clear, group leaders run hoses from nearby houses or find tanks for water storage and connect electric wires to nearby posts. Their experience as construction workers and handymen is useful at this time. With ingenuity, they make water and electricity available to ease the lives of ritual participants and welcome visitors from across the city.[4]

The forty-four-day-long celebration reaches its dramatic climax on Holy Saturday, the penultimate day of the season. That day news reporters and members of the broader Hermosillo community visit the ritual grounds to see the *chapayecas* in their gaudy regalia and the *saila maso*, or deer dancer, come to life. Many of them are residents of Hermosillo who otherwise would not set foot in these neighborhoods. Upon their arrival, visitors encounter a well-raked field, the scent of wet earth, and the aroma of firewood smoke emanating from the kitchen were women prepare food for the visitors. Early in the morning, before visitors arrive, the youngest participants pick up the bottles, aluminum cans, and many Styrofoam plates and glasses left behind the night before. Soon afterward, a water truck sprays the field for dust control. This act, and the police patrolling the periphery, are deemed a contribution from the city now that the festivity is a massive public event. On the clean and wet field, participants delineate the path leading to the church with cottonwood twigs that are brought from the outskirts of town, where a few cottonwood trees can still be found. The green leaves stand out against the brownish-gray of the dusty soil, indicating the ritual space that should not be trespassed by visitors.

By setting up the *conti vo'o* and erecting the ramadas, participants are not only transforming an unoccupied urban space for religious purposes, they are also displaying the presence of Yaqui tradition to fellow Hermosillo residents, and exercising authority over the space. The connection between ritual place making and territorial sovereignty is a point frequently made. One group leader explains:

> Once the cuaresma begins and the crosses are raised this is our territory. When we obtain the permit from the city, they are obliged to safeguard the area surrounding the celebrations during the *semana mayor* [the last and most public week]. They send patrol cars that go around, but they know that in the space where we are holding the ceremonies, we are in command. They are in command from here [the *conti vo'o*] to the outside and we command from here inwards. If there is a problem in the plaza, we have the authority to apprehend

> the offender, call their attention at the *cruz mayor* [the main cross], and from there send them to the police station if we feel so. Because we are the maximum authority there, neither the mayor nor the governor of the state gets involved there, we have our own law in that space, which they respect.

## DISPOSSESSION AND CONTESTATION OF SPACE

The Yaqui cuaresma has been carried out in Hermosillo for nearly a century, and yet those who celebrate it have been unable to safeguard land for this purpose. Elderly people recall that until the early 1970s residents worked the cuaresma in two large open spaces at the heart of their barrios. From the original two ritual groups a few others have emerged over the years, due to increased participation and to internal political differences. Within the Yaqui community four groups are recognized as "the originals," for they have worked the cuaresma for at least three decades and always have a full cast of ritual participants. As Hermosillo continues to grow and new lands—usually desert hillsides and floodplains previously overlooked by real estate developers—are incorporated and sold by the city as private property for urban development, groups must continually locate new parcels to work their ceremonies or fight to maintain access to the grounds where they currently celebrate. Thus, over the last four decades, the Yaqui of Hermosillo have worked sixteen different land parcels across the city. Only two groups have maintained access to their original sites—albeit only to a section of them—and the rest have been progressively displaced to grounds further away from the barrios. This precarity in access to land marginalizes indigenous practices, further reproducing everyday experiences of inequality in the city (figure 4.4).

The urban Yaqui struggles for land are framed by the state's legal pathway for regularization, which facilitates territorialization in cities with a high percentage of land informality. Critically, the Mexican state provides a pathway toward land regularization that is based on a narrow definition of dominion as permanent residency, transformative use of space, and settlement of a productive nature. Prescribed upon a private property regime, this program benefited the urban poor, including many families in the Yaqui barrios, who acquired private property titles for their homes. But the ideological underpinning and legal definition of vacant land dismiss Yaqui forms of seasonal ritual space production and automatically preclude them from being considered for land tenure recognition. As Radding (1997) illustrates, since colonial times the pathway to land tenure in Sonora has been defined by a productivist and capitalist approach that recognizes only patterns of permanent and tangible spatial production. As Yaqui ritual practices escape the standards for property claiming specified in the legal codes—defined by occupancy, use,

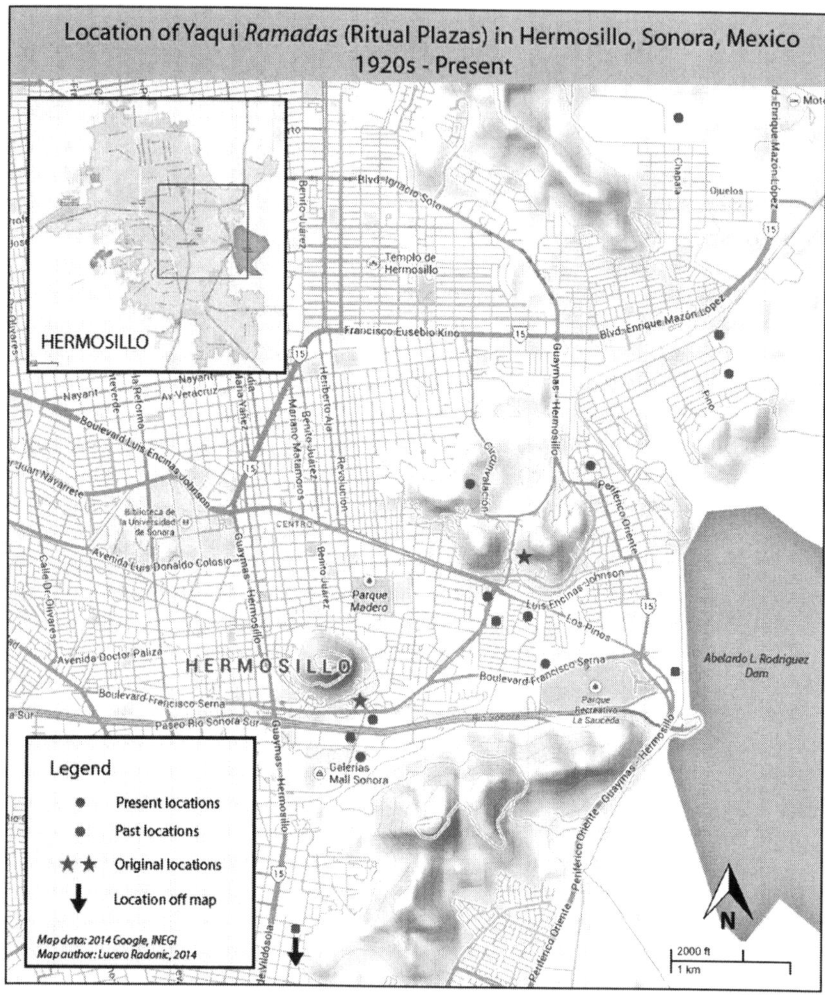


**Figure 4.4 Location of the Yaqui Ramadas of Hermosillo.** *Source*: (Radonic, 2014).

and modification—indigenous urban presence and its role in the production of urban geographies continues to be overlooked. Thus, regardless of how long they have occupied a piece of land for ritual purposes, or how much work they invest in it every year, lands used for ritual purposes are officially deemed vacant and Yaqui access is never legally secured.

Explaining how one of the first ritual grounds was lost to the regularization of land invasions, an elderly resident reflects as he points to a line of modest one-story houses: "People invaded the land during the [times of the] year when the space was seemingly empty. We would tell them 'that is not vacant, that is the space of the *chapayekas*' [referring to the ritual army of the cuaresma], but it was to no end. The government then took the concrete and brick houses to mean property." Reflecting on importance of visibility in property, he adds, "We should have fenced it off, put up a big fence."

Leaders and participants fear that if they do not obtain land tenure over their grounds, they will lose them permanently as land near the barrios is sold and built upon. In the higher part of El Coloso, ritual leaders learned that land for which they had for decades been trying to obtain rights from the municipality was in dispute. Standing in the middle of the empty field that only a month ago had been brimming with people, a middle-aged man explains to me with a hint of frustration:

> When we first arrived [to this site, over two decades ago], this space was all thorn scrub, it was full of rubble. Through the years, we improved the space. Private interests do not care about the land until we get a hold of it and clean it, only then many owners start to surface. They no longer see it as scrubland; they see it as well-located valuable lots. A piece of land they can buy, pave, and make look like Phoenix, [in nearby Arizona, US].

If the community fails to obtain permanent tenure for this ground, they anticipate they will have to occupy land at the outskirts of town; this is seen as undermining the celebration, as well as their own history and legitimacy as urban residents. To be far away from the barrios is to be far away from the people who support the celebrations by preparing the holy figures of saints and virgins, coming at night to pray and sing, or bringing food for those participating. In addition, to be at the margins of town means to be out of sight of the larger Hermosillo community.

After nearly two decades of internal factionalism, several groups have come together to advocate for property rights over lands upon which to continue celebrating their religious ceremonies without threat of eviction. In their request for land, they are framing the cuaresma in the multicultural lexicon of *usos y costumbres*, or "uses and customs." Within this framework, there are three central arguments often raised by group leaders. First, that the ritual army and church officials constitute a structure of customary authorities with the power to govern over ritual spaces during the cuaresma. Second, that the cuaresma has been part of Hermosillo's intangible cultural patrimony for the last century, which indicates traditional occupation at the urban scale, despite recurrent displacements within the city. Third, they maintain that seasonal occupation and ephemeral construction is part of their traditional place-making practices, and therefore should be understood as a form of customary possession conducive to land tenure. As multiple Yaqui leaders articulate, outside the ritual season these parcels may look like vacant lots, but for the cuaresma the space is materially and symbolically transformed through Yaqui occupation and labor—cleaning, constructing, praying, marching, and standing guard.

In their mobilization of *usos y costumbres*, they keep in sight how the urban reality of their barrios has permeated tradition, grounding Yaqui practices in Hermosillo's socio-environmental context. For example, the ceremonial ramadas are acknowledged as erected on a seasonal basis, but with recycled materials and ornamental clippings in addition to the customary mesquite and reed used in the pueblos. Similarly, the erection of the *conti vo'o* is described as the delimitation of a seasonal sacred space as well as a drug-free terrain (with marijuana admittedly in a gray zone of permissibility). The *chapayeka* army is highlighted for containing an ensemble of masks—from the Mexican television host Eugenio Derbez to the King Pig of the hit video game Angry Birds—that reveal the contemporary existence of Yaqui culture. By articulating discourses on *usos y costumbres* with the social dynamics of their marginal urban barrios, they are subverting discursive articulations of essentialized indigenous identities and territories centered on earth-bonds and ruralness (Perreault & Green, 2013). Furthermore, they are claiming their right to be indigenous in their native city, thus contesting the ongoing settler colonialism that threatens to further marginalize residents from their city.

## CONCLUSION

Ethnographic fieldwork among the Yaqui communities of Hermosillo makes evident the critical importance and interconnection between real estate development and demands over the right to the city of indigenous peoples. This specific case study reveals that in articulating the indigenous beliefs and practices of their ancestors in their everyday life—through the production of ritual grounds and the manufacturing of ritual artifacts—urban Yaquis seek to shape the social geography of their industrial hometown, thus claiming a right to the city.

This chapter illustrates how urban environments are constituted as part and parcel of indigenous territories—in practice if not yet in the law. This is a process that occurs through collective place-making practices and property claims. Urban indigenous people, however, continue to face the effects of the *terra nullius* doctrine, which was first mobilized by colonial powers to rationalize occupation and appropriation of indigenous lands in the New World (Miller, LeSage, & López Escarcena, 2010). In contemporary times, some spaces that have important public functions for indigenous minorities continue to be designated as vacant lands eligible for government appropriation and subsequent privatization, as urban Yaquis rarely hold legal property titles. This situation points at a new form of settler colonialism now applied to capital expansion in the urban frontier. The hyperbolic application of this term to the contemporary urban terrain highlights the perpetuation of neocolonial representations of space in modern cities. In these examples, indigenous place making and Yaqui right to the city are largely omitted from urban historiographies and urban planning. An ethnographic analysis of indigenous experiences in the urban diasporic context illustrates the iterative process of marginalization, but it also highlights the creative endurance of residents in the face of historical and structural inequalities.

The global demographic trend toward urbanization produces assemblages that articulate the political economy of real estate development and the politics of indigeneity. In Latin America, indigenous urbanization is a widespread phenomenon. The percentage of indigenous populations living in cities ranges from 10 percent in Paraguay to nearly 65 percent in Chile (Del Popolo, Oyarce, & Ribotta, 2009). Given this seemingly irreversible trend, indigenous and nonindigenous leaders and policy makers must operate in a sociopolitical landscape where resource claims grounded in traditional indigenous homelands intersect with emerging claims over urban homelands and rights to the city.

## NOTES

1. I would like to thank Dr. Thomas E. Sheridan for his constant guidance throughout my fieldwork and his insightful advice as I began analyzing the data I collected in Hermosillo. I am also thankful to Megan Sheehan and Angela Storey for their feedback on earlier versions of this chapter. The research was funded by the Inter-American Foundation, the Arizona Archaeological and Historical Society, the Smithsonian Institute for Museum Anthropology, the Carson Fellowship, and the Confluence Center for Creative Enquiry.

2. While both barrios have similar histories and current demographic characteristics, I focus primarily in El Coloso as it is here where I conducted most of my ethnographic fieldwork.

3. The church houses the plaster images of virgins and saints, and is intended as a space for prayer and somberness. Immediately to the east of the church, an earth mound is raised to serve as headquarter for the ritual army. At the other end of the plaza, the fiesta ramada is dedicated to the deer and *pascola* dances. This ramada usually hosts nights of festive hullaballoo amidst prayers, coffee, cigarettes, and a bit of alcohol for the dancers. A kitchen space—a hearth surrounded by wood piles, large pots, and bags with provisions and utensils—is set up close to the fiesta ramada to provide sustenance for ritual participants and attendees. During the last days of Holy Week, about a dozen vendors set up their stands at the outer periphery of the plaza with authorization from the army chiefs. In the pueblos, the central plazas have a

permanent church. In contrast, with one exception, all buildings for the cuaresma in Hermosillo are temporary ramadas.

4. In previous years, electrical wires were illegally connected from nearby posts while water was obtained from houses close by running a series of rubber hoses. Today, the city grants the group authorization to run their own connections from public lighting. To get water, the group continues to run a hose from different private sources as they are made available, but now the water is stored in 150-gallon tanks often provided by politicians seeking votes.

## BIBLIOGRAPHY

Aboites, L. (1987). *Irrigación revolucionaria.* Ciudad de Mexico: Centro de Investigaciones y Estudios Superiores en Antropología Social.

Anand, N. (2012). Municipal disconnect: On abject water and its urban infrastructures. *Ethnography, 13*, 487–509.

Crenshaw, K. (1989). Demarginalizing the intersection of race and sex: A Black feminist critique of antidiscrimination doctrine, feminist theory and antiracist politics. *University of Chicago Legal Forum, 1*(8), 139–167.

Dabdoub, C. (1980). *Breve historia del valle del Yaqui.* Ciudad de Mexico: Editores Asociados Mexicanos.

de la Peña, G. (2006). A new Mexican nationalism? Indigenous rights, constitutional reform and the conflicting meanings of multiculturalismn. *Nations and Nationalism, 12*(2), 279–302.

Del Popolo, F., Oyarce, A.M., & Ribotta, B. (2009). Indígenas urbanos en América Latina: Algunos resultados censales y su relación con los Objetivos de Desarrollo del Milenio. *Notas de Poblacion (CEPAL), 86*, 101–140.

Espinoza Sauceda, G., Escalante Betancourt, Y., Gallegos Toussaint, X., López Bárcenas, F., & Zúñiga Balderas, A. (2001). *Los Derechos indígenas y la reforma constitucional en México.* Ciudad de Mexico: Centro de Orientación y Asesoría a Pueblos Indígenas A.C.

Ferguson, J. (2009). *Expectations of modernity: Myths and meanings of urban life on the Zambian Copperbelt.* Berkeley, CA: University of California Press.

Fixico, D.L. (2001). Foreword. In S. Lobo & K. Peters (Eds.), *American Indians and the urban experience* (pp. ix–x). New York: Altamira Press.

González Galván, J.A. (2002). La validez del derecho indigena en el derecho nacional. In M. Carbonell & K. Pérez Portilla (Eds.), *Comentarios a la reforma constitucional en materia indígena* (pp. 37–50). Ciudad de Mexico: Instituto de Investigaciones Jurídicas, Universidad Nacional Autónoma de México.

Hernandez, A. (2002). Indigenous law and identity politics in Mexico: Indigenous men's and women's struggles for a multicultural nation. *Political and Legal Anthropology Review, 25*(1), 90–109.

Hu-Dehart, E. (1984). *Yaqui resistance and survival: The struggle for land and autonomy, 1821–1910.* Madison, WI: University of Wisconsin Press.

Instituto Municipal de Planeamiento [IMPLAN]. (2006). *Hermosillo. Programa de Desarrollo Urbano*. I.M.d.P. Urbana, ed. Hermosillo, Sonora, Mexico: Municipio de Hermosillo.

Instituto Nacional de Estadística y Geografia [INEGI]. (2010). *Censo Nacional de Población y Vivienda*. Ciudad de Mexico, Mexico: INEGI.

Lefebvre, H. (1996 [1967]). Right to the city. In E. Kofman & E. Lebas (Eds.), *Henri Lefebvre: Writing on cities* (pp. 61–184). Oxford, United Kingdom: Blackwell.

Lobo, S., & Peters, K. (Eds.). (2001). *American Indians and the urban experience*. Walnut Creek, CA: Altamira Press.

López Bárcenas, F. (2001). *Legislación y derechos indígenas en México*. Ciudad de Mexico: Centro de Orientación y Asesoría a Pueblos Indígenas AC.

Miller, R.J., LeSage, L., & López Escarcena, S. (2010). The international law of discovery, Indigenous peoples, and Chile. *Nebraska Law Review*, *89*(4), 820–884.

Murphy, M. (2006). *Sick building syndrome and the problem of uncertainty: Environmental politics, technoscience, and women workers*. Durham, NC: Duke University Press.

Padilla Ramos, R. (1995). *Yucatan, fin del sueño Yaqui: El tráfico de los Yaquis y el otro triunvirato*. Hermosillo, Sonora, Mexico: Instituto Sonorense de Cultura.

Painter, M.T. (1971). *A Yaqui easter*. Tucson, AZ: The University of Arizona Press.

Pérez Portilla, K. (2002). La nación mexicana y los pueblos indígenas en el artículo 2o. constitucional. In M. Carbonell & K. Pérez Portilla (Eds.), *Comentarios a la Reforma Constitucional en Materia Indigena* (pp. 51–66). Ciudad de Mexico, Mexico: Instituto de Investigaciones Jurídicas, Universidad Nacional Autónoma de Mexico.

Perreault, T., & Green, B. (2013). Reworking the spaces of indigeneity: The Bolivian ayllu and lowland autonomy movements compared. *Environment and Planning D: Society and Space*, *31*, 43–60.

Peterson, E., & Andersen C. (2013). *Indigenous in the city: Contemporary identities and cultural innovation*. Vancouver, Canada: University of British Columbia Press.

Radding, C. (1997). *Wandering peoples: Colonialism, ethnic spaces, and ecological frontiers in Northwestern Mexico, 1700–1850*. Durham, NC: Duke University Press.

Radonic, L. (2014). *Claiming territory and asserting indigeneity: The urbanization of nature, its history and politics in Northwestern Mexico* (Doctoral dissertation, University of Arizona, Tucson, Arizona, United States). Retrieved from http://hdl.handle.net/10150/333339.

Ramirez, R.K. (2007). *Native hubs. Culture, community, and belonging in Silicon Valley and beyond*. Durham, NC: Duke University Press.

Safransky, S. (2014). Greening the urban frontier: Race, property, and resettlement in Detroit. *Geoforum*, 56, 237–248.

Spicer, E. (1940). *Pascua: A Yaqui village in Arizona*. Chicago, IL: University of Chicago Press.

Spicer, E. (1980). *The Yaquis: A cultural history*. Tucson, AZ: University of Arizona Press.

Wainwright, J. (2008). *Decolonizing development: Colonial power and the Maya.* Malden, MA: Blackwell Publishing.

Watson, M.K. (2010). Diasporic indigeneity: Place and the articulation of Ainu identity in Tokyo, Japan. *Environment and Planning A*, *42*, 268–284.

Watson, M.K. (2014). *Japan's Ainu minority in Tokyo: Diasporic indigeneity and urban politics*. New York, NY: Routledge.

# Chapter 5

# Traditions of the Oppressed

## *Popular Aesthetics and Layered Barrio Space against the Erasure of Gentrification in Austin*

Ben Chappell

As a novice anthropologist researching Mexican American custom car style in Austin, Texas—the same city where I was a graduate student—I assured myself and my advisers that I crossed a proper "border" when I traveled from the University of Texas campus to fieldwork across town.[1] My project focused on how the aesthetic practices of lowrider car clubs intersected with social life and with the politics of space in the city. The research involved taking part in the activities of one such club, including regular meetings at a carwash, cruising on weekend nights, and occasional events like competitive car shows and holiday picnics in a park. To get to know the context of ordinary life that formed the backdrop of lowriding, I moved to a residential neighborhood just east of the large interstate highway that bisected the city. This was a part of Austin that had one of the highest concentrations of Mexican-descended denizens in the country, a barrio known by some residents at the time as "the Eastside." In the book that I eventually wrote about conducting fieldwork in the early 2000s, I described entering the Eastside from downtown on Cesar Chavez Street, a major east-west thoroughfare:

> After crossing the elevated lanes of IH-35 and leaving behind the big hotels and convention center of downtown, pass the pawnshop and the Terrazas Branch Library, then the old house that is now Austin Spoilers and Tint Shop, advertising *Polarizado de Autos*. This strip has changed considerably … now you might see an upscale boutique and a continuum of real estate operations: to the left, a very hip office with new-economy décor promising the "good life" through condos, then close by on the right, a thrown-up poster-board sign offering "fast cash" for your home. (Chappell, 2012, p. 9)

Strike up a conversation with someone familiar with the area "back in the day," and the observations could go on—the Mexican buses loading and unloading passengers at the back of a nondescript lot, a roll call of favorite taquerias and beer lounges, some perhaps long gone. Such a conversation in the past few years might touch on Jumpolin, one of many homegrown enterprises along Cesar Chavez Street, a store that specialized in Mexican-style piñatas and party supplies, including rental equipment such as popcorn machines and inflated "jump houses." Jumpolin was popular in the community and made its colorful presence known as part of the distinctive street scene of the Eastside.

In February 2015, the owner, Sergio Lejarazu, had received several eviction notices after a real estate development firm bought the property in October and immediately applied for permission to demolish it. Lejarazu hired a lawyer and kept paying rent because he knew his lease was good until 2017. On February 12, however, Lejarazu arrived at work to find the store demolished, with all of his stock inside. Reporting on the story revealed that the real estate firm had been eager to demolish because they had rented out an adjacent building for a tech entrepreneur party during the huge South by Southwest multimedia festival, scheduled for March. To meet city codes requiring parking space for the event, they needed the lot where Jumpolin stood. Thus, a neighborhood business went down in dust.

In news reports on the Jumpolin controversy, the firm F&F Real Estate Ventures argued that they had followed due process, and portrayed Jumpolin's owner as operating outside the rules of property and tenantship. A representative of F&F Real Estate Ventures elaborated on this position in an interview with a local online journal, days after the demolition, insinuating the illegitimacy of Jumpolin and portraying its demolition as a clean-up operation. He said: "Probably their livelihood was selling helium and stolen bicycles. . . . They weren't making a living selling piñatas; they were selling something else. I don't want to speculate what that is. Say you have a house that was infested by roaches, you have to clean that up" (Planas, 2015).

Two years later, the store reopened at a new location, substantially further east on the same street. Lejarazu said, "I am so happy to be back. . . . We have support from a lot of people in the community. . . . We belong to the east. This is our place" (Hall, 2017).

The spatial confinement and isolation of people of color in segregated neighborhoods is a central theme of modern U.S. urbanization. Yet, over generations and in spite of the de jure and de facto forms of segregation associated with the designation and enforcement of their spatial location, people have made segregated areas into collective homes, places rich with memory and meaning. Recently, however, economic development has brought demographic change through the process known as "gentrification," as residents of a formerly segregated area find themselves displaced by the shifting economics of real estate. This, too, is a familiar feature of urban social dynamics in the United States. In cities around the country, gentrification has been amplified recently as mobile information workers and entrepreneurs take a renewed interest in urban cores as desirable settings in which to live and work. Demand for urban spaces has been compounded by aesthetics favoring "authenticity," such that areas where people of color had been concentrated because they were once deemed to be undesirable spaces take on a new luster for purchase and investment (Aoki, 1993). Historically, unequal distributions of wealth put the original residents of gentrifying neighborhoods at a disadvantage, leading to their displacement as property values rise. As these long-running processes intensify, so too does resistance to them (Caterine, 2016).

In the years since my fieldwork, the 78702 ZIP code, which encompasses Austin's Eastside, saw a 212 percent increase in property values, ranking it as one of the top-twenty most gentrified neighborhoods nationwide, according to one study (Devadanam, 2018). The fact that gentrification was already a concern of residents in 2000, and before that, calls to mind Walter Benjamin's eighth thesis on the concept of history, "The tradition of the oppressed teaches us that the 'state of emergency' in which we live is not the exception but the rule" (1940, p. 257). While some may be inclined to focus on the benefits of rising property values "in the long run," and dismiss the traumatic effects on long-time residents as mere growing pains, that is not the view held by many of those residents themselves. University of Texas scholars completed a door-to-door study of "people who stayed" in a gentrifying area of East Austin, surveying those who had lived at the same address between 1999 and 2015. The researchers found that a clear majority held a negative view of developments in their neighborhood, citing not only rising costs of living, but also the issue of becoming "no longer a people of color neighborhood" (Tang & Falola, 2018, p. 6).

What is lost in such a transformation? In this chapter, I argue that in order to appreciate the displacements of gentrification, we must take instruction from the first phrase of Benjamin's thesis, and pay attention to "the traditions of the oppressed." In fact, to take the popular memory of the pre-gentrification residents of the Eastside seriously is to begin to understand their displacement as part of a larger history, one in which the structural conflicts over resources and space that make up urban politics, conflicts that function in racialized class terms, connect to the history of Mexicans in Texas. This history has been illuminated by prior scholars who have taken precisely those traditions of the oppressed, the vernacular cultural knowledge of the denizens of Greater Mexico, as an archive for their studies (Limón, 2012, p. 129). Situating the Eastside within that history not only helps explain what is specifically at stake in this neighborhood's gentrification, but also shows the conflict of gentrification to be a clash of distinct ideas of what urban space is. On one hand, real estate markets treat space as the fungible raw material of development; and on the other, the production of space is a gradual, accruing process through which layers of memory accumulate.

As José Limón has argued in his long-term engagement with the work of Américo Paredes, the historical circumstances of racialized capitalism must be considered in order to best understand vernacular culture. Conversely, the vernacular cultural productions of people oppressed by any historical order must be considered in order to understand those circumstances and how they work (Limón, 1994, p. 179). In this vein, my point of departure is that the cultural forms of a "tradition of the oppressed" acquire distinctive affective force through their popular aesthetics and social embeddedness. The continuation of these forms through performance has material effects on the political and cultural landscape of a city in what I have called in previous work a *performance of space* (Chappell, 2012, p. 205).

In what follows, I offer glimpses of change in the Eastside with an eye for the traditions of the oppressed. Paying attention to socially embedded, popular aesthetics can bring to light distinctive productions of space, ones that clash sharply with the dominant production under capitalism (Lefebvre, 1992). The latter projects a homogeneous, humanist space in which places are commodities available to anyone for the right price, to be used as the buyer sees fit. My argument, then, sets up a conflict between two kinds of spatial production: one forms collective homeplaces through the historical occupation of parts of the city. The other commodifies sites through the processes known as gentrification. This conflict of community and commodity is nothing new, nor are the categories perfectly discrete. But as gentrification's displacements and resistance to them intensify, it remains vital to recognize that small-scale, popular, even banal cultural forms are archives that should inform our understanding of contested urban existence.

## EASTSIDE, TEXAS

The contested relationship of Mexican-descended people to place in Texas has a long history, to say the least. Texas was once a part of Mexico, but migration of whites from the Southern United States and Texas independence established Anglo rule by the middle of the nineteenth century. With this Anglo rule came slavery, which had been abolished in Mexico. Anglo residents of Austin raised concern in 1854 that Mexicans in the city might have a bad influence on enslaved people, giving them a "false sense of freedom." A mob action arose to run what they called the "rascally peons" out of town, and by 1860 only twenty people with Spanish surnames remained in the entire county, each vouched for by a white person (Lack, 1981, p. 11). In ensuing decades, the Mexican population of Austin grew back as part of the more general story of migration from Mexico to the United States, with large numbers crossing the border during the tumult of the Mexican Revolution from 1810 to 1820. People of Mexican descent established enclave communities in Austin, including an area in the Southwest of downtown around a chili canning factory that came to be known as "Little Mexico," and another neighborhood along the Colorado River known as Rainey Street—now a busy restaurant district.

The area east of downtown became the "Eastside" as a result of a master plan that the city of Austin commissioned from private consultants in 1928 (Koch & Fowler, 1928) (figure 5.1). One issue that the plan addressed was the "problem of segregation" between the races. In 1928, the problem was not that there *was* segregation, but rather how to establish and maintain it efficiently. The nonwhite populations of Austin, including the Mexican Americans in the areas I just described, as well as African Americans who had settled in various "freedom town" neighborhoods after emancipation, were dispersed throughout the city, making it difficult to maintain public facilities such as schools, libraries, parks, and swimming pools under the "separate but equal" doctrine that had yet to be challenged in court.

Thus, the 1928 plan called for the area east of downtown to be designated for nonwhite residents. This was realized by a series of "push and pull" measures, including the construction of race-specific public housing, the relocation of community institutions such as the Our Lady of Guadalupe Catholic Church, and discriminatory banking and real estate practices. By the time the multilane Interstate 35 highway was built through the center of Austin after the Interstate Highway Act of 1956, this highly visible, if permeable, concrete boundary between white and nonwhite Austin merely marked a social boundary that was already well established and felt.

The demographics of the city have shifted unevenly in the course of this history, as Austin has become one of the fastest-growing metropolitan areas in the United States, currently growing at a rate of 3 percent. The World Population Review lists the current population of Austin at 964,254, with over 2 million in the larger metro area (Austin, Texas Population, 2019). This is up from 656,562 inhabitants in 2000, around the time I began fieldwork. The Mexican-descended population is difficult to track in census figures, due to the ambiguity of the "Hispanic origin" ethnic category. Consulting 1990 census figures when I first began to study in Austin, I was struck that many respondents self-identified as "Hispanic-origin other" from among the race options. In its own presentation of census demographic data, the city of Austin deals with the socially salient "Hispanic-Latino" category by distinguishing

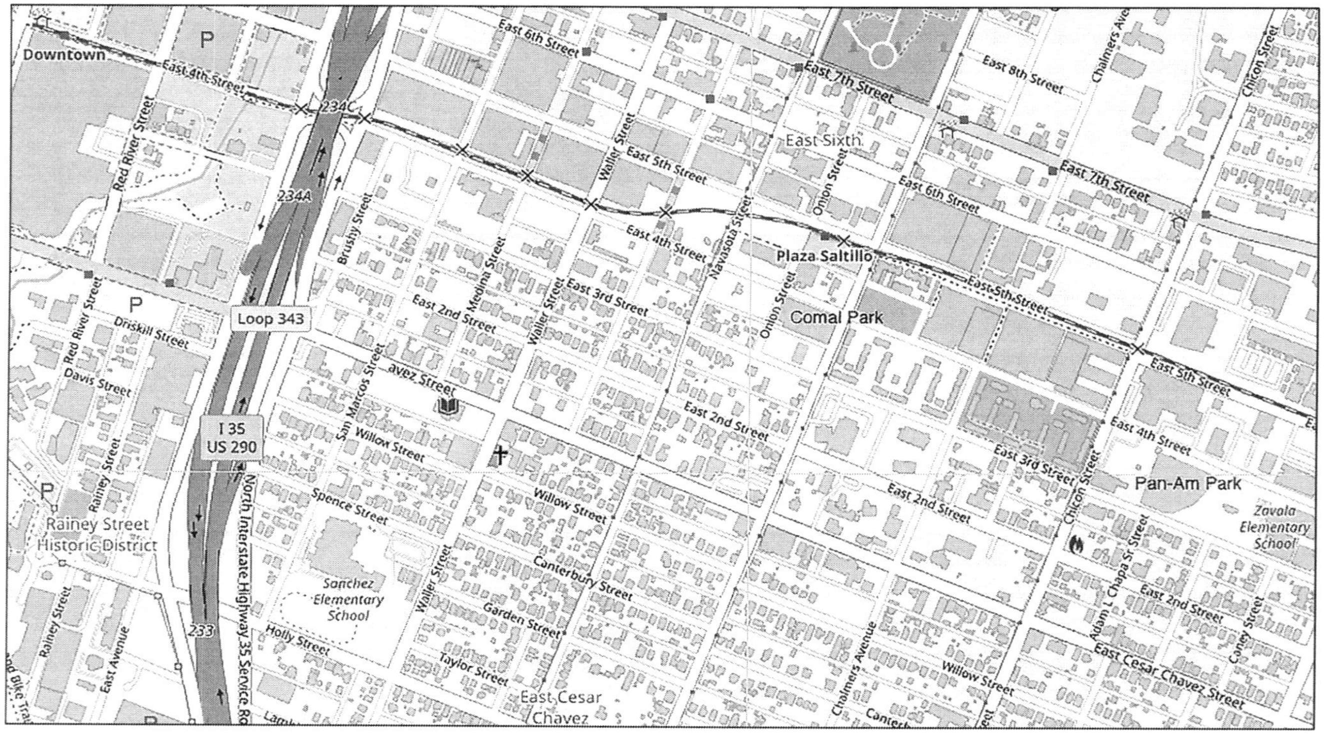


**Figure 5.1 Map of the Eastside Neighborhood in Austin, Texas.** *Source*: openstreetmap.org.

that count from "Anglos," or "Non-Hispanic White" (Robinson, 2011a). Over the course of three censuses, from 1990 to 2010, Anglos have steadily grown in real numbers, but their portion of the Austin population has declined from 61.7 percent to 48.7 percent. Meanwhile, those counted as Hispanic-Latino in the same censuses rose from 22.8 percent of the population to 35.1 percent. In the same period, African Americans in Austin declined from 11.9 percent of the population to 7.7 percent, with a decline of 4,000 people from 2000 to 2010 (Robinson, 2011a).

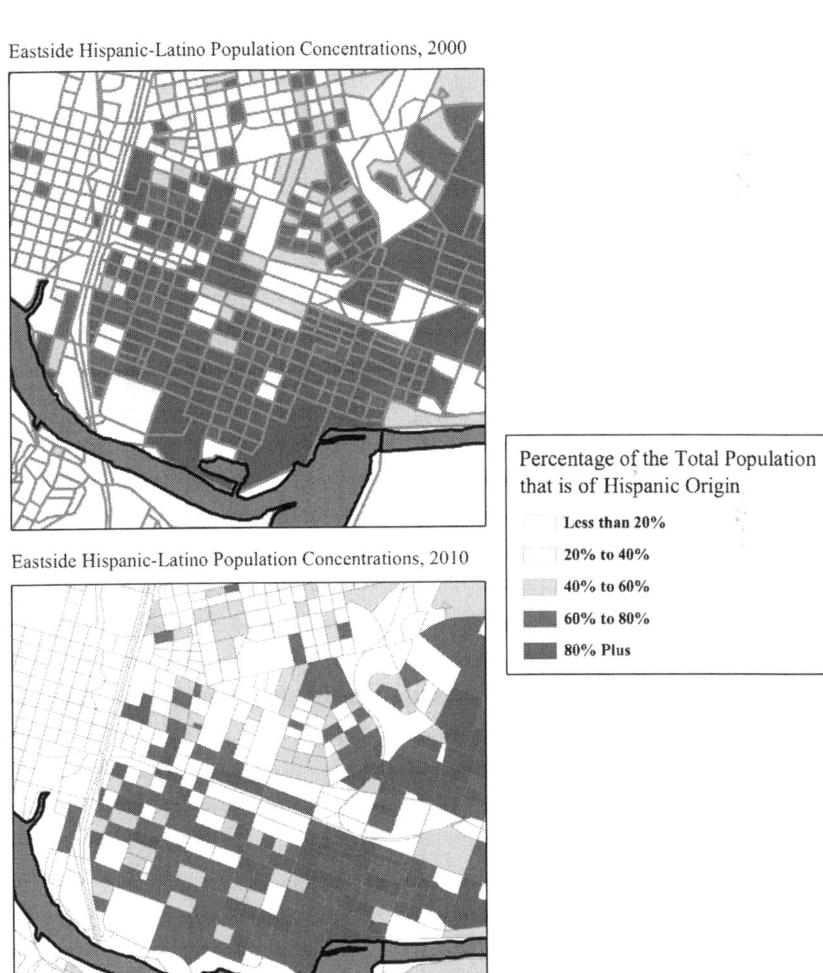


**Figure 5.2 Details from the Map "Changing Hispanic Landscape: Hispanic-Latino Concentrations, 2000 and 2010."** *Source*: www.austintexas.gov.

Despite growth in the Hispanic-Latino share of Austin's population overall, the traditional barrio of the Eastside has seen a dramatic drop in "Hispanic-origin" residents, as depicted in a map of Hispanic-Latino concentrations by census blocks (figure 5.2). In 2000, almost every block of the Eastside had 80 percent or more residents claiming Hispanic origin. By 2010, most of the same areas registered as 60 percent or more Hispanic origin, with several blocks dipping below that (Robinson, 2011b). This is what is commonly referenced in Austin as the "demographic changes" of the Eastside, a whitening or Anglocization that many area residents see as the effect of gentrification.

## BARRIOLOGY

The formation of the Eastside was an instance of a historical process that scholars such as Raul Homero Villa (2000) have called "barrioization." This process occurred in many cities around the nation and is marked by the formation of Mexican American communities, or barrios, through measures of displacement, segregation, containment, and policing of those populations. Yet, Villa argues that as destructive as the processes of barrioization can be, and as much as they represent anything but the agency and choice of their residents, something else happens in the history of barrios. In the process of being conducted into these spatially defined ethnic-local communities, people somehow find a way to live. As they do so, they produce traditions of the oppressed, and the vernacular cultural productions that result from their particular experiences of space constitutes barrioization. Villa calls these cultural productions and the knowledge of them "barriology," a specific place-based form of knowledge that accrues collectively as an area designated for containment becomes the location for other forms of sociality, including family, friendships, and new forms of identity based on practices and experiences specific to the area. Barriology, I argue, is a repertoire of traditions of the oppressed that needs to be taken seriously.

This has been the focus of my research over the past fifteen years of conducting ethnographic fieldwork on Mexican American vernacular cultures. The first project, through which I got to know the Eastside and the spatial stakes of popular aesthetics, culminated in my book on lowrider car style. This style of custom-modifying and driving cars is a popular aesthetic form associated with Mexican Americans in U.S. cities (figure 5.3). In my book, I tracked ways that the form was identified with barrio places like the Eastside, and how the movement of lowrider cars and their drivers was subject to intensive surveillance and policing in the race- and class-riven context of Austin in the early 2000s (Chappell, 2012).

**Figure 5.3 A Lowrider on the Eastside.** *Source*: Photo by the author.

One pivotal location for this field research was on the Eastside, a park known as Fiesta Gardens to many locals, officially "Edward Rendon, Sr. Park at Festival Beach" to the city, and Chicano Park to residents. It was here that lowriders would gather most Sunday nights when it was warm, to show off their latest adornments and socialize. Recently, I had the opportunity to reminisce about this scene from a distance in space and time as I browsed the YouTube website for a song I had heard responding to the gentrification of the Eastside. Locating "What Happened to Austin," I scrolled casually through the comments, noticing one post that read "I Heard It for the First Time on Sunday at Chicano Park." The song, by barber and hip-hop MC Lench Martinez, opens with a clip of a news broadcast covering the destruction of Jumpolin, accented by tolling bells and a grim, minor-key hip-hop track. Martinez's lyrics mark the transformation of his neighborhood, grieving the loss of the "beautiful city, my beautiful home," without ignoring that deprivation was part of barrio history:

It was all about peace and progress
Way before you called it Cesar Chavez
It was First Street
And the worst street
Bunch of *mexicanos* on a seven-day work week
Selling *raspas*, corn and *piñatas*
Back when all the *casas* were owned by *la raza*

There were rascals running down Haskell
Now it's full of *vatos* on bikes with satchels
Are you mad, bro?
How you think we feel?
Kick us out the *barrio* and now you want to rebuild. (Martinez, 2016, used with the author's permission)

In a video for the song, Martinez appears situated in specific Eastside sites, standing in the street in front of the A. B. Cantú Pan-American Recreation Center, in the park behind the center, and cruising down a residential street in his classic car while he delivers a tour in verse:

The fields right there where my grandpa played
Cristo Rey church where my grandma prayed
Santa Rita courts where my fam all stayed
Back when Little Joe used to jam all day. (Martinez, 2016)

For the chorus, however, Martinez stands on the Hillside stage behind the center that former residents call "Pan-Am." That stage is the site for community events such as the summer Hillside concert series of live music. Its walls are decorated with a mural by artist Raul Valdez, a work rich with Chicana/o and Mexican themes, including an image of the Aztec Templo Mayor of Tenochtitlán, scenes of the Spanish conquest, folkloric dancers, a custom car, and Emiliano Zapata.

Unlike some other murals throughout the Eastside on privately owned buildings, which increasingly have been subject to being painted over, the Hillside murals garner some protection from being part of the city's Cultural Heritage Collection rather than privately owned—indeed, the city has invested over $50,000 in a restoration of the murals (Castillo, 2012). The space of the stage that the painted walls surround is also thick with memory for some Eastside residents—not only because of the extensive community involvement, both when the walls were originally painted in 1978 and during the restoration by the artist in 2012. Through some of my fieldwork contacts, I was able to correspond with Lench, who informed me that the Hillside stage was also sacred ground to him. This went back to the 1980s, when the Eastside was traumatized by warring cliques and events that went undocumented but remained unforgettable, like what lowriders recalled as "the Easterday Shootout" at Chicano Park. According to Lench, it was on the Hillside stage that the well-known politician Gonzalo Barrientos asked Lench's father to mediate a truce between the rival sets.

Most of this history was not visible to me when, as a field researcher living on the Eastside, I attended Hillside concerts, showing up on my bike on summer evenings. The rich sociality that converged around the stage, though, was evident in the weekly concerts, a kind of community event that was both routine and special. Neighborhood residents set their lawn chairs up on the hill or parked their cars on the street behind Pan-Am rec center. The night I went, the band was introduced as *Grupo Adicción*, formerly known as *Los Hermanos Cruz*. The MC of the evening worked to animate the crowd with general shout-outs—"Hello Austin! We're here in the capital city! Hello Eastside!"—and specific greetings: Gabriela Cruz, the Garzas, Anthony who is celebrating his nineteenth birthday.

After I settled onto the grass to listen, a middle-aged man and woman spread their blanket nearby, and before long he wordlessly offered me one of their beers. We ended up chatting about my bike as the band took a break and the MC called out neighborhoods: "We got anyone from 4th Street? Willow? Govalle? Eastside?" People cheered their street, but one guy back by the parked cars cheered every single one. His enthusiasm climbed higher when a 70s Monte Carlo on rims pulled onto the side street with its sound system hitting, and the guy yelled "Eastside! We got a lowrider here!" Turning away from the stage, I could see the softball field at the west end of the park, and the girls' team that had been practicing was wrapping things up as a boy who had jumped the fence from Hillside danced a cumbia with the center fielder. As the band wrapped up and I said goodbye to my neighbors, we agreed to look for each other the next week.

## SENSES OF PLACE

The layers of sedimented historical meaning that accrue in a place through its use as a meeting point and common ground for the surrounding community situate space as a living, unfolding history. Steve Feld and Keith Basso, in their influential statement on "senses of place" as phenomena that can be apprehended ethnographically, write:

> Senses of place: the terrain covered here includes the relation of sensation to emplacement; the experiential and expressive ways places are known, imagined, yearned for, held, remembered, voiced, lived, contested, and struggled over; and the multiple ways places are metonymically and metaphorically tied to identities. We begin by asking how people are dwelling and how ethnographic accounts of their modes of dwelling might enrich our sense of why places, however vague, are lived out in deeply meaningful ways. (Feld & Basso, 1996, p. 11)

Places like the Eastside may be "vague" in a sense of offering structures of feeling (see Williams, 1977) rather than more directly articulated reasons for their significance, especially in a moment long after the gentrification process has begun, in which Anglos can be overheard saying things like "Did you know this used to be a Latino area?" Practiced identities of place may also be vague and hard to put a finger on, and yet they may be articulated precisely. For example, when I first arrived in Austin, I was told by an acquaintance that "if you look at the area east of the highway, you just know you don't want to be there," illustrating the way other people at the University talked about the Eastside.

Though senses of place are notoriously difficult to define, the phrase speaks to an experience people have with a collective homeplace, an accumulation of layered social space. There is more to this than the "development" of an area as places get built, made, and elaborated according to the plans of a "developer." Instead, everyday practice and the traditions of the oppressed generate social space as a "back-formation from practices," or what Lauren Berlant calls "environment" (2007, p. 759). For Berlant, an environment is not only spatial but temporal, a kind of space "whose qualities and whose contours in time and space are often identified with the presentness of ordinariness itself, that domain of living on, in which everyday activity; memory, needs, and desires; diverse temporalities and horizons of the taken-for-granted are brought into proximity" (Berlant, 2007, p. 759). This moves toward what Nigel Thrift (2008) has termed a "non-representational" approach to space, emphasizing its emergent materiality, which may be experienced or felt without being directly contemplated, such that "just because it lacks explicit articulation, is not therefore without a grip" (p. 16). The grip of the social space of the Eastside is what grabs listeners who know the neighborhood and feel changes in the sense of place.

The richness of environments that have been formed through repeated and ordinary practices becomes clear in the memory of material presentness. This is how displacement registers as a loss, and contrasts with the humanist conception of space that presumes places to be blank until owned. That idea of blank space is expressed in much of the discourse of "development," and therefore the process of gentrification, in which the various territories of the city are simply backgrounds for the projects of individual property-owning agents. Someone needs space for their tech entrepreneur party, or their block of lofts, or their niche business that will make the area more interesting, fun, and profitable. They find the space and take it where they can. This relation to space is determined primarily by historical, unequal distributions of capital. Thus, Jumpolin falls and, even if neighborhood residents were not sure what to call the changes in their neighborhood before this point, they understand that some material presence has gone. The grip of Jumpolin's new absence is part of the aesthetic response that people registered to Lench's song.

The market-humanist notion of place-making proffers space as a universal material, presumptively available to all—we occupy it, construct particular formations of space to serve our interests, reflect our individuality, or offer consumable versions of individuality for other subjects. This is very closely aligned with the model of urbanism that we can recognize as part and parcel of neoliberal capitalism and the process of gentrification. In the humanist frame, the idea behind gentrification is a kind of cultural effervescence made possible by liberal markets. It begins with the prospect that space in general, and urban space in particular, is a blank slate. In other words, the city is there for whomever will use it. Uses that reflect investment are a signal of improvement. Such a concept, empowered with capital according to historical, racialized, and uneven distributions, unconsciously takes on the form of coloniality—where the city is not a blank slate, it must be made blank in order for the effervescent creativity of capitalism to make itself known. The market-humanist production of space thus mirrors the historical concept of *terra nullius*, the empty land waiting to be improved by colonists and settlers. This parallel to long-running histories of colonialism has not been lost on activists who resist it (PODER, 2003). Space in its market production is not so much infused with history, as it is opportunity. But in an unequal society, opportunity is the encounter between cleared space and wealth, the results of prior accumulations. The barrio space that is layered with meaning through the ordinary and special practices of the traditions of the oppressed works differently—meaning accumulates among people already present in the space through their shared ordinariness of experience. Rather than taking possession of a place in order to make it into something, they inhabit the place and co-emerge with it as a "community."

## PLACE IN PLAY

On another day during fieldwork I passed by the ball field at Pan-Am, across the park from Hillside (figure 5.4). I saw two teams of adult men facing off on the dirt field, one in green and gold caps and shirts with a jester motif. Watching a few pitches, I quickly realized this was not the recreational "slow pitch" form of the game that I often think of as softball. The pitcher, apparently in his fifties, was throwing the ball hard and, when the opportunity came, the other men fielded and ran the bases aggressively.

I would eventually come to know this competitive, fast-paced game the way the players refer to it, simply as "fastpitch." I also would learn that Mexican American communities spread throughout the railroad network that supported them with employment have maintained a fastpitch tradition since the 1940s. Inside the Pan-Am community center are some traces that fastpitch

**Figure 5.4 The Softball Diamond at Pan-Am Park.** *Source*: Photo by the author.

has left on the community, in a mural by Martin Garcia titled *Las Acciones del Pasado Aseguran el Éxito Hacia el Futuro* ("Actions from the Past Ensure Success in the Future"). There, images of a ballfield and specific individuals representing memorable teams mark layers of memory that thicken the space for those who were there for the cyclical gatherings that the game occasioned, through weeknight leagues and all-day weekend tournaments. When pausing to pay attention to a recreational game that is not likely to make the news, it becomes evident how years of practice, memory, imagery, and talk enliven the space. All of these repeated and ordinary practices are conditioned by poetic and aesthetic patterns that make certain games, certain phrases, and certain ways of being together seem to fit the context.

It is not unusual for a community to commemorate their sports heroes, since sport is a ubiquitous cultural form in the United States, an unscripted drama that gets performed repeatedly, staging epic struggles on a weekly or seasonal basis. Unlike professional sports perceived from a distance, though, or high-investment youth club sports played in dedicated complexes and requiring travel, Eastside fastpitch happened close to front porches, close enough to watch in the course of an ordinary week. Because Pan-Am park, the "fields where my grandpa played," is also fully embedded in the community, families could watch games from across the street, and players stepping up to bat could see the crowd gathering for a Hillside concert and hear a lowrider's music playing as it rolled by. The affective power that Lench draws on in his song comes from referencing the particularity of the place that Pan-Am park represents, this dense environment of memory and practice, rendering a sense of the value the place holds, a value that is not captured in real estate or property tax assessments. To view land use as "just business," and displacement as inevitable, progressive change evacuates the environment to make it fungible, just another "property" among others.

## CONCLUSION

The traditions of the oppressed call us to recognize that what appears to the new arrival as a blank slate is in fact crisscrossed with affectively engraved traces of people's multiple paths that meet in urban space (Massey, 2005). They further attest to the need for "greater attention to the ways in which cultural citizenship is a *visceral experience* by focusing on 'structures of belonging'" (Diaz-Barriga, 2008, p. 136, emphasis added). In this chapter, I have chosen to look for such viscerality in popular aesthetics that register in material space, entertainment, and play. My selection of recognizable practices, easily observable in public, also does not even begin to account for all the barriological modes of dwelling that together constitute the Eastside. Not least, for example, one could delve deeply into the "church where my grandma prayed" and other spaces of barriological practice. This is not to argue that the features of landscape and ephemeral practice presented here are any more important than what is more readily recognized as spatial politics. Activists and social movements on the Eastside, such as the People Organized in Defense of Earth and her Resources (PODER), and leaders such as PODER director Susana Almanza, are well aware of the value of their homeplaces, and my arguments here should only be taken as a call to support such movements (PODER, 2003). Furthermore, as gentrification continues to accelerate and the clash of productions of space is ongoing, grassroots organizing has won considerable gains, such as bringing to the city resolutions on "the right to stay," conceived through the availability of affordable housing (Goard, 2018).

Legislative measures can be drag on, however, and the deliberative process of formal politics sometimes delivers remedies that have been negotiated down to a scale that is insufficient to slow the ravages of capital-rich real estate trade. The accumulation of historical ties to place is also slow and gradual but no less valuable for it. To honor such ongoing histories, we must attend to the traditions of the oppressed.

## NOTE

1. I am grateful to Lench Martinez for permission to quote and discuss his song "What Happened to Austin" at length. Support for the research discussed in this chapter was provided by the Wenner-Gren foundation (grant #6600), a grant from the University of Kansas General Research Fund, and a Big XII Fellowship, for which I am indebted to John Hartigan, director of the Américo Paredes Center for Cultural Studies at the University of Texas, for his invitation to study in Austin.

## BIBLIOGRAPHY

Aoki, K. (1993). Race, space, and place: The relation between architectural modernism, post-modernism, urban planning, and gentrification. *Fordham Urban Law Journal, 20*, 699–828.

Austin, Texas Population. (2019). World population review. Retrieved from http://worldpopulationreview.com/us-cities/austin-population/.

Benjamin, W. (1940). Theses on the philosophy of history. In H. Arendt (Ed.), *Illuminations* (Harry Zohn, Trans., pp. 253–264). New York: Schocken Books.

Berlant, L. (2007). Slow death (sovereignty, obesity, lateral agency). *Critical Inquiry, 33*(4), 754–780.

Castillo, J. (2012, September 22). Bold and colorful once again, mural at East Austin outdoor theater comes into focus. *Statesman*. Retrieved from https://www.statesman.com/news/20120922/bold-and-colorful-once-again-mural-at-east-austin-outdoor-theater-comes-into-focus.

Caterine, J. (2016, April 15). Fighting to stay: A culture of resistance is growing in neighborhoods that find themselves on the verge of displacement. *The Austin Chronicle*. Retrieved from https://www.austinchronicle.com/news/2016-04-15/fighting-to-stay.

Chappell, B. (2012). *Lowrider space: Aesthetics and politics of Mexican American custom cars*. Austin, TX: University of Texas Press.

Devadanam, S. (2018). This Austin ZIP code ranks among the most gentrified in the nation. *Culture Map Austin*. Retrieved from http://austin.culturemap.com/news/real-estate/03-29-18-most-gentrified-zip-code-east-austin-78702/.

Diaz-Barriga, M. (2008). *Distracción*: Notes on cultural citizenship, visual ethnography, and Mexican migration to Pennsylvania. *Visual Anthropology Review, 24*(2), 133–147.

Feld, S., & Basso, K. (Eds.). (1996). *Senses of place*. Santa Fe, NM: School for Advanced Research.

Goard, A. (2018). City council looks to turn the tide of gentrification in East Austin. *KXAN*. Retrieved from https://www.kxan.com/news/local/austin/city-council-looks-to-turn-the-tide-of-gentrification-in-east-austin/1026461299.

Hall, K. (2017). East Austin: Jumpolin piñata store returns two years after controversial demolition. *Austin American-Statesman* (updated September 22, 2018).

Retrieved from https://www.statesman.com/news/20170823/east-austin-jumpolin-piata-store-returns-2-years-after-controversial-demolition.

Koch & Fowler. (1928). *A city plan for Austin, Texas.* Austin, TX: City Plan Commission.

Lack, P.D. (1981). Slavery and vigilantism in Austin, Texas, 1840–1860. *Southwestern Historical Quarterly, 85*(1), 1–20.

Lefebvre, H. (1992). *The production of space* (D. Nicholson-Smith, Trans.). Malden, MA: Wiley-Blackwell.

Limón, J.E. (1994). *Dancing with the devil: Society and cultural poetics in Mexican–American South Texas.* Madison, WI: University of Wisconsin Press.

Limón, J.E. (2012). *Américo Paredes: Culture and critique.* Austin, TX: University of Texas Press.

Martinez, L. (2016). What happened to Austin? *Brown South Entertainment.* Retrieved from https://youtu.be/W1m03-DlHu0.

Massey, D. (2005). *For space.* Thousand Oaks, CA: Sage.

Planas, R. (2015). Destroying a family-owned piñata shop totally backfired against this company. *Huffington Post Latino Voices.* Retrieved from https://www.huffingtonpost.com/2015/03/20/pinata-shop-austin_n_6905968.html.

PODER—People Organized in Defense of Earth and her Resources. (2003). *SMART growth, historic zoning, and gentrification of East Austin: Continued relocation of native people from their homeland.* Austin, TX: S. Almanza, S. Herrera & L. Almanza.

Robinson, R. (2011a). City of Austin demographic profile. Retrieved from https://www.austintexas.gov/sites/default/files/files/Planning/Demographics/city_of_austin_profile_2010.pdf.

Robinson, R. (2011b). Changing Hispanic landscape: Hispanic-Latino concentrations, 2000 and 2010. Retrieved from http://www.austintexas.gov/sites/default/files/files/Planning/Demographics/hisp_change00_10.pdf.

Tang, E., & Falola, B. (2018). *Those who stayed: The impact of gentrification on longstanding residents of East Austin.* Austin, TX: University of Texas Institute for Urban Policy and Analysis.

Thrift, N. (2008). *Non-representational theory: Space, politics, affect.* London, England: Routledge.

Villa, R.H. (2000). *Barrio logos: Space and place in urban Chicano literature and culture.* Austin, TX: University of Texas Press.

Williams, R. (1977). *Marxism and literature.* Oxford, England: Oxford University Press.

# Chapter 6

# They Always Promise Toilets

## *Electoral Politics and Infrastructural Inequality in Postapartheid Cape Town*

Angela D. Storey

Characterized by a stark contrast between mansions nestled into the leafy edges of Table Mountain and informal settlements stretched across the Cape Flats, Cape Town remains one of the most unequal cities in the world (UN-Habitat, 2016).[1] Promises of equity and justice surrounding the first postapartheid elections in 1994 have eroded over time with the persistence of socioeconomic inequality. Alongside this decay, participation in elections has steadily subsided, transitioning from the astonishing turnout of 1994's long but celebratory voting lines to a more sedate ritual of citizenship practice (Gordon et al., 2018). Marking twenty years of democracy, the national and provincial elections of 2014 were characterized by residents of peripheral and impoverished urban informal settlements more by feelings of frustration than those of promise. This chapter examines how residents of Cape Town's informal settlements expressed discontent with persistent urban inequality around the 2014 elections, and, particularly, how these frustrations were often grounded in discussions of infrastructure.

Building from scholarship examining shifting urban belonging and terrains of infrastructural inequality in South Africa, I argue that narratives about infrastructure and elections provide a way to see the material and political contours of peripheral citizenship. As residents take advantage of opportunities for material improvement, rework and blur lines of service access, and contest the centrality of electoral process to democratic belonging, they narrate a postapartheid democracy in which urban inequality has become everyday politics. Highlighting the ways in which residents critique and challenge democratic processes, while also sometimes engaging in them, I utilize the concept of refusal (McGranahan, 2016; Simpson, 2014, 2016; Weiss, 2016) to explore complex interactions between peripheral citizens and centralized processes of governance.

In examining the experiences of marginalized residents in the context of persistent urban inequality, I draw from the work of scholars emphasizing the importance of urban peripheries in re-crafting understandings of citizenship (Brown, 2015; Holston, 2009), and calls to examine citizenship from a politics of everyday life (Robins, Cornwall, & von Lieres, 2008). I connect this to recent ethnographic work examining how urban politics are increasingly articulated through the exclusions of infrastructural systems, exploring how these material connections provide important ways to examine belonging in profoundly unequal global cities (Anand, 2017; von Schnitzler, 2016). These approaches prompt us to examine how normative conceptualizations of democratic participation overlook the experiences of marginalized urban communities and to ask how such notions might be reshaped when grounded in local experience.

## BACKGROUND AND METHODS: IN THE PERIPHERIES OF CAPE TOWN

Informal settlements were first thought to be short-term solutions to a post-apartheid housing crisis, but quickly became inescapable parts of the urban landscape (Huchzermeyer & Karam, 2006). Leslie Bank describes South Africa's urban spaces as "fractured" (2011), reflecting the patchwork of places excluded from development alongside those far to the opposite—stately houses behind high walls in gated communities, in contrast with expanses of tin-roofed shacks along busy roads. Nearly 20 percent of city households live in informal dwellings (City of Cape Town, 2017)—self-constructed homes, often of tin and thin plywood—with this number growing (City of Cape Town, 2017; Housing Development Agency, 2013). Life within informality illustrates extreme racial disparity: according to the last national census, nearly half of the city's black households live in an informal dwelling, while only 1 percent of the city's white population do as well (City of Cape Town, 2012) (figure 6.1).

Cape Town is a markedly segregated city, based upon both race and class. This is apparent within official statistics on access to formal housing and infrastructure, employment levels, or educational access, and is readily visible within the city's public spaces. When walking on Kloof Street, in the dramatic upcurve of Table Mountain that leads from downtown to the affluent neighborhoods above, restaurants and shops will be filled largely with white customers and tourists but staffed by workers of color who likely traveled an hour or two to arrive that morning. This is similarly the experience when visiting Constantia Village, a busy shopping center in the city's wealthy Southern Suburbs, where the predominantly white population is mirrored in

**Figure 6.1 Map of Cape Town, South Africa.** *Source*: Openstreetmap.org.

the shoppers and in the selection of stores. To walk through a shopping mall in Khayelitsha, however, is to see a very different tableau, one reflecting the fact that 98.6 percent of residents identify as black, as well as the area's precipitously high unemployment rate (City of Cape Town, 2013). My whiteness allowed me to traverse city spaces in ways necessarily framed by my social privileges and contextual limitations. This movement was important for understanding a small part of Cape Town's severe divisions and revealed ways in which the city's structural inequalities were entrenched and normalized through the homogeneity of mundane spaces and encounters.

In a city of more than 4 million (City of Cape Town, 2017), the suburb of Khayelitsha perches at the interior edge of the city. Included in the metropolitan area during postapartheid reorganization, the area was initially built in the 1980s for black workers excluded from the city under apartheid's race-based residency laws (Cook, 1992). In 2014, Khayelitsha was home—officially—to nearly 400,000 people (City of Cape Town, 2013). Khayelitsha includes many neighborhoods of formal homes, financed either privately or publicly, but 54 percent of the area dwellings are informal structures, some located in the backyards of formal dwellings and many more situated in the suburb's dozens of informal settlements (City of Cape Town, 2013) (figure 6.2). Although government financing has resulted in the construction of millions of formal homes across the country postapartheid, the backlog for housing

**Figure 6.2 A Broad Informal Settlement in Khayelitsha, 2015.** *Source*: Photo by Shachaf Polakow.

lists in Cape Town is estimated to be over sixty years at recent construction rates (Maregele, 2017).

In Khayelitsha, informal settlements experience a range of infrastructural access. The city of Cape Town has set goals of informal settlement provision for water at the rate of one common tap for every twenty-five households, and toilets at the rate of one toilet for every five households (de Lille, 2013). Even in areas in which this target is met, this level of provision results in significant burdens to individuals, households, and communities to meet daily needs, and some modes of provision are seen as undignified and inappropriate. For areas in which service goals are not met, hundreds of people might share a single water tap (ISN, 2010) and several dozen may utilize one chemical toilet (SJC, 2013). The provision of infrastructure to informal settlements is the obligation of municipalities and public entities in South Africa, and thus modes of service provision vary by location, funding, and political will, among other factors.

My ethnographic research in Cape Town has included work in a number of informal settlements between 2010 and 2019, with a significant focus on three informal settlements near one of Khayelitsha's main roadways. The data at the core of this chapter was collected in 2013 and 2014 during fourteen months of fieldwork and is contextualized by an additional seven months of research conducted over the intervening years. Data has been collected primarily via participant observation and interviews, conducted both within informal settlements and with a variety of local organizations based in Khayelitsha—social movements, nonprofit organizations, street committees, political parties, youth movements, and others—all of which were working to gain municipal improvements to basic service access. Research within informal settlements was conducted following meetings with and approval from local social movements, street committees, and/or neighborhood groups within each site. The in-depth, semi-structured interviews discussed in this chapter were conducted with eighty-six residents of three selected informal settlements, and held in community centers, homes, or public space, reflecting the needs and preferences of the interviewee. Participant observation included attendance at local events, meetings, marches, trainings, walking tours of communities, and time spent in individual households, among other sites. This included observation at election sites in five areas of the city with voters before and after attending the polls on election day, as well as informal discussions with residents, party officials, and candidates regarding the influence of the election on the possibilities for infrastructural improvements.

During the period discussed in this chapter, surrounding the 2014 election, the informal settlements on which this research focuses experienced a wide array of different service forms for electricity, water, and sanitation, with variation in provision within and between sites. The areas were also home to a broad set of politicized groups, including social movements, community-based groups, political parties, and locally elected committees. These differences in infrastructural provision and political engagements within a small area offered the possibility for wide-ranging discussions with residents surrounding conceptualizations of inequality, belonging, and politics.

## "LOOK BUSY": THE MATERIAL POLITICS OF INEQUALITY

One morning in late January 2014, I sat in the small office of a community-based social movement in Khayelitsha, talking about a light pole. Our conversation centered upon a series of new streetlights that had recently been built by the city of Cape Town along this main roadway, their metal sides bright in the day's summer sunshine and the lights themselves lit but looking dull midday. Tata Silu,[2] an activist and amaXhosa resident of the nearest informal settlement, chortled dismissively when I asked after the unexpected construction of the shiny new light poles. "Yeah," he said, by way of a full explanation, "the elections are coming."

This accounting for the city's actions was given consistently by residents of informal settlements when talking about service-related work completed in the months leading up to the May 2014 national and provincial elections. Many continued on to say that the city intended for construction to be a way to "look busy" before the elections, implying that actual infrastructural improvements were less important to the city than the possibility that people would perceive them—and, by proxy, the party in control of the city government—as working to improve access to water, sanitation, electricity, or other basic services.

The selection of streetlights as a particular infrastructural improvement was not lost on residents; the location of the lights along a busy roadway proved hyper-visible both to residents and to anyone passing through this major artery. Other such projects pointed out by residents as part of the "looking busy" logic leading up to the election included projects of similarly high visibility, such as road repaving. This sat in contrast to the many needed modes of service that were not as visible, such as toilets, taps, and electricity boxes—smaller items often set in the midst of, or within, homes. While frustrating as a sole improvement, improved lighting has been a campaign of social movements in Khayelitsha as a way to decrease violence (Mortlock, 2017), and the city of Cape Town has stated that insufficient public lighting is linked to the area's high crime rate (Charles, 2019). The lighting improvement was necessary in the particularity of its usage while, simultaneously, being a highly symbolic marker of the many everyday violences in this same site that went wholly unaddressed by the municipality. This kind of piecemeal approach to upgrading infrastructure has been readily identified by informal settlement residents in Cape Town as inadequate for improving safety in the absence of significant structural change (Brown-Luthango, Reyes, & Gubevu, 2017).

At the time of the installation of the lamp posts, Cape Town was the only major metropolitan area in South Africa under the control of the country's main opposition party, the Democratic Alliance (DA). The city was also located within the only province then led by the DA. The DA's purported success in running Cape Town thus became a foundation for their provincial reelection campaign in 2014 and a main example of their governance capabilities used to support their national aspirations against the African National Congress (ANC), South Africa's postapartheid revolutionary movement become twenty-year ruling party. The DA had captured control of Cape Town in the last provincial elections, in 2009, on a slim margin, and sought to retain that control, in part by appealing to black voters. The DA struggled to gain black voters and were widely seen as representing the concerns and interests of white and coloured[3] communities (Mottiar, 2015). Indeed, Khayelitsha was one of the areas of the city—along with other majority-black suburbs, such as Nyanga and Philippi—that remained strongly ANC in the 2009 elections, following national patterns of race-based voting postapartheid (Mottiar, 2015). During the 2014 campaign, the DA sought to appeal to black voters by highlighting improvements made to service access and the funding dedicated to the poorest citizens (Africa, 2015). The pressure on Cape Town's governance as a hyper-visible national model, and the challenges of overcoming past patterns of voting, meant that the city did, indeed, need to "look busy" (figure 6.3).

While Ta-Silu and many others that I spoke with in Khayelitsha saw the streetlights as a sign of the city's inescapably partisan electoral campaigning, the streetlights were a material improvement in an area with significant needs. And, like other modes of limited infrastructure provided by the government, they quickly became part of local assemblages of service access that worked around binaries of formal/informal, legal/illegal, and public/private provision. Thando, another local social movement activist, laughed at dismissive comments made about the city and the "look busy" explanation for projects such as the lights. But, he argued, they have been so nice and made it easy to open these new poles. He explained that some households had already released the maintenance access point at the base of their nearest pole and were using that connection to bring free electricity into their shacks. Despite two decades on this site, the informal settlement that Thando pointed out—and in which he and Ta-Silu both lived—had yet to gain legal electricity connections for the vast majority of households. Significant time and resources were thus spent by households to gain temporary modes of access to electricity, sometimes

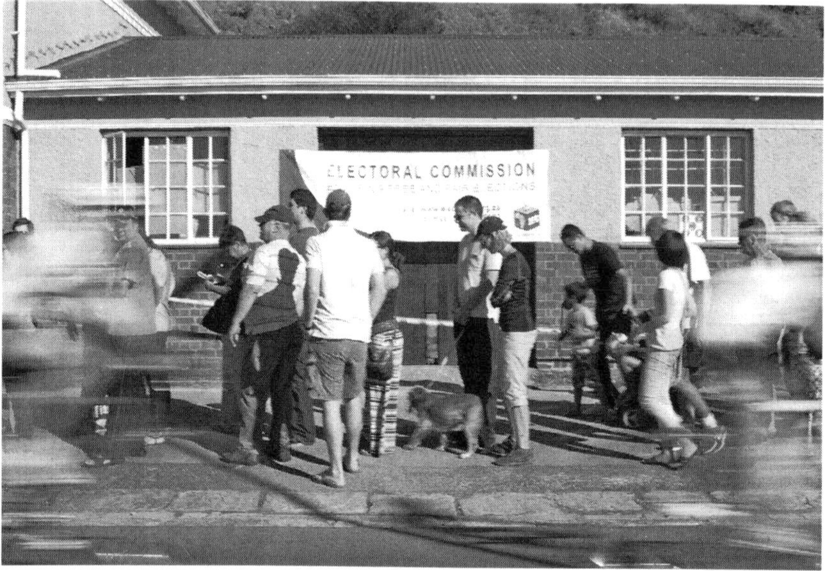


**Figure 6.3 Cyclists Blur Past Voters Lined Up Near Muizenberg, Cape Town.** *Source*: Photo by Shachaf Polakow.

directly from power poles but often purchased through arrangements with the nearest formal houses or electricity-provided informal settlements. These extended connections were not especially reliable—the lines are often broken, fried, or purposefully cut to steal the wire, and households selling electricity connections frequently asked for additional money part way through a month to retain the link—so a new opportunity for a proximate connection was readily utilized.

The streetlights were not, in their everyday usage, the symbols of infrastructural progress that the city might have imagined them to be for residents-as-voters, if the rationale for their construction did follow the logic of "looking busy" before the elections. Instead, the streetlight's presence and use became part of the logics of making-do that characterize urban informality globally. In profoundly unequal cities, where significant portions of the population are excluded from formal infrastructural systems, socio-material relations emerge that provide access to daily needs (Anand, 2017; Dubbeld, 2017; Simone, 2004). These partial and make-do infrastructures are intensely political—daily reminders of both urban exclusions and the labor required by excluded communities to survive under conditions of infrastructural violence (Rodgers & O'Neill, 2012). Here, residents strategize around public and private systems to gain access, crafting modes of "people's power"—connections that work around active structural exclusions (Dawson, 2010). Such assemblages and linkages are framed as not only necessary in the absence of formal and full provision, but also as overtly political: a people's connection is not just one that reworks formal systems of access, but also one that traces a politics of reclamation and grassroots redistribution meant to counter persistent inequality.

Such socio-material politics are ubiquitous in Khayelitsha's informal settlements—there is no escaping the drooping electricity wires of extended connections or the patched together taps fixed by neighbors, just as one cannot escape explanations of political logics or actions based in the lived knowledge of the city's entrenched inequality. As Nikhil Anand (2017) argues for residents of Mumbai who rework access to water around formal structures and lines of political power or bureaucracy, new forms of citizenship are crafted in the infrastructural interstices of the city.

## "THEY KICK US AWAY": REFUSING ELECTORAL POLITICS

The elections were a constant topic of discussion in interviews I conducted with residents of informal settlements in Khayelitsha during the months before and after the 2014 elections. Often conversations involved party politics: a few residents voiced support for opposition parties, and others professed ongoing dedication to the ANC. The ANC would end up again sweeping this area of Cape Town and retaining national control but would fail to re-take the Western Cape Province (Mottiar, 2015). Ta-Silu emphasized the temporary interest in Khayelitsha by the city—seen as proxy for the DA—in our discussion of the streetlights, and many other residents expressed frustration with the inadequacy of both of these major political parties, and electoral politics as a whole, to address entrenched infrastructural inequalities. A neighbor of Ta-Silu's said, evocatively, that political parties "make people their step-ladders, then when they are up they kick us away."

Down the road from Ta-Silu and Thando, residents of another informal settlement had struggled for decades to gain access to reliable and dignified forms of sanitation. They were provided by the city with a kind of toilet known as the "bucket system." These units were named to reflect their simple structure: a plastic container with a ring seat atop it, placed inside a plastic or concrete shell.[4] Here such toilets were commonly shared at the rate of two households per unit. The bucket system may be the most reviled sanitation system in the country, widely associated with the apartheid government's political exclusions and its dehumanizing practices. Such systems remain in use despite national deadlines set—and missed—to eradicate the use of bucket toilets by 2006, and then by 2015 (October, 2017). Indeed, the province in which Cape Town is located has actually reported an increase in the provision of bucket toilets to informal settlements in recent years (Lepule, 2018).

Like the electrical work-arounds that included extended connections from the streetlights up the road, here individuals and families sought to access modes of sanitation beyond the bucket system in any way possible. This included participation in a variety of social movement campaigns, community-based work, and street protests. It also included the creation of relationships of exchange or payment with households in nearby areas with access to different modes of sanitation. A few residents even chose to defecate in open spaces instead of using the bucket system, explaining in interviews the horror at using such toilets—both in their apartheid connections and due to the propensity of bucket toilets to cultivate maggots. In talking about bucket toilets with residents, discussions wove together the politics of material use and the multiple politicized actions of the community to seek alternative provisions from the city.

Less than two weeks after the 2014 elections, I interviewed Phaphama. An amaXhosa man in his mid-thirties, Phaphama had lived in this area of Khayelitsha for more than fifteen years, moved here by the city as a result of municipal construction on the site of his previous informal settlement. In our lengthy interview, he detailed the repeated infrastructural promises made and broken by city officials and candidates from multiple parties. Barring the construction of a formal house, the most urgent need for the area was to be rid of the bucket toilets, in Phaphama's view, and that of many of his neighbors. Promises made for the construction of full-flush toilets were so common here that I heard repeatedly from residents, when asking after what they knew of infrastructural plans, that *everyone*—every politician, every city worker, every development organization—promised them toilets. Frustration over the bucket toilets' ongoing presence in his community permeated our discussion, and midway through, Phaphama told a story about recent electoral campaigning. He said:

> Even now, before the elections, there was a people who was coming here in (this informal settlement) from the different parties, to come to canvass for a vote. A lot of people then said to them, "OK, you can talk to the bucket system, they can go and vote for the party. Get out from my house!" . . . And then (the canvasser) . . . asks "Why? Why are you so rude to me?" (And the resident replies) "Here, look here, I have been staying with this bucket system for 30 years. So I am fucking sick and tired of all the promises. Get out. Because you are going to promise, even you. . . . No, I am not under anybody (any party), I am sick and tired of all of you. . . . I won't vote for anyone.

Here, ire boiling over, the user of the bucket system ends the political canvasser's overtures by not only rejecting the party but also the system of voting as a whole. Promises have become the mere matter of elections and not the basis of actual change. The bucket system, no longer just an unsanitary toilet, becomes a political actor of its own accord, the only potential audience for further promises.

Government is manifest in the lives of South Africa's poor primarily through forms of often inadequate service delivery, which are seen as evidence of the incomplete project of democratization (Dubbeld, 2017; Etzo, 2010). A resident from an informal settlement across the road from Phaphama's site told me: "I'm seeing no changes. All of these years I've been alive, I see no changes. I've been voting, voting, voting but I'm still staying in a shack." Although residents describe citizenship as an experience of waiting, they have not become what Auyero calls "patients of the state" (2012), those waiting for the state to enroll them in processes of governance. In critiquing electoral processes, residents craft a politics of refusal, appraising and rejecting the sufficiency of state-sanctioned roles. Refusal, as theorized by Simpson (2014, 2016), emphasizes the ways in which we may reimagine subject-making processes between, around, and through the refusals of states to recognize some groups, alongside the refusal of groups to recognize the state. Building from work within Kahnawà:ke Mohawk activism and communities, Simpson frames the necessity of engaging refusal as not a synonym of resistance but as a position in which actors reject the possibility of states as all-encompassing, or as sufficient. Such an approach identifies refusals as generative stances in which relations between actors are made in new ways (McGranahan, 2016) and in which new political spaces can be opened (Weiss, 2016).

Refusal becomes an important frame for seeing the actions of informal settlement residents in that it acknowledges both the exclusions of the state and the ways in which individuals and groups declare the state itself to be insufficient. The positions of residents mark elections themselves as inadequate, but also declare that the scope of political action does not fully capture their locus. The actions of informal settlements residents certainly include social movement and protest actions (Brown, 2015), but also active reworkings of postapartheid political norms that valorize democratic process as inherent forces for social improvement. Many see the relationship of voting as one that reinforces marginality, in which inequality is the product of democracy. As one man in Khayelitsha said to me around the 2014 elections, "We vote, but things dissatisfy us. It looks like we are voting for poverty now." This refrain echoes the statement of some South African social movements of informal settlement residents, like Abahlali baseMjondolo (AbM), that has at times advocated to reject voting. As AbM leader S'bu Zikode has said:

> For years I have tried the so-called diplomacy. I have approached the high-profile members of the ruling party, and tried to make deals, deals that will liberate you and I; deals that will answer the critical questions of access to basic rights like clean water, housing, sanitation, electricity, health care and education. But all in vain! In this democracy the poor are only used for voting. Once we have voted we are only lied to and undermined and ignored. (Zikode, 2008, p. 119)

Despite widespread discontent, many people in Khayelitsha did end up voting. Even some people who told me that they would not vote did, after all, end up casting ballots. Reasons were diverse: pressure from family or friends, concern that the absence of a voting stamp in their ID book might prevent access to jobs or social services, or worry about the visible absence of a tell-tale inked finger over the days following the election. It is possible that some of these voters chose to attend the polls but to "spoil" their ballot, an approach encouraged during that election by previously high-ranking ANC members dissatisfied with the party's actions (Africa, 2015). However, the act of voting does not counter the critiques voiced in narratives such as that of Phaphama. If he chose to vote, he did so not as a docile citizen enacting a limited, state-granted form of political agency, but as member of a community that actively politicized the modes of exclusion and inequality seen as irresolvable through voting alone.

Rejecting voting itself, in action, could have dire consequences in the lives of individuals already experiencing multiple exclusions. Indeed, acts of resistance can open an individual or community up to the focus of the state or its actors, even when the action is meant to reject enrollment in the state (Weiss, 2016). I heard anecdotes from community members that ward council offices deprioritized residents for publicly funded jobs when they were known to be members of other political parties, or not to have voted. While unsubstantiated, the power of such gossip to raise concern about access to much-needed work would reasonably animate an individual's choice to vote. As Holston argues, insurgent and entrenched forms of citizenship are inextricably caught up together, each destabilizing the other (2009) (figure 6.4).

For Phaphama and his neighbors, their politics were grounded in an unshakable understanding of their marginalization within the city, their position at the losing end of a vast chasm of social stratification. The daily reminder of this inequality, manifest in the requirements to use a bucket toilet, or to invest significant time or labor to identify alternatives, provoked a peripheral politics of refusal, one that sought to balance between the precarious poles of resistance and survival.

In recent years, infrastructure has become increasingly emphasized in scholarship linking socio-material relations and power (Bakker, 2003;

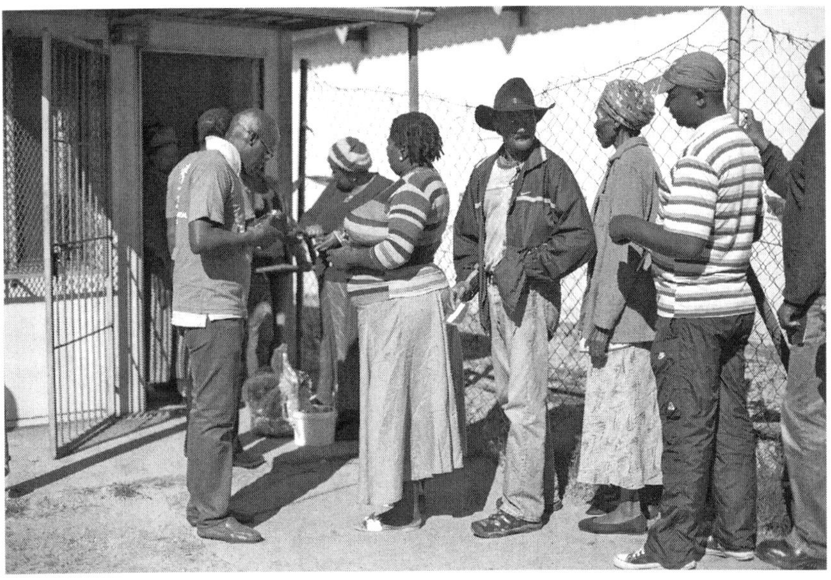

**Figure 6.4 Voters Wait to Enter a Polling Station in Khayelitsha, Cape Town.** *Source*: Photo by Shachaf Polakow.

Castro, 2004; Graham & Marvin, 2001; Howe et al., 2015; Larkin, 2013; Star, 1997). In South Africa, this work has emphasized the techno-political work of prepaid water and electricity meters (Dawson, 2010; von Schnitzler, 2016), the impacts of privatization and commodification under neoliberal policies (McDonald & Ruiters, 2005; Storey, 2014), and the ethics of innovation and protest (Robins, 2014). To understand a politics grounded in the infrastructural everyday—one tied tightly to the choices and labor that Phaphama, Ta-Silu, and Thando must negotiate—is to rethink citizenship at urban peripheries "from the perspective of citizens themselves" (Robins et al., 2008, p. 1085).

Ethnography offers an impactful set of methods through which to understand lived inequality and micro-relations of power, situating the everyday in the context of scales that move from neighborhood to city, and nation to globe. To see what peripheral citizens themselves see is to take seriously the complexity within which political actions interact with layers of marginalization. This requires holding together actions of democratic defiance and participation, or of state engagement and opposition, that characterize post-apartheid social movements (Oldfield & Stokke, 2007). A politics of refusal frames actions not within a binary, but as a lens through which everyday life itself can be understood as a deeply political terrain of contestation calling into question the sufficiency of postapartheid democracy.

## CONCLUSION: INFRASTRUCTURAL POLITICS OF URBAN INEQUALITY

Elections are caught up in the promises of infrastructure. For residents of Khayelitsha's informal settlements, wider political currents divert around the frustrations of their daily infrastructural needs. Here, the mundane is the matter of politics—a politics of urban inequality that saturates the everyday lives of residents. New streetlights are not a marker of infrastructure to come nor a small promise fulfilled by elected parties. Rather, they are a new piece added to larger material assemblages, made political through everyday use. Read as symbols of progress and promise by candidates and officials, the streetlights are stripped of this resonance once plunged into the wider sets of reworking and making-do characteristic of informality. Instead, pieces of the assemblage seen locally to reflect postapartheid exclusion are signified as markers of rampant inequality. Bucket toilets stand in for the extension of apartheid logics into the democratic everyday—the persistence of residential segregation and marginalization, and the seeming inability of elections or elected officials to change this. Residents of Khayelitsha know quite clearly that their use of temporary, inadequate, and unhygienic services exists within the same city in which many wealthier, often white residents live in easy affluence, provisioned in their suburban homes with sewage systems, flush toilets, and running water. The cycle of promises for improved service access to informal settlements mark for their residents not movement toward dignified infrastructural provision, but, rather, define their position as a community for whom promises are the devalued currency of postapartheid democracy.

Elections become a site of contradiction and complexity in terms of experienced political subjectivity: they remain the hallmark of democratic citizenship, the lauded and necessary foundation for inclusion in the rights of the state, but, likewise, are a painful reminder of material and socioeconomic changes yet to be made. Elections are at once celebratory and painful, hopeful times and evidence of promises unfulfilled.

While the postapartheid state is often made synonymous with the ANC, residents of Khayelitsha have—quite uniquely—experienced the failures of both the ANC and of opposition parties to meet basic service needs, revealing what many see as the inadequacy of the democratic process to fulfill promises of redistribution. Making the connection between infrastructure and politics is unsurprising at a local, municipal, or national level. Cape Town has particularly been marked in recent years by public contestation over access to basic services, with significant increases in protest actions here—as around the country—over inadequate provision (McFarlane & Silver, 2017). The 2011 local elections were punctuated by media coverage of construction by the city of unenclosed toilets for residents of Makhaza, in Khayelitsha;

when the resulting media spectacle identified similar toilets in municipalities controlled by the ANC, the incidents became known as the "toilet election" (Rakodi, 2011). In 2013, protests around a form of chemical toilet provided to informal settlements included the dumping of human waste in a series of public spaces, including on the cars of DA officials, at the international airport, and at the provincial offices. The series of events came to be known as the "poo protests" and intersected with significant social movement activism locally (Mottiar, 2015; Robins, 2014). Finally, the international publicity of Cape Town's water crisis in early 2018 brought to a head several years of seemingly inadequate planning in reaction to drought, and resulted in the declaration of a "Day Zero" in which many water taps would be turned off in order to force conservation (City of Cape Town, 2018).

Across South Africa, infrastructure is hyper-politicized. In Khayelitsha, however, these politics are not only those of media spectacle, electoral drama, or poor planning. Infrastructural assemblages created and used within informal spaces—patched together, reworked, always inadequate—are understood by residents through their daily usage to be markers of an elusive postapartheid citizenship inextricably caught up within material and economic development. Whether absent, promised, in-progress, completed, broken-down, or decaying, infrastructure serves as a koan of development's inescapable potentiality. For residents of informal settlements, the very known and obvious absences of infrastructural connections marks them as not only unequal in material terms, but, likewise, in political terms. The daily experiences of limited access to water, electricity, and sanitation services, and the work needed to patch together what access can be had, reiterates to residents that their presence in the city and the state is not equivalent to that of affluent residents within the city's more central suburbs, producing a marked and critical urban citizenship at the periphery.

## NOTES

1. My heartfelt thanks to the communities and organizations with whom I have conducted research in Khayelitsha, and to my wonderful colleague in Cape Town, Minah Koela. Versions of this chapter were presented at the 2019 American Anthropological Association meetings and the 2014 European Association of Social Anthropology meetings. This research was generously funded by a Dissertation Fieldwork Grant from the Wenner-Gren Foundation (#8612), with additional support from the School of Anthropology, the Bureau of Applied Research in Anthropology, the Social and Behavioral Sciences Research Institute, and the Confluence Center for Creative Inquiry at the University of Arizona. I would also like to sincerely thank advisers, colleagues, and friends who have commented on this chapter at various points, particularly Megan Sheehan, Kimberly Kelly, Anru Lee, and Tad Park. Endless thanks to

my husband, Shachaf Polakow, for his amazing photographs included in this volume and incredible support.

2. All names used are pseudonyms. Tata Silu (*tata*, isiXhosa for father, is added as a sign of respect) is shorted to Ta-Silu.

3. The term "coloured" denotes an official racial category in South Africa, a multiracial descendent group located primarily in the Western Cape Province.

4. The bucket toilets were maintained through a private contract under the city of Cape Town, with a company arriving—on average, according to the community members—twice a week to empty the waste from the units. Dismay with the particular actions of the company, and their hiring practices, layered onto frustrations with the toilets themselves: it was difficult to get the company to listen to citizen concerns and the city was locked into a contract with the company already, so had little room—and, seemingly, interest—in changing the arrangements. This contract was one of many for service provision to informal settlements; indeed, the rush to neoliberal provision of services had made the city increasingly treat citizens as customers (Storey, 2014).

## BIBLIOGRAPHY


Africa, C. (2015). Reproducing toxic election campaigns: Negative campaigning and race-based politics in the Western Cape. *Journal of African Elections, 14*(1), 124–148.

Anand, N. (2017). *Hydraulic city: Water and the infrastructures of citizenship in Mumbai*. Durham, NC: Duke University Press.

Auyero, J. (2012). *Patients of the state: The politics of waiting in Argentina*. Durham, NC: Duke University Press.

Bakker, K. (2003). *An uncooperative commodity: Privatizing water in England and Wales*. Oxford, England: Oxford University Press.

Bank, L. (2011). *Homes spaces, street styles: Contesting power and identity in a South African city*. London, England: Pluto Press.

Brown, J. (2015). *South Africa's insurgent citizens: On dissent and the possibility of politics*. London, England: Zed Books.

Brown-Luthango, M., Reyes, E., & Gubevu, M. (2017). Informal settlement upgrading and safety: Experiences from Cape Town, South Africa. *Journal of Housing and the Built Environment, 32*, 471–493.

Castro, J.E. (2004). Urban water and the politics of citizenship: The case of the Mexico City Metropolitan Area during the 1980s and 1990s. *Environment and Planning A, 36*, 327–346.

Charles, M. (2019, August 16). City of Cape Town admits poor lighting spurs crime. *IOL,* 2019. Retrieved from https://www.iol.co.za/capeargus/news/city-of-cape-town-admits-poor-lighting-spurs-crime-30858080.

City of Cape Town. (2012, December). *City of Cape Town—2011 Census—Cape Town*. Strategic Development and GIS Department (SDI&GIS).

City of Cape Town. (2013, July). *City of Cape Town – 2011 Census Suburb Khayelitsha.* Development and GIS Department (SDI&GIS).

City of Cape Town. (2017). 2016 community survey Cape Town trends 1996 to 2016. Research Branch, Organisational Policy and Planning Department. Retrieved from http://resource.capetown.gov.za/documentcentre/Documents/Maps%20and%20statistics/2016%20Community%20Survey%20Cape%20Town%20Trends.pdf.

City of Cape Town. (2018, January 17). Day zero now likely to happen–New emergency measures. Statement by the City's Executive Mayor Patricia de Lille. *City of Cape Town.* Retrieved from http://www.capetown.gov.za/Media-and-news/Day%20Zero%20now%20likely%20to%20happen%20%E2%80%93%20new%20emergency%20measures.

Cook, G.P. (1992). Khayelitsha: New settlement forms in the Cape Peninsula. In D.M. Smith (Ed.), *The Apartheid city and beyond: Urbanization and social change in South Africa* (pp. 125–135). London, England: Routledge.

Dawson, M. (2010). The cost of belonging: Exploring class and citizenship in Soweto's water war. *Citizenship Studies*, *14*(4), 381–394.

De Lille, P. (2013, June 5). Cape Town's record on sanitation delivery: The facts. *PoliticsWebSA.* Retrieved from http://www.politicsweb.co.za/news-and-analysis/cape-towns-record-on-sanitation-delivery-the-facts.

Dubbeld, B. (2017). Democracy as technopolitical future: Delivery and discontent in a government settlement in the South African countryside. *Anthropology Southern Africa, 40*(2), 73–84.

Etzo, S. (2010). 'The unfinished business of democratization': Struggles for services and accountability in South African cities. *Democratization, 17*(3), 564–586.

Gordon, S., Struwig, J., Roberts, B., Mchunu, N., Mtyingizane, S., & Radebe, T. (2018). What drives citizen participation in political gatherings in modern South Africa? A quantitative analysis of self-reported behavior. *Social Indicators Research, 141*(2), 791–808. https://doi.org/10.1007/s11205-018-1851-1.

Graham, S., & Marvin, S. (2001). *Splintering urbanism: Networked infrastructures, technological mobilities, and the urban condition.* London, England: Routledge.

Holston, J. (2009). *Insurgent citizenship: Disjunctions of democracy and modernity in Brazil.* Princeton, NJ: Princeton University Press.

Housing Development Agency. (2013). Western Cape informal settlements status (2013). Johannesburg. Retrieved from http://www.thehda.co.za/uploads/files/HDA_Western_Cape_Report.pdf.

Howe, C., Lockrem, J., Appel, H., Hackett, E., Boyer, D., Hall, R., Schneider-Mayerson, M., Pope, A., Gupta, A., Rodwell, E., Ballestero, A., Durbin, T., el-Dahdah, F., Long, E., & Mody, C. (2015). Paradoxical infrastructures: Ruins, retrofit, and risk. *Science, Technology, and Human Values, 41*(3), 547–565.

Huchzermeyer, M., & Karam, A. (2006). The continuing challenge of infromal settlements: An introduction. In M. Huchzermeyer & A. Karam (Eds.), *Informal settlements: A perpetual challenge?* (pp. 1–16). Cape Town, South Africa: University of Cape Town Press.

Informal Settlement Network (ISN). (2010). *Barcelona household enumeration report*. Gugulethu, Cape Town, South Africa: Barcelona Community Leadership, and Community Organisation Resource Centre.

Larkin, B. (2013). The politics and poetics of infrastructure. *Annual Review of Anthropology, 42*, 327–343.

Lepule, T. (2018, June 17). Western Cape use of bucket toilets rose over past year. *Weekend Argus*. Retrieved from https://www.iol.co.za/weekend-argus/graphic-western-cape-use-of-bucket-toilets-rose-over-past-year-15515079.

Maregele, B. (2017, October 2). Waiting period on Cape Town's housing list is 60 years, Khayelitsha meeting told. *GroundUp News*. Retrieved from https://www.groundup.org.za/article/waiting-period-cape-towns-housing-list-60-years-khayelitsha-meeting-told/.

McDonald, D.A., & Ruiters, G. (2005). Theorizing water privatization in Southern Africa. In D.A. McDonald & G. Ruiters (Eds.), *The age of commodity: Water privatization in Southern Africa* (pp. 13–42). London, England: Earthscan.

McFarlane, C., & Silver, J. (2017). The political city: "Seeing sanitation" and making the urban political in Cape Town. *Antipode, 49*(1), 125–148.

McGranahan, C. (2016). Theorizing refusal: An introduction. *Cultural Anthropology, 31*(3), 319–325.

Mortlock, M. (2017, May 20). Limited street lights a major cause of high crime rates in CT townships. *EWN*. Retrieved from https://ewn.co.za/2017/05/20/sjc-demands-more-street-lights-across-cape-townships.

Mottiar, S. (2015). The democratic alliance and the role of opposition parties in South Africa. *Journal of African Elections, 14*(1), 107–123.

October, A. (2017, November 9). Government is 11 years past deadline to end bucket system. *GroundUp*. Retrieved from https://www.groundup.org.za/article/government-11-years-over-deadline-eradicate-bucket-system/.

Oldfield, S., & Stokke, K. (2007). Political polemics and local practices of community organizing and neoliberal politics in South Africa. In H. Lettner et al. (Eds.), *Contesting neoliberalism: Urban frontiers* (pp. 139–156). New York: Guildford Press.

Rakodi, C. (2011, June 7). Local government matters: The 'toilet elections' in South Africa. *University of Birmingham International Development Blog*. Retrieved from https://iddbirmingham.wordpress.com/2011/06/07/local-government-matters-the-toilet-elections-in-south-africa/.

Robins, S. (2014). Poo wars as matter out of place: 'Toilets for Africa' in Cape Town. *Anthropology Today, 30*(1), 1–3.

Robins, S., Cornwall, A., & von Lieres, B. (2008). Rethinking 'citizenship' in the postcolony. *Third World Quarterly, 29*(6), 1069–1086.

Rodgers, D., & O'Neill, B. (2012). Infrastructural violence: Introduction to the special issue. *Ethnography, 13*(4), 401–412.

von Schnitzler, A. (2016). *Democracy's infrastructure: Techno-politics and protest after apartheid*. Princeton, NJ: Princeton University Press.

Simone, A. (2004). People as infrastructure: Intersection fragments in Johannesburg. *Public Culture, 16*(3), 407–429.

Simpson, A. (2014). *Mohawk interruptus: Political life across the borders of settler states*. Durham, NC: Duke University Press.

Simpson, A. (2016). Consent's revenge. *Cultural Anthropology, 31*(3), 326–333.

Social Justice Coalition (SJC). (2013). *Report of the Khayelitsha "Mshengu" toilet social audit: April 22–27, 2013*. Cape Town, South Africa.

Star, S.L. (1999). The ethnography of infrastructure. *American Behavioral Scientist, 43*(3), 377–391.

Storey, A. (2014). Making experience legible: Spaces of participation and the construction of knowledge in Khayelitsha. *Politikon: South African Journal of Political Studies, 41*(3), 403–420.

United Nations Human Settlements Programme (UN-Habitat). (2016). *Urbanization and development: Emerging futures. World cities report 2016*. Nairobi, Kenya: UN-Habitat. Retrieved from http://wcr.unhabitat.org/wp-content/uploads/2017/02/WCR-2016-Full-Report.pdf.

Weiss, E. (2016). Refusal as act, refusal as abstention. *Cultural Anthropology, 31*(3), 351–358.

Zikode, S. (2008). Sekwanel! Sekwanele! (Enough is enough!). *Journal of Asian and African Studies, 43*(1), 119–124.

*Part III*

# DIFFERENCE AND PROXIMITY

## Chapter 7

# Spaces of Migration and the Production of Inequalities in Santiago, Chile

Megan Sheehan

Despite recent efforts to mitigate economic disparities, Latin America remains the most unequal region in the world (Hoffman & Centano, 2003).[1] As residents confront the daily reality of persistent and historically rooted inequalities based on gender, racial, social, and economic status, increasing flows of regional migration flourish (International Labour Organization, 2017). Starting in the 1990s, Chile's strong economy began to attract migrants from other Latin American nations. As a growing number of migrants settle in the Chilean capital of Santiago, they face bureaucratic challenges to obtaining rental housing—even when they have their documents and residency status. Largely excluded from formal markets, migrants often seek housing through informal strategies. As social networks channel new arrivals into available housing, neighborhoods with clustered migrant populations develop rapidly. Everyday practices—like those involved in regulating and seeking housing—inscribe inequalities on cityscapes, spatializing migration and shaping migrant experiences of Santiago.

This chapter highlights one lived experience of inequality that migrants face in Santiago—that of housing. This quotidian experience of inequality intersects with the ways in which migrant settlement patterns are understood by Chilean residents of Santiago. Even as the logics of making-do shape where migrants reside in the city, the cumulative effect of their presence and the resulting neighborhood transformations become emblems used by Chileans in discussing spatial associations and housing conditions linked to migration. As notions of migratory spaces circulate in public discourse, these sites are reified, creating a geography of urban migration that is both imagined and enacted by a cacophony of uncoordinated and independent actors within Santiago. This chapter follows in several sections. First, I outline the structures that produce housing disparity for migrant residents in Santiago. Next, I show how migrants mobilize varied resources to negotiate discrimination and structural exclusion as they seek housing, and, finally, I illustrate how Chileans understand and talk about migrant settlement in Santiago. In this chapter, I argue that these three elements—macro structures framing inequality, everyday experiences of housing, and circulating discourses of living conditions—coalesce in a self-reinforcing manner. The cumulative power of uncoordinated actions is evident as property owners ask for specific rental requirements, migrants look for an access point for housing, and Chileans share perceptions about their changing city, highlighting the ways in which multiple agents acting independently combine to produce urban assemblages—in this case, Santiago's precarious spaces of migration.

## CONFRONTING INTERSECTIONAL INEQUALITIES IN MIGRATION IN CHILE

Since the early 1990s, migration to Chile has increased exponentially (Godoy, 2019; INE, 1992, 2002, 2012). Peruvian migration was the primary driver behind the early growth in transnational population (Martinez Pizarro, 2003; Stefoni, 2003), but migratory flows became more diverse in the late 2000s, with noted settlement from Colombia, Bolivia, Ecuador, the Dominican Republic, and Haiti (DEM, 2016). Between 2015 and 2019, however, the unprecedented influx of Venezuelan migrants has transformed the reality of migration in Chile. While foreign-born residents represented just 0.8 percent of the total population in 1982 and 2.3 percent in 2012, migrants now account for 7 percent of the population (DEM, 2014; Godoy, 2019; INE, 1982, 2012). As of June 2019, there were nearly 1.3 million Venezuelan migrants in Chile (Godoy, 2019), and the Chilean government predicts that 300,000 more Venezuelans will arrive in 2020 (Reyes & Vera, 2019).

Chile's strong economy—under a staunchly neoliberal model—and demand for inexpensive, unskilled labor frame migration to Chile, prioritizing swift incorporation of migrants into the workforce. Most migrants occupy low-paid positions (Bellolio & Errázuriz, 2014; Stefoni, 2011), and 16 percent of all migrants in Chile work as domestic laborers (Cano & Soffia, 2009). Migrants also find employment as sales personnel, street vendors, wait staff, kitchen assistants, landscapers, construction workers, street sweepers, parking attendants, and in professional positions (Bellolio & Errázuriz, 2014). While official estimates of irregular migration do not exist, the vast majority of migrants have residency and work documents and most migrants with lapsed documentation are still eligible to legalize their status (Doña-Reveco & Levingson, 2012; Stefoni, 2011). Three periods of regularization, including one in 2018, further reduced the number of migrants without up-to-date documents (Tumba, 2018). However, new, more restrictive entry requirements for Haitian and Venezuelan migrants and a new migration law passed in 2019 may exacerbate irregular migration (Ramos, 2019; Reyes, Caro, & Jara, 2019; Vedoya & Navarrete, 2019).[2]

Migrants often face inequalities both in their country of origin and in Chile. Each migratory flow to Chile highlights unique push and pull factors, illustrating a range of strategies of making-do in the face of global economic inequalities. These factors include the high demand for Peruvian domestic laborers, who earn comparatively high salaries; the initial visas given to Haitians as a relief effort after the 2010 earthquake and subsequent chain migrations; and the dramatic new influx of Venezuelans fleeing challenging national circumstances. Mirroring the "kaleidoscope of inequalities that afflict Latin America" (Gootenberg, 2010, p. 22), migrants face numerous articulations of racial, gender, economic, labor, health, and quality of life disparities over the course of their transnational experiences. Addressing the impact of challenges faced by migrants, sociologists Nicolás Rojas Pedemonte and Claudia Silva Dittborn note, "Even when migrants have visas and are documented, they continue to be extremely vulnerable to abuses and to hostilities on the part of a society that does not fully recognize them as subjects with rights" (2016, p. 40). Despite state-afforded documents, rights, and services, migrants continue to encounter exclusions and disparities enacted both interpersonally and in more systematic, often racialized, ways.[3] The inequalities and exclusions that migrants face overlap and co-occur, illustrating the intersectional complexity framing and amplifying everyday challenges.

Culturally understood boundaries and the power relationship between social groups (Tilly, 1998) provide important context for understanding the relational nature of inequalities in Latin America. That said, this work follows Gootenberg's (2010) shift toward framing disparities as "'indelible inequalities,' which underscores the human agency and culture at play in their creation and perseverance, their complexity and camouflage beyond stark categorical divides, and their fluid and peopled possibilities of change" (2010, p. 5). While inequalities are difficult to address, they are not inherent. Likewise, relational categories that Tilly (1998) emphasizes are fluid in practice, often individually enacted, and notably present as racial, cultural, and class categories are permeable and coalesce over time in Latin America (c.f. de la Cadena, 2000; Hale, 2006; Poole, 1997; Wade, 2010).

Ethnographic narratives suggest that even while categorical inequalities may be reinforced (Tilly, 1998), the everyday reality is much more nuanced, as migrants deploy a range of ordinary tools and informal strategies to negotiate structural disparities and to mitigate the impact of inequalities. Highlighting the transformative power of uncoordinated—albeit cumulatively powerful actions—Asef Bayat argues that "the urban disenfranchised, through their quiet and unassuming daily struggles, refigure new life and communities for themselves and different urban realities on the ground" (2013, p. 5). In this way, marginalized urban residents may participate in the "quiet encroachment of the ordinary" (Bayat, 2013), such that their informal strategies of networking and accessing housing create new urban norms. Without setting out to change the face of the city, the cumulative outcome of migrants pursuing informal housing strategies is transforming Santiago's center. The everyday work involved in producing, negotiating, and addressing experiences of inequality bears tangible urban impacts that can be read from—and into—the shifting spatial arrangements of city life.

This chapter draws on more than 24 months ethnographic fieldwork conducted in Santiago, Chile, between 2009 and 2019. I conducted 16 months of continuous research in 2012 and 2013, in which my primary field sites included a migrant hiring hall, an agency that aids migrants, and a public plaza where migrants frequently gather. In 2019, I returned to Santiago for three months of follow-up research, focusing on understanding the implications of Venezuelan migration in the neighborhoods where they settle. The data presented in this chapter draws from semi-structured interviews conducted with migrants in Santiago (n = 139) and with Chilean residents (n = 43) across the different periods of fieldwork, as well as a structured questionnaire (n = 96) administered to Peruvian migrants in 2016 detailing the use of urban sites. Interview data is contextualized by field notes chronicling long-term participant observation, and insights gained from "go-alongs" (Kusenbach, 2003) in which I accompanied migrants in their travels through the city. The breadth of this data enables an analysis of the changes over time as well as of the similarities in themes that emerge in the different forms of data, affording a textured perspective on migration in Santiago.

## ACCESS AND INEQUALITY IN THE HOUSING MARKET

The city of Santiago dominates Chile's economic, educational, and social spheres, and more than 7 million people—approximately 40 percent of the national population—reside in the bustling metropolitan area (INE, 2017). Santiago's development exemplifies aspirations of modernity, order, and global integration. From luring European architects to plan nineteenth-century versions of the city to the current incorporation of skyscrapers, LEED-certified buildings, bike share programs, below-ground highways, extensive metro service, and proliferating malls, the city has worked to brand itself as a thriving urban hub.[4] The *New York Times* described the city as "an electrifying place of vibrant contrasts, with lush new parks, renovated Beaux-Arts neighborhoods and blocks of glamazon-thronged galleries and cafes clustered around 'Sanhattan,' the soaring financial district" (Jones, 2009), and later awarded the city its top spot on the coveted "Places to Go in 2011" list (Singer, 2011). This effective city branding (Çağlar & Glick Schiller, 2018; McCann & Ward, 2011) obscures the inequalities and socioeconomic differences that divide the city. Over the last three decades, population growth in the urban peripheries have prompted new subcenters, increasing the reliance on transportation and fostering greater class segregation (de Mattos, 2004). New public spaces are increasingly linked to commerce and have the potential to reshape urban citizenship, exacerbating divisions along class lines and fostering an "implosion of modern public life" in which fear, stereotypes, and segregation lead to increasingly divided cities (Caldeira, 2000, p. 323).

Amid these urban changes, migrant settlement is also altering the city. Two-thirds of all migrants live in Santiago (Garces, 2007; INE, 2017), and migrants primarily live in central districts of the city—downtown Santiago, Recoleta, Independencia, and Estación Central (figure 7.1)—often occupying rooms in subdivided houses (Ducci & Rojas, 2010; Fernandez, 2009; Garces, 2015; Stefoni, 2008). This central location affords migrants access to ready transportation, migrant-targeted services, call centers, internet, food booths with Peruvian food, and imported products (Ducci & Rojas, 2010; Garces, 2015; Stefoni, 2008). While such neighborhoods are often dubbed "ethnic enclaves" (c.f. Portes & Jensen, 1987; Portes & Manning, 2014), Pessar's (1995) call to rethink the underlying assumed unity of enclaves prompts new questions: How are settlement patterns and spatial associations produced? Who and what relationships enable or constrain their production? Exploring these questions in light of migrant settlement in Santiago enables ethnographically grounded analysis of the complex terrain of bureaucratic requirements, discriminatory practices, social networks, and personal resources that individual migrants negotiate on a daily basis.

Property law frames the marginalization of migrant populations seeking rental housing. In Chile, the rental market embodies a neoliberal ethos, and the law prioritizes the rights of property owners. During the Pinochet dictatorship (1973–1988), two legal statutes (n° 18.101 and n° 964) replaced earlier laws, largely eliminating regulations on standards for housing quality and protections for renters. Under these laws, landlords may request any guarantee that they deem expedient.[5]

Property owners frequently insist that migrants demonstrate definitive residence—a visa category typically attained only after two full years of residency. Additionally, landlords often request a multitude of other guarantees, which may include: a financial backer or cosigner, a month's rent as a deposit, another month's rent as an additional guarantee, a third month's rent to be

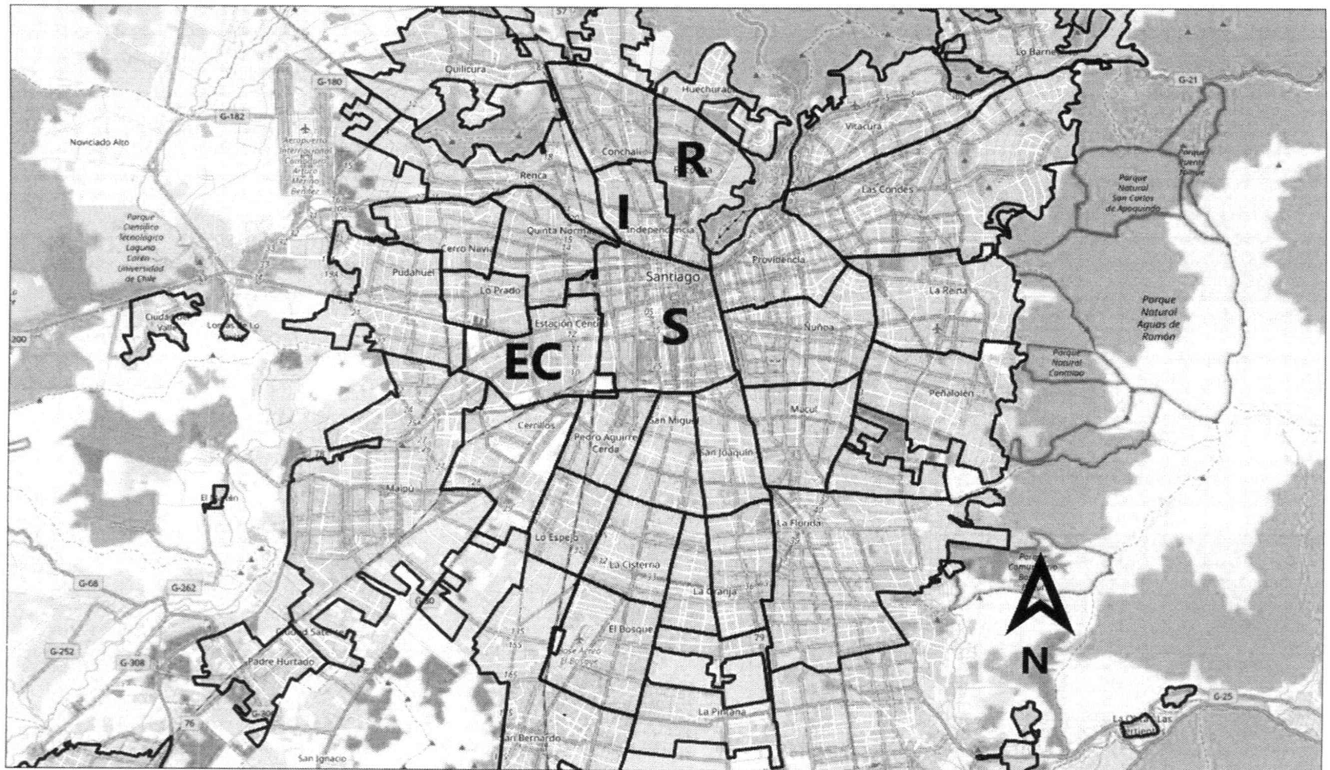


**Figure 7.1 Map of Santiago, with the *Comunas*, or Municipal Districts, Outlined.** The *comuna* of central Santiago (S) is where the largest population of migrants live; 28 percent of residents in the *comuna* are migrants (INE 2017). The *comuna* of Estación Central (EC), Independencia (I), and Recoleta (R) all have significant migrant populations. *Source*: Map by author and map data © OpenStreetMap contributors.

paid up front, a signed work contract, and proof of a bank account—which is its own particular challenge to acquire (personal communication, Instituto Católico Chileno de Migración, January 11, 2017). These requirements are often impossible for migrants to meet, and function as a barrier to formal housing agreements, thus producing migrants—even those with visas—as marginal urban residents who must locate housing through informal channels and in precarious sites. As individual landlords and property owners require separate norms for specific groups of individuals—necessitating the investment of significant time and resources while further elaborating exclusions along national, racial, ethnic, linguistic, and gendered divisions—they produce a stratified new form of the urban milieu (Kilanski & Auyero, 2015). In short, rental statues funnel migrants disproportionately into substandard housing arrangements, reproduce housing inequality, and further structural violence.

The many rental stipulations required by landlords in the largely unregulated rental market exacerbate the economic precarity of individuals working in lower-paying service and commerce positions, highlighting how multiple overlapping inequalities combine to further marginalize migrants. In 2016, I administered a questionnaire to 96 Peruvian migrants living in Santiago. Two-thirds of respondents reported living in housing conditions marked by overcrowding, substandard conditions, and informality. Fifty-six percent of the respondents reported living in one-room of a partitioned house or apartment. Moreover, more than three-quarters of the migrants living in subdivided rooms were sharing their room with an average 4.5 people.[6] A similar study found that 73 percent of migrants reported living in rented rooms, with the majority of these located in *cités*, or tenements (Fernandez, 2009, p. 9). Drawing on national survey data, Rojas Pedemonte and Silva Dittborn suggest that 33 percent of migrants—compared to 14 percent of Chileans—live in conditions recognized as overcrowded, exceeding 2.5 people per room (2016, pp. 36–37). In her work on migrant health in Santiago, Lorena Núñez describes these infamous tenement conditions: "In a space the size of a gymnasium, flimsy dividers, made of [plywood], were used to create [twenty] small and ceiling-less cubicles. … Two toilets, two showers providing only cold water" (2008, p. 117). Overcrowded one-room residences, shared bathrooms, and limited cooking facilities characterize migrant housing in Santiago. Many migrants report that their housing conditions in Chile are worse than those in their country of origin (Rojas Pedemonte & Silva Dittborn, 2016, p. 37). These precarious conditions epitomize the material reality of systematic exclusion and lived inequalities. The flourishing of these residences are a tangible outcome of the property laws, the ways in which legal statutes are used by property owners to create barriers to formal housing, and the limits of economic and social resources that migrants draw upon to mitigate the impacts of bureaucratic precarity.

## NAVIGATING HOUSING DISPARITIES THROUGH PERSONAL RELATIONSHIPS

I interviewed Olivia[7] on a rainy winter day in 2013. A single mother of a six-month-old baby girl, Olivia recounted her story as we drank hot tea to ward off the chill. Over the previous month I had gotten to know Olivia during her frequent visits to the migrant shelter and hiring hall where my research was based. Like many migrants, Olivia came to the hiring hall in an effort to find steady employment. However, her lack of access to childcare hampered her success in landing a full-time job and she had to make-do with income from sporadic household cleaning gigs. During her pregnancy, Olivia made the difficult choice to leave the financial and housing stability afforded by her partner's job. In light of an abusive situation, she opted to move out in the hope of offering her baby a more peaceful environment. It was hard to find housing at a price that she could afford, compounded, she felt, by the fact that potential landlords could see she was visibly pregnant. After weeks of searching, a friend of hers who had just found a room invited her to share the space.

Olivia's new home was a rough-hewn plywood enclosure, one "room" in a row of eight, built on a dormant construction site. She explained that the owner of the land was waiting on funding for the development of a high-rise apartment building. The owner lived abroad and had left a migrant caretaker to look after the vacant lot. The caretaker had overseen the division of a large concrete-walled garage into plywood structures, allowing eight families to live on the site, sharing one bathroom. Olivia described the enclosure: "[It's like a] prefabricated house, like, made of newsprint or of cardboard. Plywood. Practically transparent. It is not comfortable. With everything you can't clean it like one would like to. But at least, nobody bothers me, like used to happen at the last place. Some places there are people who all the time make it uncomfortable even to sleep." In discussing her challenges finding adequate housing where she and her baby could live in peace, Olivia was acutely aware of the disparities in the housing market and the unequal conditions that she faces in comparison to Chilean residents. She continued:

> The majority of houses that one goes to here, or those that I have seen in Chile, in Santiago aren't like this. The places that we, more precisely, that migrants rent, they live like this. We live like this. It's like what you see is more people together, mainly because we have to save [money]. It could be said that I would like more hygienic, more everything, to rent an apartment, but . . . .

Olivia's discussion trailed off before she added as an afterthought, "There are too many people, it's overcrowded." This narrative highlights the complex and intersecting ways that migrants navigate overlapping constraints: the challenge of finding stable employment; the intersectional vulnerability to physical and emotional abuse; and the lived reality of poor housing conditions.

Moreover, Olivia assesses the housing conditions that she faces in comparison with her experiential knowledge of Chilean households. In her years working in domestic labor, she has entered many Chilean households, and her recent work has drawn her to less-privileged sectors of the city to clean for the day, working for families who cannot afford regular household help. Olivia, like many other migrant domestic laborers, experiences the extremities of inequality as she cleans family after family's tiled, private bathroom, then returns home to wait in line for her chance to use the roughly cemented and dirty bathroom. Inequality becomes tangible, marked in housing materials, heated warmth, and privacy. Disparities are experienced in highly personal ways, and these contrasting housing conditions offer both material and intimate dimensions of relational inequalities.

Social connections through family, friends, partners, employer contacts, third party introductions, and chance are the primary ways migrants identify residences. Challenges to finding housing encourage migrants to strategically call upon their social networks to gain access to informal housing options. This process results in the swift proliferation of clustered settlements of migrant populations. In contrast to intentional and collective acts, movements, and engagements, the actions of individuals addressing their own needs in light of systematic exclusions can bear powerful impacts when taken in composite. These strategies of making-do in the housing market epitomize Bayat's notion of the "quiet encroachment of the ordinary" (2013). Migrants searching for housing in Chile do not set out to impact the lived, social, and symbolic city spaces, and yet, collectively, migrant housing patterns are transforming the experience and meaning of Santiago's urban milieu.

## CONFRONTING PAPER BARRIERS IN THE SEARCH FOR HOUSING

In July 2019, I first met Sara, a Venezuelan woman in her mid-twenties. She had arrived in Chile about a month before, and eagerly responded to an online recruitment post that I had circulated on social media. We met in a small, central plaza, and I interviewed her as a free public salsa-dancing class whirled around us. After an hour and a half interview, we talked for two more hours, with Sara enthusiastically relating how the Venezuelan community thrived in her neighborhood. A couple of weeks later, I met up with Sara to learn how to make *arepas*—a corn patty that is a staple of Venezuelan and Colombian meals. I met Sara at the metro station, and she explained that a friend of hers was interested in being interviewed. We headed to an imposing block of new high-rise apartment buildings. As Sara knocked on her friend's door, she abruptly turned around with a worried expression on her face. "I need to warn you that it is just one small room." Having been in many of Santiago's new high-rise buildings, I assured Sara that this was not a surprise. Almost immediately, the two boys of the family, aged nine and five, opened the door and animatedly welcomed us into the studio apartment. The space was approximately six meters by six meters, and half of the living space was taken up by queen-sized mattresses piled on each other. Sara's friend, Julia, introduced herself and explained that they have to pile things together during the day so that the boys have space to play.

In the interview, Julia noted that they were very lucky to have found this place. She recounted how her husband had migrated first to Chile, sharing tight living quarters with a cousin and several other Venezuelans. After a year of working, he borrowed additional money to bring Julia and the boys to Chile. He had sought out housing and was only able to find a single room in a subdivided house in a neighborhood located at a distance from the central transit arteries. Julia noted in despair that the room had a dirt floor and was always damp, making the transition to life in wintery Santiago more challenging. After six months with Julia working as well, they were able to find their current studio apartment by responding to an online advertisement. Julia noted that she felt fortunate that the owner only asked for two months of rent and proof of her husband's residency status and employment, noting that most property owners: "ask you for two months of a guarantee, they ask for one month in advance, they ask you, or, for an infinite amount of money and requirements. And like everyone who has recently arrived, they ask for proof of the last six months of [retirement and healthcare] contributions, they ask you . . . in other words, another thing almost so that they [don't have] to rent to you."

As Julia spoke about their challenges finding decent housing, Sara worked rhythmically, patting out *arepas* from the cornmeal on her perch in the petite kitchen corner of the apartment. Meanwhile, the boys went from jumping around on the mattresses to knocking over the precarious tower of folded laundry to driving trucks across the window ledge. Looking across the apartment's gaping courtyard (figure 7.2), I could see children regularly appear in three other windows, likely confined by their own small environs. At one point after the interview, Julia gazed at her boys, sighed, and confided that she still wondered if they would be better off returning to Venezuela—to their spacious, two-story house and yard where the boys would play soccer in the

**Figure 7.2 Photo Taken from High-Rise Apartment Building in Santiago.** *Source*: Photo by author.

warm sun. But then she immediately added that they had been very fortunate to find a decent property owner who did not ask for the kinds of documents that often keep friends and family from accessing housing.

Sara also noted how lucky she had been to find housing, chiming in with her story. She recounted how she and two friends whom she had met on the journey from Venezuela had decided to look for a place together. After a week of disqualifications due to their limited resources and lack of bank accounts, cosigners, and visas, they were put in touch with a Venezuelan property broker, who strategized with them what documents could be used to establish legitimacy in the eyes of a property owner. With Sara's certified university diploma—itself a hard-earned and expensive document—and three months of up-front rent—lent to the trio by a brother who lives in Canada—the property broker was able to get them a compact, one-bedroom apartment around the corner from Julia's building. The negotiating of documents versus more months of up-front rent was commonplace. Several individuals whom I interviewed noted that, in place of the requested documents to validate their application for a property, they provided between six and eight months of up-front rent—essentially handing over their reduced life savings to secure a place to live. The use of property brokers, often more established migrants, is commonplace among Venezuelans seeking to identify the best strategy for making documentary claims of bureaucratic legibility and economic reliability.

As the conversation wound down and the *arepas* cooked, the boys eagerly pointed out all the apartments displaying Venezuelan flags, and Julia estimated that three-quarters of the buildings' residents are Venezuelan. Later, as we left the apartment, Sara spoke with a janitor whom we met in the elevator. He was an electrical engineer from Venezuela who had arrived two months ago and was still getting his documents—educational, visas, work permits—in order to look for better opportunities.

These two experiences of Santiago's housing market illustrate multiple and overlapping inequalities. As migrants navigate the housing market, they face intersectional dimensions of inequality that are fluid and self-reinforcing. The narratives here reveal the many actors, relationships, interactions, and meanings navigated in each search for housing. Each housing narrative shows how agents navigate complex, shifting terrains, drawing on sets of resources and relationships to negotiate critical disparities to mitigate the impacts of substandard living conditions on their health, safety, and well-being. In a similar fashion, the ways in which parts of the city are associated with migration also reflect shifting terrains and multiple actors. Associations of migrant populations, neighborhoods, and housing conditions coalesce both through the clustered settlement of migrants in certain sectors and through the ways in which these settlement patterns are discussed. The spatialized inequalities inscribed in migrant housing patterns are normalized as migrants seek out housing through informal channels—due to discriminatory practices and bureaucratic exclusions.

## IMAGINING URBAN GEOGRAPHIES OF MIGRATION

Migrant experiences of housing inequality are interpreted through layers of discourse and Chilean stereotypes about migration. As notions about who lives where and in what condition circulate, they craft representational cartographies of migration. Discourses and debates over migrant use of urban spaces and presence in particular neighborhoods are critically important to how these spaces are imagined and constructed. In her work on gentrification in a multiethnic neighborhood in Washington, DC, Gabriella Modan argues, "the way we talk about the places we live has material implications for how those places change and develop" (2007, p. 7). Iterative discussions about neighborhoods and migration shape how these areas are understood, and the spatial associations that emerge from these circulating discourses effect the subsequent ways in which people interact with these sites. In this way, the circulation of spatial discourses is a key component of the construction of urban space. Discourses do work as words and narratives "index space in multiple ways—linking transnational spaces, creating safe spaces and community for marginalized citizens, . . . and spatializing class and race" (Low, 2017, p. 122). As migrants must seek housing through informal channels and live with other migrants in precarious housing arrangements, public discussion of these housing conditions furthers spatial associations linking migration, specific neighborhoods, and the stigma of substandard housing.

Social scientists argue that the quiet encroachment of migrant presence in Santiago's urban center garners a "notorious visibility" that is produced through public discourse (Garces, 2007, p. 2; see also: Ducci & Rojas, 2010; Fernandez Tapia, 2009; Stefoni, 2004). As Rojas Pedemonte and Silva Dittborn note: "The increas[ing numbers of migrants], the territorial concentration of the population in certain cities and districts, and the arrival of new racialized migratory flows . . . is such that national public opinion perceives that the country is 'filling' with migrants" (2016, p. 10). Individuals interviewed frequently noted the feeling of being overwhelmed by migration, often pointing to the increase in Haitian arrivals between 2014 and 2018. The racialization of migrant populations has intensified in recent years, explicitly positioning migration as a problem (Correa Téllez, 2016; Stefoni, 2016; Tijoux, 2011), such that different national groups are often understood as linked to specific stereotypes and associations—ones that are also tied to certain sectors of the city (Arriagada, 2016).

In interviews conducted in 2019 with directors of neighborhood councils, the racialized and stigmatized perceptions of neighborhoods in central Santiago were a recurring theme. Gerardo, an older man who had lived in the neighborhood for forty years and who had directed the neighborhood council for many years recounted how his downtown sector was changing.

> People always talk about how small-scale drug trafficking is a real problem, when in reality, Santiago doesn't have those problems, or at least this neighborhood doesn't. But the visibility that is associated with it because they're black,

> because they're foreigners, they speak differently. Because of this the streets are empty, the streets of Santiago are abandoned, neighbors don't use them or the public parks either, the people hide away in their houses.

Gerardo vehemently disagreed with the way the neighborhood was perceived, as well as with the alleged safety concerns. He went on to describe an instance in which anti-immigrant signs were posted in the neighborhood. In response, he quickly mobilized a group of volunteers to remove the signs. Gerardo has little control over how migration is associated with his neighborhood, but working with a group of dedicated neighbors, he has ensured an openness in the neighborhood council and programming that addresses the needs of all the neighbors. That said, discussions of spaces like his neighborhood are many and are shared freely. Posts on social media, friends swapping impressions of the city, jokes that reference particular sites, and news stories mentioning specific neighborhoods are all ways in which ideas about spaces circulate, with each point of contact further shaping the association.

Media portrayals and word-of-mouth descriptions about migrant experiences of precarious housing create widespread public awareness. Chilean understandings of the housing conditions faced by migrants are not typically based on firsthand experience. However, Chileans interviewed frequently brought up the topic of the *cites* or tenement-style housing. Chileans who knew migrants often have indirect knowledge of living conditions beyond the ubiquitous media depictions of the *cites.* As I interviewed Inés, a Chilean employer of a migrant domestic laborer, she recounted her knowledge about her domestic laborer's housing:

> She told me that she pays $80,000 Chilean pesos (US $125) for a room with a shared bathroom, and the room only fits a twin bed and that's it. I find it incredibly expensive. I offered her [a room] because I have one there, that room that you see out back, one of those comfortable rooms with a bathroom, but she prefers her independence and I prefer that she gets out and has a change of scenery, relaxes a bit.

Inés's concern and empathy for her employee stood out in this conversation, and in contrast to most interview data which emphasizes graphic descriptions of challenging conditions, Inés also recognized why the woman she employs opted for this living arrangement. Writing about the very real health consequences of the *cites*, Núñez argues that the housing unit where she worked "resembled a small-scale shantytown, a kind of precarious neighbourhood hidden behind an anonymous door of a run-down building in downtown Santiago" (2008, p. 117). While it is true that these housing arrangements are understated from the exterior (figure 7.3), their frequent—and

**Figure 7.3 The *Comuna* of Santiago is a Mix of Newer High-Rise Apartment Buildings (Seen in the Background) and Older Housing Stock (in the Foreground).** Many older houses in Santiago are subdivided and rooms within them are rented, being transformed into *cites*. Photo by author.

provocative—news coverage has played a strong role in the spatial associations made between migration and certain sectors of Santiago's historic urban core (Ducci & Rojas, 2010; Torres & Garces, 2013). Given the scale of the current flows from Venezuela, recently completed high-rise apartment buildings are likely the new face of migratory housing in Santiago.

Interviews with Chileans epitomize deep divisions in public discourse over migration's impact on the urban sphere. Chilean portrayals position migrants alternatively as victims of exploitative housing market, as harbingers of a positively glossed multiculturalism—often noted in the burgeoning Chilean interest in Peruvian restaurants—or as subjects who pose a threat to Santiago's order. Such representational connections travel and find an audience that is not limited only to Chileans who frequent the city center or who interact with migrants themselves. During fieldwork, I traveled to a well-heeled and insulated subdivision in the foothills of the Andes to interview Silvia, a Chilean businesswoman. When I asked her about migrant presence in the city, she immediately rattled off a list of the "urban problems" that she linked to migration. "The Peruvians live all together in some houses which they leave fucked up, it's this crazy situation that I don't like it. And when they are drunk, they become crazy, with alcohol they become crazy." Silvia worked near the financial district, and her daily travels did not bring her near to the central areas of Santiago. However, an absence of direct experience in the center of the city did not prevent Silvia from holding strong impressions of migrant impacts on the urban sphere. Silvia's reflection suggests the durability and wide circulation of spatial associations linked to migrant housing, highlighting how the experience of, or a direct connection to, a site is not necessary to form a strong association between the space and notions of who belongs there.

Spatial associations coalesce as they circulate. Teresa Caldeira examines how spatial notions of crime build up, highlighting the dispersed ways in which such associations take shape: "Prejudices and derogations not only are verbal but also reproduce themselves in rituals of suspicion and investigation at the entrances of public and private buildings. As people's thoughts and actions are shaped by the categorical reasoning of the talk of crime, its influence spreads, affecting social interactions, public policies, and political behavior" (Caldeira, 2000, p. 39). Just as the process of walking through a metal detector shifts how a person understands both the space they are entering as well as the space they left behind, so too can anti-immigrant flyers intangibly construct a spatial association. In this way, small daily practices, conversations, social media posts, and news stories accumulate ideas and perceptions of spaces. Over time, these proliferating discourses coalesce, taking the form of a malleable spatial association. Caldeira goes on to argue, "the new urban morphologies of fear give new forms to inequality, keep groups apart, and inscribe a new sociability that runs against the ideals of the modern public" (2000, p. 335). As spatial associations regarding migrant use of Santiago neighborhoods form, they work iteratively to shift how people engage with these areas. The dispersed and cumulative effects suggest that increasing socio-spatial divides will continue to develop.

The Chilean commentaries here emphasize the power that discourses have to shape perceptions of particular urban sites even in the absence of an experiential connection with the site. The iterative circulation of housing and neighborhood discourses produce spatial associations, tying stigma, and exclusion to specific urban spaces and crafting norms about who belongs in certain spaces (Modan, 2007; Secor, 2004). As these associations continue to circulate, they shape expectations of these spaces, indicative of Lefebvre's "representational space" (1991), which consist of the abstract ideas, thoughts, images, and visions of physical sites. The representational spaces produced in these debates become a new and flexible framework through which Chileans create further social distinctions, assert national boundaries, and challenge migrant belonging.

## CONCLUSION

The ethnographic examples shared here shed light on the many actors, relationships, interactions, and meanings linked to housing. The largely unregulated housing market affords property owners broad leeway to establish their own criteria for leasing, fostering a paradox in which migrants with residency visas may be excluded from formal leases. Limited economic resources can be mitigated by social, cultural, or economic capital as those migrants with more extensive networks of family, friends, and acquaintances—particularly well-connected ones—are more successful in securing housing. Additionally, those who lack an address find it more challenging to secure jobs, bank accounts, and bureaucratic documents—often working around this by using a friend's or nonprofit agency's address, again increasing their dependence on another entity. Informal housing and challenges to finding housing increase migrant vulnerability to gendered and intimate partner abuse, seen in Olivia's story. Finally, some migrants, like Julia and Sara, are able to negotiate housing arrangements by leveraging the strategic advantage of different types of documents—residency papers, letters from employers, certified diplomas—paired with outside financial resources. Each housing narrative illustrates how agents navigate complex, shifting terrains, drawing on sets of resources and relationships to negotiate critical disparities in securing housing and to mitigate the impacts of substandard living conditions on their health, safety, and well-being.

In a similar fashion, the ways in which urban spaces take on meaning—here meanings associated with migration—also reflect flexibility, shifting terrains, and multiple actors. Associations of migrant populations, neighborhoods, and housing conditions coalesce both through the accumulated settlement of migrants in certain sectors and through the ways in which these settlement patterns are discussed. The spatialized inequalities inscribed in migrant housing patterns are normalized through processes of quiet encroachment (Bayat, 2013) that proceed as migrants seek out housing through informal channels—due to discriminatory and bureaucratic exclusions. Additionally, circulating discourses of migrant housing and neighborhood locations also work to spatially inscribe inequality as a normative pattern of migrant urban life. There is a flexibility and fluidity to these spatial associations, just as they are dialectically produced and productive, they are also capable of change. The understandings of who belongs in which spaces are constantly changing, seen in instances of gentrification (Modan, 2007) as in instances of transnational migration (Dávila, 2004). Peruvian migrants have been stereotyped and linked to central city spaces; however, these spatial associations are currently contested. Increasing settlement by Venezuelan, Haitian, and Colombian communities prompt new debates about who belongs where. These emerging spatial articulations are again redrafting central Santiago, further highlighting the many ways that migration works to transform urban spaces.

## NOTES

1. I would like to thank the generosity of the many research participants who opened their homes to me and shared their stories with me. I also wish to thank Patricio Carrasco Echeverria for his invaluable research assistance and insightful suggestions. I am grateful to Angela Storey and Anru Lee for their constructive feedback during the revision process. Finally, this work would not be possible without funding from Fulbright IIE, Lehigh University, and the College of St Benedict/St John's University.

2. As of January 2020, it is unclear when the new migration law will take effect. While the law was approved in August 2019, it was pending the development of a plan for its implementation (Reyes et al., 2019). The implementation plan was not finished prior to the October 2019 social movements which resulted in a change of cabinet and political uncertainty in Chile (Tinsman, 2019).

3. The "new immigration" (Martinez, 2003) also marks a demographic shift from largely European and Argentinean migrants to the current arrival of mostly Andean migrants (Stefoni, 2003). As in other Latin American nations, previous migratory waves to Chile were often associated with "racial improvement" via *blanquemiento*, or whitening, a deliberate move away from bodily, material, and cultural markers of indigeneity (Hale, 2006; Wade, 2010). Currently, the increase in intraregional migration is producing a more diverse population in Chile, a nation in which almost two-thirds of the population self-identify as with their European ancestry (Latinobarómetro, 2010). In light of increasing Latin American migration, combined with the active resurgence of Chilean indigenous, ethnic, and racial groups advocating for recognition and rights, discussions of racial and ethnic difference have taken on greater prominence in national discourse, countering hegemonic conceptions of the nation and its history (Postero, Risør, & Prieto Montt, 2018).

4. The protests that made national and international news in October 2019 critique the notions of a Chilean economic "success story" and the trappings of Santiago's branding as neoliberal modern city (Tinsman, 2019).

5. While the new migration law that was approved in August 2019 will replace these earlier laws, the new law has yet to take effect (Reyes et al., 2019). As of January 2020, it is unclear when the new law will be rolled out.

6. It is important to note that this survey had a small sample size (n = 96) and focused exclusively on Peruvian migrants—at the time, the most populous migrant group in Chile.

7. All names are pseudonyms.

## BIBLIOGRAPHY

Arriagada Luco, C. (2016). Barrios Centrales Emergentes y Discriminación de los Inmigrantes Minorías Visibles. In M.E. Tijoux (Ed.), *Racismo en Chile: La piel como marca de la inmigración* (pp. 129–140). Santiago, Chile: Editorial Universitaria.

Bayat, A. (2013). *Life as politics: How ordinary people change the Middle East.* Palo Alto, CA: Stanford University Press.

Bellolio, A., & Errazuriz, C.H.F. (2014). *Migraciones en Chile: Oportunidad Ignorada.* Santiago, Chile: Ediciones Libertad y Desarrollo.

Çağlar, A., & Glick Schiller, N. (2018). *Migrants and city-making: Dispossession, displacement, and urban regeneration.* Durham: Duke University Press.

Caldeira, T.P.R. (2000). *City of walls: Crime, segregation, and citizenship in São Paulo.* Berkeley, CA: University of California Press.

Cano, V., & Soffia, M. (2009). Los estudios sobre migracion internacional en Chile. *Papeles de Población, 15*(61), 129–167.

Correa Téllez, J. (2016). La inmigración como 'problema' o el resurgir de la raza. Racismo general, racismo cotidiano y su papel en la conformación de la Nación. In M.E. Tijoux (Ed.), *Racismo en Chile: La piel como marca de la inmigración* (pp. 35–48). Santiago, Chile: Editorial Universitaria.

Dávila, A. (2004). *Barrio dreams: Puerto Ricans, Latinos, and the Neoliberal city.* Berkeley, CA: University of California Press.

De la Cadena, M. (2000). *Indigenous mestizos: The politics of race and culture in Cuzco, Peru, 1910–1991.* Durham, NC: Duke University Press.

De Mattos, C. (2004). Santiago de Chile: Metamorfosis bajo un Nuevo Impulso de Modernización Capitalista. In C. De Mattos, M.E. Ducci, A. Rodríguez, & G. Yáñez (Eds.), *Santiago en la Globalización: ¿Una Nueva Ciudad?* (pp. 17–46). Santiago, Chile: Ediciones SUR.

DEM (Departamento de Extranjería). (2014). Migración en Chile: 2005–2014. Retrieved from http://www.extranjeria.gob.cl/.

DEM (Departamento de Extranjería). (2016). Visas otorgadas período 2011–2016. Retrieved from http://www.extranjeria.gob.cl/estadisticas-migratorias/.

Doña-Reveco, C., & Levinson, A. (2012). Chile: A growing destination country in search of a coherent approach to migration. *Migration Policy Institute.* Retrieved

from http://www.migrationpolicy.org/article/chile-growing-destination-country-search-coherent-approach-migration.
Ducci, M.E., & Rojas Symmes, L. (2010). La pequeña Lima: Nueva cara y vitalidad para el centro de Santiago de Chile. *EURE, 36*, 95–121.
Fernández Tapia, C. (2009). Síntesis estudio de caracterización de comunidades peruanas en comunas de la zona norte de Santiago. *Cultura-Urbana, 6*, 1–17.
Garcés, A. (2007). Entre lugares y espacios desbordados: Formaciones urbanas de la migración peruana en Santiago de Chile. *Serie Documentos, 2*, 5–22.
Garcés, A. (2015). *Migración Peruana en Santiago: Políticas, espacios y economías*. Santiago, Chile: RIL Editors.
Godoy, G. (2019). Según estimaciones, la cantidad de personas extranjeras residentes habituales en Chile superó los 1,2 millones al 31 de diciembre de 2018. *INE (Instituto Nacional de Estadística)*. Retrieved from https://www.ine.cl/docs/default-source/default-document-library/estimaci%C3%B3n-de-personas-extranjeras-residentes-en-chile-al-31-de-diciembre-de-2018.pdf?sfvrsn=69145bd2_0.
Gootenberg, P. (2010). Latin American inequalities: New perspectives from history, politics, and culture. In P. Gootenberg & L. Reygadas (Eds.), *Indelible inequalities in Latin America: Insights from history, politics, and culture* (pp. 3–22). Durham, NC: Duke University Press.
Hale, C. (2006). *Más Que un Indio: Racial ambivalence and neoliberal multiculturalism in Guatemala*. Santa Fe, NM: School of American Research.
Hoffman, K., & Centeno, M.A. (2003). The lopsided continent: Inequality in Latin America. *Annual Review of Sociology, 29*, 363–390.
INE (Instituto Nacional de Estadística). (1982). *Censo*. Santiago, Chile.
INE (Instituto Nacional de Estadística). (1992). *Censo*. Santiago, Chile.
INE (Instituto Nacional de Estadística). (2002). *Censo*. Santiago, Chile.
INE (Instituto Nacional de Estadística). (2012). *Censo*. Santiago, Chile.
INE (Instituto Nacional de Estadística). (2017). *Censo*. Santiago, Chile.
International Labour Organization. (2017). Labour migration in Latin America and the Caribbean: Diagnosis, strategy, and ILO's work in the region. Retrieved from http://www.ilo.org/wcmsp5/groups/public/-americas/-ro-lima/documents/publication/wcms_548185.pdf.
Jones, F.O. (2009, October 22). Santiago, Chile, is hardly sleepy anymore. *New York Times*. Retrieved from https://www.nytimes.com/2009/10/25/travel/25next.html.
Kilanski, K., & Auyero, A. (2015). Introduction. In J. Auyero, P. Bourgois, & N. Scheper-Hughes (Eds.), *Violence at the urban margins* (pp. 1–20). New York, NY: Oxford University Press.
Kusenbach, M. (2003). Street phenomenology: The go-along as ethnographic research tool. *Ethnography, 4*(3), 455–485.
Latinobarómetro. (2010). Chile. Retrieved from http://www.latinobarometro.org/latOnline.jsp.
Lefebvre, H. (1991). *The production of space*. Malden, MA: Blackwell Press.
Low, S. (2017). *Spatializing culture: The ethnography of space and place*. New York, NY: Routledge.

Martinez Pizarro, J. (2003). *El Encanto de los Datos: Sociodemográfica de la inmigración en Chile según el censo de 2002*. Santiago, Chile: CEPAL – SERIE Población y desarrollo.

McCann, E., & Ward, K. (2011). *Mobile urbanism: Cities and policymaking in the global age*. Minneapolis, MN: University of Minnesota Press.

Modan, G. (2007). *Turf wars: Discourse, diversity, and the politics of place*. New York, NY: Wiley.

Núñez, L. (2008). *Living on the margins: Illness and healthcare among Peruvian migrants in Chile* (Doctoral dissertation). Leiden University, The Netherlands.

Pessar, P. (1995). The elusive enclave: Ethnicity, class, and nationality among Latino entrepreneurs in greater Washington, DC. *Human Organization, 54*(4), 383–392.

Poole, D. (1997). *Vision, race, and modernity: A visual economy of the Andean image world*. Princeton, NJ: University of Princeton Press.

Portes, A., & Jensen, L. (1987). What's an ethnic enclave? The case for conceptual clarity. *American Sociological Review, 52*, 768–771.

Portes, A., & Manning, R. (2014). Immigrant enclave: Theory and empirical examples. In D.B. Grusky (Ed.), *Social stratification: Class, race, and gender in sociological perspective* (pp. 710–720). New York, NY: Routledge.

Postero, N., Risør, H., & Prieto Montt, M. (2018). Introduction: The politics of identity in neoliberal Chile. *Latin American and Caribbean Ethnic Studies, 13*(3), 203–213.

Ramos, N. (2019). Chile exigirá visa de turistas a venezolanos, aumenta lugares para otorgar visa especial. *Reuters*, June 22. Retrieved from https://lta.reuters.com/articulo/migracion-chile-venezuela-idLTAKCN1TN0IQ-OUSLT.

Reyes, C., Caro, I., & Jara, A. (2019, August 13). La sala del Senado aprobó en general el proyecto de ley de Migraciónes. *La Tercera*. Retrieved from https://www.latercera.com/politica/noticia/la-sala-del-senado-aprobo-general-proyecto-ley-migraciones/781732/.

Reyes, C., & Vera, A. (2019, July 1). Chadwick advierte que 300 mil venezolanos tendrían intención de ingresar a Chile en los próximos meses. *La Tercera*. Retrieved from https://www.latercera.com/politica/noticia/chadwick-advierte-organismos-internacionales-proyectan-300-mil-venezolanos-tendrian-intencion-ingresar-chile-los-proximos-meses/723962/.

Rojas Pedemonte, N., & Silva Dittborn, C. (2016). *La Migración en Chile: Breve Reporte y Caracterización*. Santiago, Chile: Observatorio Iberoamericano sobre Movilidad Humana, Migraciones y Desarrollo.

Secor, A. (2004). 'There is an Istanbul that belongs to me': Citizenship, space, and identity in the city. *Annals of the Association of American Geographers, 94*(2), 352–368.

Singer, P. (2011, January 7). Santiago: The 41 places to go in 2011. *New York Times*. Retrieved from https://www.nytimes.com/2011/01/09/travel/09where-to-go.html.

Stefoni, C. (2003). *Inmigración peruana en Chile: una oportunidad a la integración*. Santiago de Chile: Editorial Universitaria.

Stefoni, C. (2008). Gastronomía Peruana en las Calles de Santiago y la Construcción de Espacio Transnacionales y Territorios. In S. Novick (Ed.), *Las migraciones en*

*América Latina: políticas, culturas y estrategias* (pp. 211–228). Buenos Aires, Argentina: Consejo Latinoamericano de Ciencias Sociales.
Stefoni, C. (2011). *Perfil Migratorio de Chile.* Santiago, Chile: Organización Internacional para las Migraciones.
Stefoni, C. (2016). La nacionalidad y color de piel en la racialización del extranjero. Migrantes como buenos trabajadores en el sector de la construcción. In M.E. Tijoux (Ed.), *Racismo en Chile: La piel como marca de la inmigración* (pp. 65–78). Santiago, Chile: Editorial Universitaria.
Tijoux, M.E. (2011). Negando al 'otro': El constante sufrimiento de los inmigrantes peruanos en Chile. In C. Stefoni (Ed.), *Mujeres inmigrantes en Chile: ¿Mano de obra o trabajadoras con derechos?* (pp. 15–42). Santiago, Chile: Ediciones Universidad Alberto Hurtado.
Tilly, C. (1998). *Durable inequality.* Berkeley, CA: University of California Press.
Tinsman, H. (2019). La democracia chilena: Las protestas y las herencias de la dictadura. North American Congress on Latin America. Retrieved from https://nacla.org/news/2019/11/19/la-democracia-chilena-las-protestas-y-las-herencias-de-la-dictadura.
Torres, O., & Garcés, A. (2013). Representaciones sociales de migrantes peruanos sobre su proceso de integración en la ciudad de Santiago de Chile. *Polis, 35*, 2–18.
Tumba, E. (2018, Sepember 24). ¿Cuántos inmigrantes irregulares hay en Chile? *El Mostrador.* Retrieved from https://www.elmostrador.cl/noticias/opinion/2018/09/24/cuantos-inmigrantes-irregulares-hay-en-chile/.
UN-ECLAC (United Nations Economic Council). (2017). *Social panorama of Latin America 2016.* Santiago, Chile: United Nations.
Vedoya, S., & Navarrete, M.J. (2019, January 16). Los puntos esenciales del proyecto de migración que pasaron su primera prueba legislativa. *La Tercera.* Retrieved from https://www.latercera.com/nacional/noticia/los-puntos-esenciales-del-proyecto-migracion-pasaron-primera-prueba-legislativa/488533/.
Wade, P. (2010). *Race and ethnicity in Latin America* (2nd ed.). London, England: Pluto Press.

# Chapter 8

# Privilege and Space

## *An Analysis of Spatial Relations and Social Inequality in Mexico City Through the Lens of Golf*

Hugo Ceron-Anaya

How does a centrally located parcel of land stay invisible in a large city? Moreover, how could people within this site also be made invisible to others using the space? While conducting ethnographic research on wealth and privilege in Mexico City golf clubs, the themes of the production of visibility and invisibility kept emerging in my notes. Early in my research, I struggled to identify the exact location of one of the city's most prestigious golf clubs, despite growing up in its vicinity. Through aerial mapping, I located the course which abuts a major artery where I passed countless times without ever noticing the golf club. During my research, it became clear the invisibility of the club was intentionally produced, hiding away socioeconomic disparities. Such spatial seclusion is a central characteristic of most Mexico City golf clubs, rendering them "invisible" to outsiders.

When I gained access to interview individuals within some of these golf clubs, this question of visibility extended from the secluded grounds housing the club to the very workers who make golf possible. While many club golfers regard caddies—the workers who assist players while on the course—as outsiders who know little about the game, ethnographic evidence shows that the caddies working to assist players both possess deep understanding of the sport and spend more time at the golf clubs than any other actor involved in the game. This perception that turns knowledgeable aides into clueless outsiders is reinforced by confining the off-duty caddies to spaces secluded by architectural and "natural" barriers, producing a recursive form of invisibility.

My ethnography began as an analysis of class inequalities in contemporary Mexico. I focused this research on golf because of this sport's upscale character in Mexican society (Nutini, 2008; Rodriguez, 2014; Saliba, 2003). My original objective was to understand how daily interactions reinforce social hierarchies among affluent individuals. This research took me to the interior of golf clubs where lush vegetation, stately mature trees, vivid green grass, spacious halls, attentive service, and comfortable facilities revealed how class hierarchies influence a wide range of mundane practices. I observed how club members' perceptions of fashion, sense of humor, notions of honesty and morality, and basic verbal interactions created social distance and divide between themselves and the clubs' employees (Ceron-Anaya, 2019). The golf courses' built environment of construction, design, and sculpted landscaping further enhanced this distance by rendering club employees invisible, thus laminating social and material inequalities through the maintenance of privilege.

Such organization of space communicates social hierarchies and status as the spatial productions of visibility and invisibility work to obscure disparities in wealth, in turn reproducing and justifying socio-spatial articulations based on class difference. Space naturalizes what it is otherwise a historical relation of domination. This chapter addresses four key questions: Who is made visible or invisible in elite spaces? How do architectural and design features make visible and invisible different segments of the people who use these spaces? How are these concerns connected to the construction of social inequality? And finally, how are these sites constructed as everyday spaces for elite communities?

The relationship between social hierarchy, marginalization, and inequality is particularly relevant in countries marred by extreme class differences, such as Mexico (Castillo Negrete, 2017). In 2016, fifteen Mexicans appeared in Forbes' list of global billionaires. Meanwhile, Mexican workers' salaries were the lowest of any Organization for Economic Cooperation and Development member (OECD, 2017) and almost half of the population lived in poverty (CONEVAL, 2014). To better understand socioeconomic disparities in Mexico, this chapter embraces the call to "study up," taking as its focus the elite spaces in the city.[1]

This chapter is based on an ethnography of three affluent golf clubs and draws on data from 58 in-depth interviews with members of the exclusive Mexican golfing community, including club members, instructors, caddies, and golf journalists. During the summers of 2006 and 2010, I conducted five months of ethnographic research, with participants in both phases recruited using a snowball sample.[2] The first phase focused on club members and their understandings of golf and social relationships. The second period of fieldwork focused on caddies. Recorded interviews with caddies addressed the following questions: Why is golf popular among business people? How do you define a golfer? What do you think are the most important transformations golf has experienced in your lifetime? How do you define a caddy? How does a caddy learn the trade?

In the second phase of the project, a journalist connected me with his caddy friend, who facilitated an invitation to one caddies' house, the site at the golf course where caddies wait for golfer assignments. At the caddies' house, I carried out participant observation, had informal conversations with caddies, recruited participants for recorded interviews, and conducted interviews. Between interviews, I spent long periods of time waiting for more caddies to arrive, while observing the organization of social life in this part of the club. After two weeks of visiting the first caddies' house, a caddy there put me in contact with a friend of his who worked at another club. Despite the diversity of individual experiences and the varied architectural styles between clubs, interview and ethnographic data showed strong similarities in terms of spatial exclusion and a lack of visibility among these workers.

Before elaborating on the mechanisms through which dynamics of visibility and invisibility are articulated, it is necessary to explain why golf clubs are strategic sites to examine the relationship between privilege, space, and inequalities in Mexico.

## GOLF IN MEXICO

Mexican golf courses are exclusively private and semiprivate clubs. Private clubs are only open to members and their guests. Semiprivate clubs accept nonmembers on a fee-to-play basis, but commonly restrict facility access to outsiders on discretionary grounds. Similar to the rise of gated communities in Latin America (Caldeira, 2000; Janoschka & Borsdorf, 2004; Low, 2004), the privatization of space in Mexican golf clubs conveys a twofold message. It expresses a desire to create a community away from the crime rates of a large city, while communicating a class and racial statement about who should and should not be allowed to access these exclusive sites (see Ceron-Anaya, 2019, for a discussion on race and class in golf clubs).

Among Mexico's 130 million people are 27,631 registered golf players (IGF, 2017) and about 200 courses. Greater Mexico City has a population of approximately 20 million inhabitants and with 13, the largest concentration of golf clubs. The Mexican Golf Federation does not make public the distribution of registered players by geographical area. However, even if every Mexican golfer lived in Mexico City, they would only represent 0.13 percent of the city's population. This limited number of golfers directly corresponds to the game's expensive nature.

The two most exclusive clubs in Mexico City have one-time membership fees over US$100,000, while the most accessible club charges about

US$7,000 (Rodriguez, 2014; Saliba, 2003). Interviewees report a median one-time membership fee around US$20,000. This fee does not cover additional playing costs, which include annual maintenance fees, minimum monthly expenses, golf lessons, equipment, and caddy fees. Most interviewees acknowledge the high costs of the sport. For instance, Horacio,[3] an upper-middle-class club member in his late forties, remarked that in Mexico, "It is cheaper to buy an expensive car than to play golf." In a similar vein, Daniel, a junior executive in his late thirties who visits semiprivate clubs to play, indicated that he has seen acquaintances taking lessons at driving ranges (inexpensive sites to practice hitting golf balls) and getting excited about the sport. However, in almost every case, people changed their mind when, "They visit the golf shop and see the prices [of the equipment], and definitively abandon the idea of being a golfer when they realize the cost of the green fees [in semipublic clubs], because they see that they won't be able to play frequently, or play at all."

The privileged nature of the sport is particularly evident when compared with the economic reality of most Mexicans. Over half (53%) of the Mexican population lives below the poverty line (World Bank, 2017) and the average annual after tax income is only US$15,300 (OECD, 2017). At the same time, the middle class is characterized by its economic vulnerability (Atkinson & Brandolini, 2014; Teruel & Reyes, 2017). While public courses broaden access to golf in the United States and the United Kingdom (Moss, 2001; Wynne, 2002), golf in Mexico remains a pastime for the upper-middle and upper classes (Nutini, 2008). Such conditions of high affluence are precisely what makes these clubs strategic sites to examine the relationship between privilege and inequality in Mexico City. This relation goes beyond the cost of membership and the norms that go along with social belonging. The built environment of golf clubs illustrates how elite groups further solidify social hierarchies through the organization of space. Hence, the everyday experience of privileged sites, like these golf clubs, reinforces social norms of urban inequality.

## THE MATERIALIZATION OF SOCIAL FORCES

While sociologists often view space as the context for social dynamics, spatial arrangements can be constitutive of social relationships. As George Simmel long argued, a "Boundary is not a spatial fact with sociological consequences, but a sociological fact that forms itself spatially" (1997 [1903], p. 143). In other words, space and spatial arrangements are not elements independent from the social lives organized in and around them. Instead, they are the specific modes of organization of social life in any given society that determines how space is configured and distributed (Harvey, 2005; Massey, 2005). Space represents the materialization of the ideas, assumptions, expectations, and norms that regulate social interactions (Shields, 2013). Following Simmel's argumentation, "Once [a social convention] becomes a spatial and sensory object that we inscribe into nature [. . .], then [it] produces strong repercussions on the consciousness of the relationship of the parties" (1997 [1903], p. 143). Social perceptions unwittingly inform the way space is organized, which in turn reproduces the perceptions that influence spatial arrangements. Space should not be thought of as a set of objects or scenic elements that do not affect social dynamics, but rather a central dimension that reinforces and contributes to the naturalization of social life (Dinzey-Flores, 2013, 2017).

The apparent irrelevance of space turns it into a highly effective channel to reproduce social hierarchies via seemingly natural spatial layouts like a golf course. For example, a fence, a tall wall, a line of tightly planted trees, a guardhouse, or a narrow entryway into an open space, are spatial configurations that articulate social borders. These static structures stress some form of social differentiation, which translates into perceptions of belonging. The overlooked importance of space makes it the ideal conduit to reaffirm the "essential" conditions of social hierarchies, transforming social inequalities from historical struggles into naturalized hierarchies. For example, a guardhouse not only physically regulates an access point, but emphasizes the social distinction between those who can effortlessly pass it with a simple greeting and those who routinely—that is, "naturally"—need to stop and offer explanations of their intentions and objectives before passing through to the guarded space.

Spatial arrangements are a materialization of the social forces that influence our lives. People do not robotically follow spatial arrangements, but space unconsciously affects how individuals perceive and interact with the world by reminding people about the specific type of relations that regulate society in a given site and time. Streets without sidewalks play down the role of pedestrians while asserting cars' supremacy. Public spaces without seating areas downplay the meeting function of open areas, assigning them a transitory character and discouraging loitering. There are always possibilities to subvert the organization of space, such as sitting on the ground in benchless public areas. However, most people use spaces in the ways for which they are designed, such as not stepping over a fence no matter how small it is.

Space renders norms and social hierarchies visible, becoming a fundamental component in the reproduction of social relations. The distribution of spatial arrangements permits social groups to emphasize processes of differentiation, including notions of similarities and differences.[4] In the specific case of elite golf clubs, space emphasizes the social distance between members and outsiders, while facilitating among members an unwitting but steady internalization of a sense of social superiority. In other words, the organization of space around and inside elite golf clubs facilitates the reification of privilege.

## THE MATERIALIZATION OF PRIVILEGE

I grew up in the northern part of Mexico City and knew there was a golf club in the vicinity. Yet, when I started doing research on golf clubs, I found myself unable to determine the precise location of this club. I first assumed my inability to identify this site came from my insufficient knowledge of the area, so I used aerial maps to locate the club. I discovered that I had passed right by the course countless times, but never recognized the existence of the club because a tall wall prevents people from seeing it.

From the aerial maps, a startling trend captured my attention. A wide-angle view of Mexico City reveals relatively few tracts of green land, illustrating the lack of green spaces in this metropolis. Second, apart from a handful of public parks and ecological preserves, many of the green areas visible from above are golf courses. This prompted me to investigate how I could easily identify a golf course in an aerial view of the city but not notice such a tract when walking alongside it. How is it possible that a large, centrally located parcel of land stays invisible in a large city? (see figure 8.1).

Such an analysis of space and social relations was not my original research focus. However, the seeming invisibility of this club suggests that space functions as an unperceived yet solid fabric that reaffirms the city's social hierarchies. This idea was corroborated during the process of interviewing workers. While interviewing one caddy, I asked him how he explains his job to people unfamiliar to golf. He indicated that it was difficult, as few people understand the sport. He added that even people who work and daily pass by the club are oblivious to the presence of a golf course in the area. He noted, "Yeah, the first time I came to the club I arrived late, outside of the metro station [located about half a mile away]. Nobody could tell me how to get to the club." People only become fully aware of this tract of land through their participation in a set of social relations that reinforce their privilege as club members, or their subordination as workers. Thus, the club becomes part of an assemblage of privilege that operates through social, material, and spatial relationships.

After speaking with this caddy, I went to the nearby metro station and asked people for directions to the club. I asked street vendors, workers at inexpensive restaurants, and taxi drivers. Except for one taxi driver, the other workers did not know about the affluent golf course located less than a mile away. The inability of working- and middle-class pedestrians to recognize

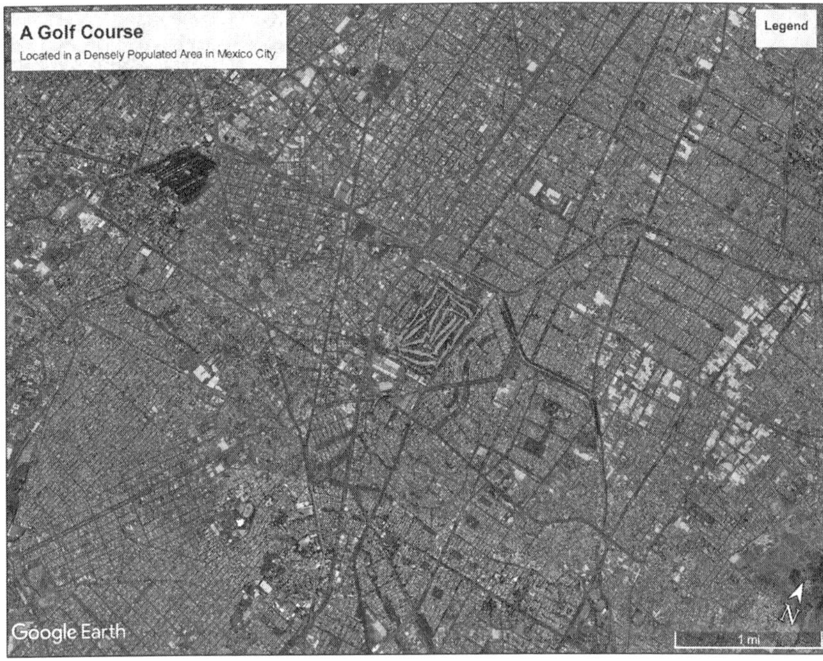


**Figure 8.1 A "Hidden" Golf Course Located in a Densely Populated Area in Mexico City.** *Source*: Map data @ Google 2019, INEGI.

this vast piece of land is not a personal failure but the result of produced invisibility. Reduced visibility secludes the club from the larger city. This emphasizes the large class distinction that exists between club members and the lower- and middle-class people outside the club, even as it removes exterior visual markers of economic disparity. I later learned that this lack of visibility is not an exclusive characteristic of one specific club. The most exclusive club in the city, located next to a central artery, uses multiple architectural barriers, including unimpressive doors, tall walls, thick bushes, and lack of outdoor name signs, to close itself off from the large number of urban dwellers passing by. Newer clubs materialize their lack of visibility by developing upscale residential areas with poor or no public transportation around them, thus preventing outsiders from passing nearby these affluent clubs. These tactics make golf clubs invisible or inaccessible to people who do not have privileged knowledge and access.

For club members, the produced seclusion of these sites adds to their desirability. Interviewees commonly used metaphors such as "hidden gem" and "oasis" to talk about the clubs, further crafting exceptional spaces not visible to all people. These comments implicitly compare these sites with the rest of the metropolis; tacitly reproducing a distinction between those who are inside the "oasis" and those who are outside. Despite variations in the architectural styles and locations, similar patterns repeat in the organization of the clubs' internal spaces. For example, the outside entrances of most clubs, particularly the central ones, were rather simple, especially when considering the hefty membership fees and status of their members. In opposition to the outside entrances' simplicity, the clubhouse doors convey an upscale feeling that incorporates global design trends. For example, in the newest club I visited, the clubhouse door looks like a large barn door—a style similar to the rustic chic currently in vogue in upmarket country houses in the United States.

In all three clubs, a smiling, polite female host offers a welcoming reception to members and guests a short distance from the main doors. The recurrent presence of these female workers marks the transitional space between the city and the club interior. Mexico City, like other metropolises, anonymizes those who move through its streets, turning affluent individuals into indistinctive city dwellers. The courteous aides' role is to welcome members in an individualized manner, assuring them of their uniqueness and distinction and interpellating them into their role as a member. These workers are not personal in their greetings. Instead, they include a combination of reverential terms such as courtesy titles (e.g., señor [Mr.] or señora [Mrs.]) before using the first or last name of the golfer. After the salutation, the worker engages in basic conversation. The club member dictates the length of the interaction by keeping a fast pace, dropping the tone of voice, or making a request, which lets the worker know that the interaction is over. The figure of the aide calms and uplifts members by re-centering social attention from external elements, such as local traffic, to the immediate needs and emotions of golfers (for a parallel analysis in Australia see Donaldson & Poynting, 2004).

After passing through the reception area, the internal spaces convey a sense of amplitude and openness. In contrast to the clubs' external lack of visibility, no structural barrier blocks the visibility of the hallways inside the clubhouses. The restaurants, bars, and most other facilities inside these buildings follow a similar pattern. Space is organized in a way to minimize obstacles and increase the possibilities that members can constantly interact with each other. Interviews conducted inside the clubhouses reinforced this factor. All included interruptions by other members who approached to greet the members I was interviewing.

Inside the clubs, only two member areas avoid the open spatial design: changing rooms and the golf course. Regarding the latter, the courses' hilly terrain, tree and shrub distribution, and the considerable distance needed between groups of players—a small, hard, fast-moving ball represents a real danger if golfers do not keep distance between them—highly restricted visibility. Club members talk about the course as "natural" spaces; a site saved from the voracious appetite of urban developers. One participant even talked about golf clubs as "ecological projects." However, this perception fails to recognize that the common characteristics found in golf clubs—for example, lush green hills, ponds, and sand traps—are reminiscent of aristocratic British taste, rather than natural elements (Klein, 1999). Hence, the lack of visibility the golf course produces is not the result of the endemic pristine vegetation, but the action of human intervention in the landscape.

The invisibility created by the golf course is erased at the bar. All clubs have a central bar known as the "nineteenth hole," situated next to the eighteenth hole (the final hole of the game). After the game is over, most groups of players stop at the nineteenth hole to drink, eat, and rest, while memorializing the just-finished game. Unlike regular restaurants where people keep the conversation between those seated together, at the nineteenth hole, members at adjacent tables frequently interact with each other. Jokes and stories about what just happened on the course are frequently narrated loud enough to let others hear them, generating laughs and interjections by other golfers present at the bar. This communal interaction lets people gain information about who is an outstanding player, who is a funny person to play with, who gets irritated when things do not go right, who maintains composure despite losing a bet, and who cheats. The conversation at the bar shares the actions that happened on the course witnessed only by a handful of members with the entire community. These observations were corroborated throughout the interviews with golfers. For instance, Fernando, a club member in his early thirties, indicated that the bar was a space marked by camaraderie. He explained that even when a member does not know all the golfers at another table there is still a feeling of community, "Because after all, you are part of the same circle, you are a member of the club, [everybody is] in the same socioeconomic situation, which creates a feeling of friendship." The interviewees generally describe the bar in terms of friendship and conviviality (for an analysis of the ways in which women members are beholden to spatial, social, and playing hierarchies such as those limiting access to the nineteenth hole, see Ceron-Anaya, 2019).

The public discussion at the bar lets members learn a great deal of information about their peers. For example, golfers hear about the witty conversation, sense of humor, shy personality, expansive knowledge of the rules, strong playing skills, dishonest attitudes, and perseverance of other members in the club. Even if a golfer has not met all the other members, he may already have heard information about a fellow club member based on the information that circulates at the bar. The nineteenth hole restores the open visibility that informs social relations among club members in most other physical areas of the clubs. This space emphasizes for whom the club is made for and, hence, the information that circulates between tables centers the attention of club members on other club members. Unsurprisingly, caddies never access this part of the club. If they want to eat or drink, they have their own space: the caddies' house.

## THE MATERIALIZATION OF SUBORDINATION

Caddies perform the vital work that enables smooth and comfortable play for club members. Caddies carry golf bags, take care of the clubs, keep track of where balls land, locate lost balls, advise players on strategy, and pass messages between groups of golfers, among other duties. Despite their pivotal role, there is an important socioeconomic divide between club members and the caddies. All caddies interviewed described themselves and their coworkers as working class. For example, during one conversation with a caddy in his mid-twenties, I asked how he explained to people unfamiliar with golf what a caddy is. He answered, "[I told them] have you ever seen on TV sports news, when they talk about golf? [Caddies] are the dudes who carry the bags, I am one of them, yeah . . . *el gato* [the lackey]. So, I am *el gato*, [laughs] we all [caddies] are *gatos*." The latter translates as "cat," which in Mexico City slang is a pejorative term that implies subjugation, obedience, servitude, and lower-class status.[5] By identifying himself and all caddies as *gatos*, this young caddy marks his profession as corresponding to a lower socioeconomic status. While not all caddies used derogatory terms to refer to their trade, all of them used allegories that conveyed impoverished origins to talk about themselves and their group.

In all the clubs that I visited, hiring a caddy was the norm. Only the most economical club in the city allows players to opt out of hiring one. Yet, even this "affordable" club grants players immediate access to these workers if they want to hire one. The first time an interviewee invited me to play in his club, a group of caddies promptly showed up carrying our clubs as soon as we stepped into the warm-up area. When we finished playing, these workers swiftly and discreetly disappeared from the course. I particularly noticed their fast exit because I tried to tip the caddy who worked for me, but he had already disappeared from view. My experience did not differ on other playing occasions. Caddies quickly appeared at the beginning of the game and rapidly vanished at the end of it, almost as if their actions were magically orchestrated.

The second time I was invited to play, I became curious about where caddies stay inside the club when they were not working. Two players informed me that caddies had their own space inside the club, called the "caddies' house," located between the beginning and end of the course (the standard design of a golf course situates the first and last hole next to each other). When we finished playing, one of the golfers pointed to a line of thick hedges saying, "that's the caddies' house, they are behind the fence." In the clubs I visited, the caddies' houses were out of the view of players, thus maintaining and conflating social and spatial distance even within a bounded site. When a member needs something from a site beyond the visual boundaries, such as talking with a caddy or getting their equipment, they commonly instruct another worker to fetch the desired person or piece of equipment. When I later spent time at the caddies' house, I saw only one female golfer briskly walk through this area while looking at the ground. In response to my inquiry, a caddy told me that she was a member who commonly walked between her house and the club, and the shortest route passed by the caddies' house. In no other instance did I observe a member approach the caddies' house. The spatial boundaries that separate workers from members reflect and reproduce the large class differences that already divide these two groups.

During my first period of fieldwork, I almost exclusively spent time with club members. My interactions with caddies focused on my needs as a player, such as advice on strategy or suggestions about which of the fourteen clubs I should use. These dynamics were interspersed with jokes and other types of humorous remarks, particularly when the caddies noted that I had difficult moments playing—hitting trees, landing the ball on water hazards, and hitting the grass instead of the ball. In subtle ways, the caddies tried to calm and uplift me—just as the receptionists did with members in the entrance of the clubhouse—by telling jokes or emphasizing the few good shots I made. These comments suggested that I was not that bad. Later, when I interviewed caddies, I learned that this form of emotional labor is a fundamental part of their job (Hochschild, 1983).[6] While their labor is a key support to members as they play, when the game is over, caddies promptly disappear from the players' view. The spatial layouts of the clubs facilitate this rapid access and exit of workers to the course by keeping the caddies' house centrally located while simultaneously hidden.

In interviews, I queried club members about their perceptions of caddies. I asked members how common it was for caddies to try to become professional players and if so, why no former caddy was competing in the best leagues in Europe or the United States. I was not interested in golfers' thoughts on professional players. Instead, I wanted to hear members' views about caddies. Most interviewees, men and women alike, offered a narrative that primarily blamed caddies for their own lack of success. The answers commonly elaborated on a lack of work ethic, discipline, morals, and perseverance to explain the fact that only a handful of caddies have tried to become professionals and no one ever reached top leagues. In a more nuanced way, some members also pointed out the limited support clubs offer caddies when these workers try to become professionals. At the end of the first period of fieldwork, my understanding of caddies remained minimal. I had only interacted with them a handful of times, and I had mainly heard neutral or negative anecdotes about these workers. The spatial segregation of caddies, which decreased their visibility, prevented me and most other members, from even collecting information to challenge unfavorable impressions about these workers with concrete stories of perseverance and discipline.

My second period of fieldwork almost exclusively focused on these workers. Time with the caddies produced a more nuanced understanding of these workers, corroborating Simmel's argument that a "boundary is not a spatial fact with sociological consequences, but a sociological fact that forms itself spatially" (1997 [1903], p. 143). For instance, unlike the elegant doors that give access to the clubhouse, the caddy entryway commonly consists of a metal door adjacent to large tinted windows. The design of this entrance allows guards behind the door to see who is ringing the bell without being seen themselves, which creates the feeling for those trying to gain entry that they are being inspected. Remarkably, this design element mirrors the layout of factories and other sites for workers.

The organization of spaces around the entrances for members and workers are radically different. The entryway for members interpellates those who pass through it as privileged members of the community. The door is a sign of belonging, and it grants full access to the space as well as a voice in its development. By contrast, the organization of the space around the entrance for caddies conveys a clear message of subordination. In a Foucauldian sense, the large tinted windows express an open need to oversee, discipline, and control the workers who enter these doors.

In the most affluent clubs, the caddies' houses are still characterized by its simplicity. They include modest changing rooms with metal lockers and benches; basic showers, urinals, and toilets; and an inexpensive eatery that sells breakfast, lunch, and snacks. This eatery includes a simple kitchen, a plain covered shed, and plastic tables and chairs. A small patio with more plastic tables and chairs completes the site. The chairs are adequate for brief rests or eating, but not comfortable seating for longer timeframes. Yet, because of the nature of their work, caddies spend long periods in this area.

In the clubs I visited, caddies are contingent workers who receive payment only when called onto the course. In other words, they are flexible, precarious labor—conditions associated with the global expansion of neoliberal capitalism (Ong, 2010). Caddies are arranged in a rotation system where each worker has an assigned number. On average, each club has sixty caddies. If one of them is not present when his number is called, he needs to wait until the list starts over again (my use of male gender pronouns is intentional, as there were no female caddies in the clubs visited). While weekends are almost always busy, the number of golfers playing during the week fluctuated significantly. This arrangement encourages caddies to always be at the caddies' house waiting for their turn to work. Some of the caddies interviewed reported that it was not unusual to spend an entire day or two waiting before they could caddy, more so during weekdays and holidays when members often leave the city.

The time I spent at the caddies' house countered the negative stereotypes that I had heard about these workers. For example, while caddies did not show excitement about the long period they needed to wait to work, they patiently showed up and waited their turn. They spend their time chatting, playing cards, or staring at their phones. Amid a neoliberal system in which they are precarious laborers, dressing up and coming to work while not knowing if they will make money that day, speaks of both work ethic and perseverance.

Similarly, the complaint about caddies' lack of morals was associated with a supposed predisposition to drink too much alcohol. I asked caddies about the issue and heard a more complex picture. One young caddy remarked, "Look, some club members keep drinking [alcohol] all the time while playing, [. . .] by the end of the game they are already tipsy. Some let us keep the opened bottles for ourselves, and, it is true, some of us like to drink." Some caddies recognized problems of alcoholism among the community. Yet, these workers also noted that if a caddy arrives drunk, he is penalized and cannot work that day. If the behavior repeats, the worker is fired. The idea that caddies do not progress in life because they have a "natural predisposition" to drink is a narrative that flourishes when the daily reality of the caddies' work hides behind architectural barriers. This lack of visibility prevents members from observing the positive traits of these workers, reinforcing instead a set of inaccurate narratives that justify the segregation of caddies.

A parallel situation happens in relationship to playing skills. Most club members perceive the caddies as workers with only a basic understanding of the game. One golfer even maintained that "most caddies are clueless about this sport." Sharing a similar sentiment, the editor of a famous golf magazine told me that instead of trying to offer advice on strategy and technique, "caddies should limit themselves to carrying the clubs and do no more than that." Despite these negative arguments, my conversations with many caddies indicated their clear understanding of the technical and strategic aspects of the sport. Moreover, several of them had low handicaps (the numeral representation of a player's potential), indicating strong playing skills. However, caddies have few opportunities to demonstrate their golfing abilities to members. In most city clubs, caddies can play as many rounds as they like on Monday, when clubs are closed for maintenance. Caddies' playing skills, one of the most critical assets in an athletic club, are thus only witnessed by other caddies and not by club members. Some members indicated that from time to time, clubs organize tournaments for caddies, inviting the entire community to attend. Yet, in recent years, the Mexico Golf Federation has held professional events on the same day of the tournament for caddies, further reducing the already limited visibility of these workers and their golf expertise.

## DISCUSSION AND CONCLUSION

My initial inability to identify the exact location of golf clubs prompted a set of questions about the seeming visibility and invisibility of a centrally located tract of land. Further ethnographic research introduced a new dimension to the production of visibility and invisibility of people in those places. The limited visibility of golf courses in this metropolis is not accidental, but rather a concerted effort to maintain a firm boundary between highly affluent individuals and the middle and working classes. The invisibility is materially organized through tall walls, thick bushes, fast-moving arteries, and upscale residential areas with no public transportation. Most people who routinely pass by these courses are unable to recognize them as golf clubs. From the outside, the treetops could just as easily be part of a playground, a park, a recreational area, a preserve, a row of backyards, or the grounds of a local business. Space, therefore, is not a set of scenic elements that barely influence social dynamics, but rather, space represents the materialization of the social forces that shape our everyday lives.

The relationship between club members and caddies further illustrates this argument. Most golfers refer to caddies as outsiders who do not understand the game, positioning caddies in rhetorical opposition to club members. In this narrative, caddies lack work ethic, ambition, desire to progress, discipline, and strategic thinking—traits supposedly associated with golfers. According to the club members interviewed, the lack of positive social and cultural characteristics is what prevents most caddies from becoming successful professional players, despite their outstanding playing skills.

Space plays a vital role in legitimizing this self-serving narrative. The invisibility of the caddies' house, for instance, allows members to disregard caddies' work ethic demonstrated by their readiness to work despite not knowing if they will earn a salary that day. The physical barriers that obscure the presence of caddies inside the club prevent golfers from accurately witnessing the long stretches these workers spend waiting for their turn to work at the premises. In a similar vein, caddies' limitations in demonstrating their playing skills, playing only on the day when club members are absent, prevents most golfers from recognizing the discipline and perseverance that many caddies possess. Caddies' effort, labor, and skills are rendered invisible, thus facilitating the maintenance of club members' derogatory narratives blaming caddies for their own exclusion.

The crafting of the built environment, including the golf club and its course and architectural building design, is an integral element of an assemblage of spatialized privilege. Such organization of space efficiently reminds people about their place in social hierarchies. An elegant entryway, a tinted window adjacent to a solid metal door, a basic waiting area, and a comfortably vast open space for resting are spatial elements that not only reflect the material conditions of existence but also represent the worth of the people who occupy them. The distinction between the small, inexpensive area reserved for caddies and the large, fashionable area reserved for members suggests an almost essential difference between golfers and workers. These spatial contrasts permit affluent members to validate ideas about the "natural" distinction between class groups. Space is certainly not the only factor defining the organization of inequalities, but it contributes to the legitimization and justification of privilege and social exclusion. It does so because spatial arrangements represent the materialization of the social forces that regulate everyday life.

This case study illustrates how class dynamics operate in conjunction with a spatial assemblage to reproduce privilege. Space and spatial arrangements play a fundamental role in the articulation of these layers, obscuring the activities and participation of some groups while augmenting the visibility and contributions of others without the need to verbalize social distinction. The power of space in the reproduction of privilege resides in its perceived triviality. The "unimportant" character attributed to space is what allows it to turn historical relations of domination into reasonable and legitimate social hierarchies. Space, thus, continuously remind people of their "natural" position in society.

## NOTES

1. Since the 1980s, scholars researching Mexico have taken up Nader's call to "study up" (1972). However, almost all of these studies have analyzed institutional settings (Anzaldua & Maxfield, 1987; Arriola, 1991; Basañez, 1990), emphasizing interactions between economic elites and the nation-state (Centeno, 1994). To these valuable body of work, my research adds an analysis of informal relations to explore concrete forms of exclusion, specific mechanisms of inclusion, and distinct power dynamics involved in the constitution of privilege.

2. Gaining access to club members, recruiting participants, and building rapport were challenging tasks. My limited connections inside the world of golf might have put some club members off. I later learned, that my experience living in Britain as a graduate student, and my vivid memories about iconic courses in Scotland—which I visited as a tourist for research purposes—generated a degree of legitimacy that helped build rapport (for an extended methodological discussion see Ceron-Anaya, 2019).

3. All names are pseudonyms and multiple details have been modified to protect the privacy of informants.

4. Spatial arrangements commonly operate in conjunction with the distribution and organization of time. For a discussion of the relationship between space and time, see Bourdieu (2001), Harvey (1989), and Massey (1995).

5. The term *el gato* originates out of the pejorative term *gata*—female cat—given to live-in domestic female workers, who—like cats—spent an important amount of time on the roofs of the employer's house, doing laundry. The term highlights another example of spatial separation of workers.

6. The term "emotional labor" describes a series of displays exhibited by workers—for example, in the retail industry—to express empathy with customers. Emotional labor is a way to transform a purely economic transaction into a seemingly affectionate relationship. In doing so, workers subordinate their own emotions and points of view to the feelings and expectations of the customer.

## BIBLIOGRAPHY

Anzaldua, R., & Maxfield, S. (Eds.). (1987). *Government and private sector in contemporary Mexico*. San Diego, CA: University of California Press.

Arriola, C. (1991). *Los Empresarios y El Estado, 1970–1982*. Mexico City, Mexico: Miguel Angel Porrua.

Atkinson, A., & Brandolini, A. (2014). On the identification of the middle class. In J.C. Gornick & M. Jäntti (Eds.), *Income inequality: Economic disparities and the middle class in affluent countries* (pp. 77–100). Stanford: Stanford University Press.

Basañez, M. (1990). *La Lucha Por La Hegemonía En México*. Mexico City, Mexico: Siglo XXI.

Bourdieu, P. (2001). *Masculine domination*. Stanford, CA: Stanford University Press.

Caldeira, T.P.R. (2000). *City of walls: Crime, segregation, and citizenshipin São Paulo*. Berkeley, CA: University of California Press.

Castillo Negrete, M.R. (2017). Income inequality in Mexico, 2004–2014. *Latin American Policy, 8*(1), 93–113.

Centeno, M.A. (1994). *Democracy within reason: Technocratic revolution in Mexico*. University Park, PA: Pennsylvania State University Press.

Ceron-Anaya, H. (2019). *Privilege at play: Class, race, gender, and golf in Mexico*. New York: Oxford University Press.

CONEVAL. (2014). *Pobreza En México*. Retrieved from https://www.coneval.org.mx/Medicion/MP/Paginas/Pobreza_ 2014.aspx.

Dinzey-Flores, Z.Z. (2013). Gated communities for the rich and the poor. *Contexts, 12*(4), 24–29.

Dinzey-Flores, Z.Z. (2017). Spatially polarized landscapes and a new approach to urban inequality. *Latin American Research Review, 52*(2), 241–252.

Donaldson, M., & Poynting, S. (2004). The time of their lives: Time, work and leisure in the daily lives of ruling-class men. In N. Hollier (Ed.), *Ruling Australia:*

*The power, privilege and politics of the new ruling class* (pp. 127–153). Melbourne: Australian Scholarly Publishing.

Harvey, D. (1989). *The urban experience*. Baltimore: JHU Press.

Harvey, D. (2005). *Spaces of neoliberalization: Towards a theory of uneven geographical development*. Germany: Franz Steiner Verlag.

Hochschild, A.R. (1983). *The managed heart: Commercialization of human feeling*. Berkley, CA: University of California Press.

IGF, I.G.F. (2017). Mexican golf federation, statistics. Retrieved from https://www.igfgolf.org/nationalmembers/mexican-golf-federation/.

Janoschka, M., & Borsdorf, A. (2004). The rise of private residential neighbourhoods in Latin America. In G. Glasze, C. Webster, & K. Frantz (Eds.), *Private cities: Global and local perspectives* (pp. 89–104). New York: Routledge.

Klein, B. (1999). Cultural links: An international political economy of golf course landscapes. In T. Miller & R. Martin (Eds.), *Sportcult* (pp. 211–226). Minneapolis, MN: University of Minnesota Press.

Low, S.M. (2004). *Behind the gates: Life, security, and the pursuit of happiness in Fortress America*. New York: Routledge.

Massey, D. (1995). *Spatial divisions of labour: Social structures and the geography of production*. London: Macmillan

Massey, D. (2005). *For space*. Thousand Oaks, CA: SAGE.

Moss, R. (2001). *Golf and the American Country Club*. Urbana: University of Illinois Press.

Nader, L. (1972). Up the anthropologist perspectives gained from studying up. In D.H. Hymes (Ed.), *Reinventing anthropology* (pp. 284–311). New York: Pantheon Books.

Nutini, H.G. (2008). *The Mexican aristocracy: An expressive ethnography, 1910–2000*. Austin, TX: University of Texas Press.

OECD. (2017). *Average wages (indicator)*. Retrieved from https://data.oecd.org/earnwage/average-wages.htm#indicator-chart.

Ong, A. (2010). *Spirits of resistance and capitalist discipline: Factory women in Malaysia*. Albay, NY: Suny Press.

Rodriguez, D. (2014, February 25). Golf, ¿un deporte sólo para ricos? *El Financiero*.

Saliba, A. (2003, 2003/07/01/). Hitting the tropical links: Growth of golf stunted by heavy price tag, limited interest. *Business Mexico*.

Shields, R. (2013). *Spatial questions: Social spatialisations and cultural topologies*. London: Sage.

Simmel, G. (1997 [1903]). The sociology of space. In D. Frisby & M. Featherstone (Eds.), *Simmel on culture: Selected writings* (pp. 137–169). London: Sage.

Teruel, G., & Reyes, M. (2017). *México: País de pobres y no de clases medias*. Retrieved from http://www.kas.de/wf/doc/kas_49928-1522-4-30.pdf?170830011442.

World Bank. (2017). *Poverty & equity data, Mexico*. Retrieved from http://povertydata.worldbank.org/poverty/country/MEX.

Wynne, D. (2002). Leisure, lifestyle, and the new middle class: A case study. London, UK: Routledge.

## *Chapter 9*

# New Cityscapes

## *Redesigning Urban Cartographies Through Creative Practices and Critical Pedagogies in London*

Chiara Minestrelli

This chapter engages in a critical analysis of urban inequalities as they are experienced at the juncture of the local and the global. I do so by discussing a collaborative project based in London, called Sonic Futures, that resulted from cooperation between the London College of Communication (LCC) and May Project Gardens, a community organization. The project was conceptualized as a way to support students in their academic endeavors by combining participatory action research[1] (Selener, 1997; Ulvik, Riese, & Roness, 2018) with hip-hop music and critical pedagogies. These theoretical aspects were coupled with gardening, a practical activity that allowed participants to reflect on several local themes within this global city, including social justice, diversity, and sustainability. As unusual as it may sound, these disparate elements worked well together, prompting participants to question social structures and the inequalities they generate, alongside considerations of well-being and community formation.

Funded by the Teaching and Learning Innovation Fund at LCC, this innovative approach to understanding urban spaces and inequalities concretized in a series of five workshops that took place between October 2018 and April 2019. The activities were open to students from both LCC and London South Bank University (LSBU), another partner in this venture. The original aim of the workshops was to support student attainment, retention, and engagement in academic activities. Yet, despite the original goal to support students who might be struggling and unprepared, the students who participated were all international students from relatively privileged backgrounds. As a consequence, while maintaining a keen interest in exploring how pedagogical practices could respond to student needs, one of the questions at the heart of the workshops shifted to reflect on the positionality of instructors and students. As we all shared some experiences of migration, this reflexivity allowed us to examine the complex urban inequalities framed by the many migratory movements visible within London. Considering the location of LCC and LSBU, we decided to concentrate primarily on the area where both universities are located: Elephant and Castle in South London, within the Borough of Southwark (see figure 9.1). The workshops made connections between past and present within this site, seeking to make sense of the ways in which resources were distributed, the means by which communities gathered, and how various urban processes produced "new (in some cases expansive, in some restrictive) notions of membership and solidarity" (Holston & Appadurai, 1999, p. 189) within this global city.

The question of urban inequality was central to the workshops and was approached from two angles. First, the workshops bore testimony to the very structures of inequalities that underlie differentiated access to spaces and resources within the global city, seen in the inability to recruit local undergraduate students from marginalized backgrounds.[2] The students who did participate were all graduate students from different regions of

**Figure 9.1 The Map Shows the Location of Elephant and Castle within Greater London.**
*Source*: Map data @ Google 2019.

the world, including Sierra Leone, Mexico, and India, with varied academic backgrounds and work experiences. Second, local inequalities were addressed overtly during the workshops, including in relation to the effects of urban development and regeneration, displacement, and environmental challenges. These discussions were problematized by considering the students' personal experiences of relocation, adaptation, integration, and their "right to the city," namely the collective right to "change ourselves by changing the city more after our heart's desire" (Harvey, 2003, p. 1). The "glocal" nature of the workshops was crafted through their specificities—the international breadth provided by the students on the one hand, and the internalization of curricula based on hip-hop pedagogies on the other. In an increasingly connected world, this dynamic was in line with broader social dynamics and held the potential to establish international connections through the centrifugal movement of the students, bringing their own experiences to London and exporting new knowledge to their home country or to future homes.

Each workshop was organized around specific themes and areas of South London, and activities were carried out in several locations: Morden, a district in the south eastern part of London which still retains a rural character, and where the community organization May Project Gardens is based; and Lamlash Gardens in Elephant and Castle, the site of the former Heygate Estate[3] (now Elephant Park). Workshop foci varied from regeneration and gentrification to migration, community building, discrimination, and intersectionality. These discussions were connected to questions around sustainability and framed through concepts related to hip-hop philosophy and gardening (Hoffman, Morales-Knight & Wallach, 2007). Student participation entailed the creation of a website, writing sessions, a music recording session at the Elephant Studios at LSBU, and the update of the digital platform where the material from the workshops was digitally stored. These activities were integrated with critical reflections on the topics covered and with active participation in the organization of a final conference held at LCC in April 2019.

This chapter explores the ways in which urban place and situated inequalities can be understood at the multiple, overlapping intersections of the global and the local. I do so through a reflective discussion of pedagogical approaches used with the Sonic Futures project, exploring the influence of global migration, urban development, and individual experience for university students in South London. I suggest that, through collaborative praxis, students, educators, and community members can take small steps toward creating the types of cities they would like to see; a kind of "radical hope" for our urban futures (Lear, 2006). I begin this chapter with an ethnographic vignette that captures the workshop's approach to education and its relation to particular spaces of the city itself.

## CRITICAL URBAN SPACES: ELEPHANT AND CASTLE IN CONTEXT

The workshop at the Lamlash Gardens in South London, located just behind the University, provides a good example of how the practical and theoretical dimensions came together during the sessions. During this walking tour, we stopped in different locations to reflect on their complex histories. We started outside Elephant and Castle's iconic shopping center, and ended at the Heygate Estates memorial wall (see figure 9.2).

Our first stop was in front of the shopping center, where I explained the history of the building, its historical relevance, and its current role as a pole of attraction for various communities in the area. The students were surprised to discover that the name "Elephant and Castle" came from the coat of arms of the Worshipful Company of Cutlers, which bears testimony to the practices and activities carried out in the area during the Middle Ages. The name is also celebrated through a small statue of an Elephant with a Castle—originally a *howdah*, a carriage located on the back of camels and used to transport people—occupying the space outside the train station, which doubles as an entrance to the shopping center. The students confessed that they had never

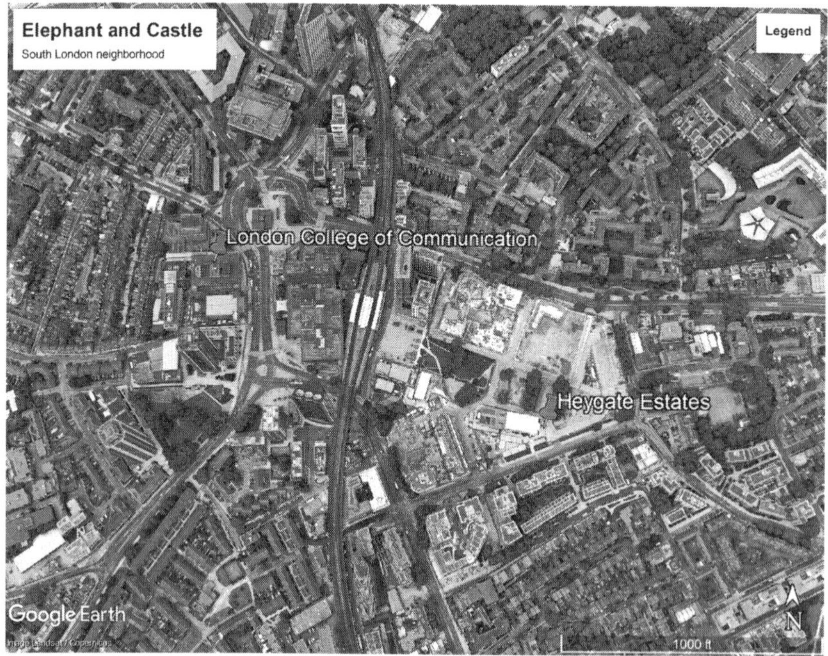


**Figure 9.2 The Map of Workshop Occurred Sites.** *Source*: Map data @ Google 2019.

**Figure 9.3 Workshop Participants Explored Lamlash Gardens.** *Source*: Photo by author.

investigated the origins and meaning of the statue, despite walking past it every day.

We then went to Lamlash Gardens where my co-moderator asked the students to identify different species of plants and insects in order to understand their role within the food chain (see figure 9.3). Experiential approaches (Kolb & Kolb, 2005) are particularly relevant when guiding students to learn about the cycles of nature, including how human beings relate to the environment and the relevance of green spaces within urban contexts. As the students were exploring their surroundings, I observed their body language. Most students had an expression of wonder on their faces, one student particularly so. Born and raised in Mumbai, India, Anika told us that she had never had the chance to be so close to nature and that this new experience gave her a deep sense of peace. To be able to observe, touch, and taste the urban environment was something new to most students. We all shared our sensations and first impressions, as well as our past experiences and understandings of nature as we all came from different countries with very different flora and fauna.

Discussions around plants and planting were integrated by a spontaneous interaction with a resident who owned a plot of land in the gardens. This resident told us that the area had changed enormously over the years due to the displacement of the local communities. She pointed to some of the impacts of

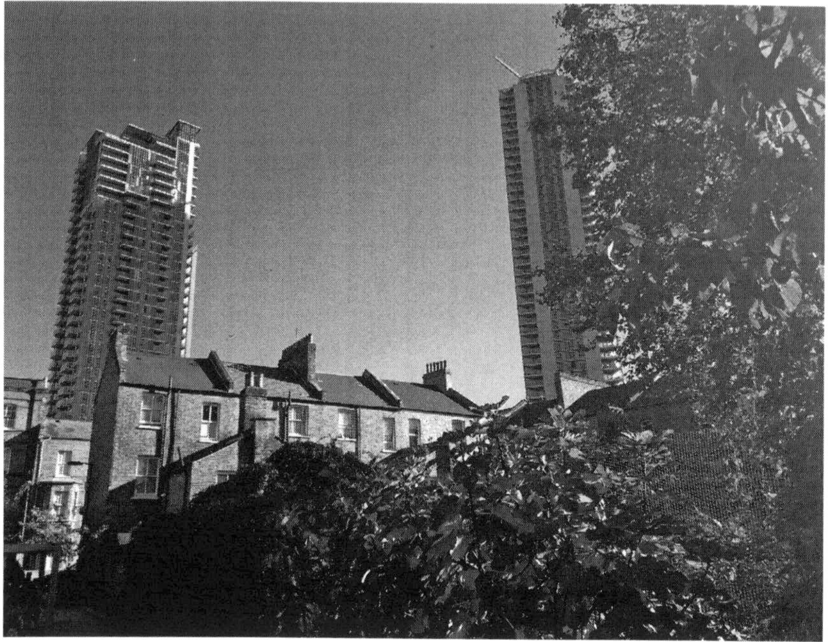

**Figure 9.4 New High-Rise Buildings Constructed on the Site of the Former Heygate Estates.** *Source*: Photo by author.

new, high-rise buildings constructed on the site of the former estate, as they block out direct sunlight (see figure 9.4).

We next moved to Elephant Park, where a commemorative wall explains the history of the Heygate Estates, an area of public housing demolished between 2011 and 2014 as part of urban redevelopment. Here, the story of hip-hop culture's birth proved to be a productive and useful example in understanding how communities are affected by urban planning processes that seem only interested in the value of economic, rather than human, capital. Chang (2005) has explored this question by narrating the role played by the Cross-Bronx Expressway in redesigning New York's cityscape after World War II. The construction of the freeway shaped the lives of those who were forced to leave their homes and relocate to areas characterized by a lack of resources and extreme poverty. This, together with other sociocultural factors, led to the origins of hip-hop. This history felt particularly impactful when standing on the site of over one thousand destroyed homes.

After a discussion on regeneration, and on access to public resources and spaces, the students shared their personal experiences and thoughts. This offered a moment in which multiple global perspectives intersected at the site of a profoundly local displacement. The urban thus becomes a set of layered locals, imbuing the city with a sense of the "glocal." These aspects are captured in student testimonies and reflections following the workshops. As Irma, a twenty-four-year-old international student from Mexico, noted:

> London is such a big, complex, diverse, fast-paced city; as a foreign woman and student living here for the first time, the workshops were a big chance to understand the complexity of the city. To walk around some neighborhoods with my peers, to do gardening, to talk to local people about gentrification; was a significant and helpful chance to not feel as a loner and small tourist in a city. I can say from my experience that it helped me in emotional aspects since it was my first time in the city and I didn't have friends living in here, but the workshops were a great chance to meet wonderful people, develop communication skills and open my mind to new perspectives of what it means—London and its people. . . . Thanks to the workshops I not only understood new standpoints of issues like gentrification, gardening, growing your own food, belonging, but also, I found my own voice and my own opinion about this. The workshops were the best therapy to know myself and how I think/felt about issues that matter and that concern me as a human, as part of a society, as a student and as a migrant in London.

## LONDON'S "SCAPES": SOCIOCULTURAL AND THEORETICAL BACKGROUND

The city of London and its suburban areas were the point of departure for the workshops and, at the same time, the conceptual "ground zero" for understanding the varied local dynamics generated within a global city. The global dimensions of the city reflect London's broad character and demographics, as well as the increasing internationalization of the higher education sector. This is, in fact, a crucial element of the economic fabric of London, as a focus on recruiting international students and engaging international topics now characterize most tertiary education institutions, including LCC and LSBU.

Definitions of the city as a locus where global and local forces come together are well established across the social sciences, with the work of Saskia Sassen (2000) providing a productive framework within which to understand the possibilities of this approach to urban worlds. Sassen's work also highlights the potential engendered by sites of memory within the city, and of sites of congregation where community organizations, or even individuals, can come together to enact alternative socio-politics. In her conceptualization of the Global City almost two decades ago, Sassen (2000) identifies the liminal space occupied by communities of immigrants—particularly relevant in London, a city in which migrants account for 36 percent of the population (Vargas-Silva & Rienzo, 2019). Sassen argues that this "postmodern frontier zone" (2000, p. 169) is a space for alternative forms of politics. Juan Camilo Cock (2011) explored this point in the case of the 2010 presidential election in Colombia, which saw the mobilization of the Colombian diaspora in London. This call to action brought together many Colombians who were asked to vote for the Green Party's candidate in Colombia while residing in London. During these elections, Elephant and Castle became one of the two symbolic sites for community gatherings in London. It is primarily the public (and private) sphere inhabited by migrants which holds traction for opportunities while being an easy target for discrimination and inequalities. As a local space actively utilized and experienced by Colombians during the Colombian election, Elephant and Castle became a symbol of community cohesion and political participation.

The workshops in the Sonic Futures project prioritized the potential of collaborative and critical pedagogies to address social inequalities within one area of a global city. While also highlighting the inequalities of London as a city, this chapter is interested in shedding light on the positive—on "radical hope" (Lear, 2006) that might be found in times of fragmentation, economic insecurity, and increasing global flows of goods and people. The British capital certainly encapsulates each of these pressures, rendering efforts to build community increasingly relevant and yet titanic.

Almost nine million people live in Greater London (Greater London Authority, 2020). Elephant and Castle is an area of South London. Fifty-four percent of the area residents are white, and significant African, Caribbean, Asian, South and Central American communities have settled here (Krausova, 2018). Another driving force behind the project was the need to understand the complex sociocultural dynamics that animate the municipality in which LCC is inserted. Elephant and Castle is indeed a "superdiverse" area, as scholar Steven Vertovec (2007) put it, with a strong Latin American presence. At the heart of the suburb sits the iconic 1965 Elephant and Castle shopping center,[4] the first of its kind in Europe, which constitutes a meeting point and hub for the many communities of immigrants who live in the area. The mall houses over sixty commercial activities owned or managed by small entrepreneurs, mainly from South America and Africa (Cock, 2011).

Due to its proximity to the city center, over the past twenty years this borough has attracted the interest of corporations, urban planners, and architects who have invested significant resources into its regeneration. Local working-class communities thus face a constant threat of expulsion and displacement due to relentless urban restoration plans and the area's fast-paced gentrification. New high-rise buildings are replacing public housing—the demolished Heygate Estates being a notable example—and an affluent population of young professionals is shaping the surrounding environment through their social demands and daily economic transactions. Persistent pockets of working class and migrant communities, as well as a growing upper-middle class, coexist in this bustling borough. These two sets of stakeholders are symbolized by a road junction in the neighborhood, one that provides gateways to many different parts of London. Situated at the iconic points of both the road junction and shopping center, LCC contributes to the demographic diversity of the area.

With almost 5,000 students, LCC is home to a highly diverse and international student population, and questions of inclusion and equality are at the core of the University's ethos. Teaching at this particular institution, I have become aware of the necessity to adapt and revise pedagogical approaches so as to ensure that learning spaces meet the needs of both students whose cultural frameworks originate outside Great Britain as well as domestic students, who also represent many different backgrounds. Recent internal statistics have shown that 37 percent of the student population at LCC is international, 48 percent is constituted by British students, and 15 percent by students from countries within the European Union (UAL, 2018/19).

The university itself has intervened in the borough's changing landscape. In 2019, LCC won a construction bid to erect a new building that will replace the old shopping center and plans to begin construction shortly. LCC's accorded plans to relocate and erect a new building where the shopping center is currently situated have exacerbated existing tensions around regeneration, thus raising questions about the role of the University in addressing inequalities. This is certainly a complex issue that cannot be unpacked by engaging in a one-sided criticism of regeneration as an absolute instrument of social displacement and discrimination. The design of the new building is in fact inspired by a communal spirit, enacted through the creation of a symbolic and physical space meant to attract and support pupils from disadvantaged backgrounds by offering more functional rooms and equipment, as well as public areas dedicated to well-being. While plans call for existing shops to be relocated to an adjacent area, with the promise to keep rents low, the news of the shopping center's planned demolition has been justifiably received with some skepticism from the local community.

## SONIC FUTURES: APPROACHES TO THEORY, METHODS, AND DATA

Mixed methods, based on a combination of practical, theoretical, and digital skills, were employed within the workshops to achieve a holistic comprehension of theory through practice. This experiential approach was valued in its potential to help students become more agentive in the learning process

(Kolb & Kolb, 2005). The workshops also adopted an approach to music not simply as an object of study, but as research and praxis (Regelski, 2005, 2009) and incorporated hip-hop-grounded critical pedagogies (Akom, 2009), which works in tandem with participatory research. Studies on hip-hop music and culture have demonstrated the potential of hip-hop as an educational tool (Dimitriadis, 2001, 2007; Hill, 2009; Low 2001; Seidel, 2011), a foundation for fostering dialogue and a platform for social change (Rose, 1994; Chang, 2005; Malone & Martinez, 2014). Akom (2009) advocates for pedagogy that places students at the center of knowledge production by turning their gaze toward the community, thinking of concrete solutions to everyday problems. This very crucial premise is at the basis of the workshop's ethical and epistemological values. A central component of the workshops was to examine how societal structures reproduce inequalities and exclude people who inhabit positions of disadvantage.

Within the workshops, questions of inequalities were approached by incorporating views that complicate well-established popular narratives on urban formations (cf. Butler, 2006) and that interrogate London's city "scapes."[5] For instance, the vignette that opens this chapter—our visit to Elephant Park, the former site of the public housing Heygate Estate—elucidates this. The estate was once a space for various communities to reside and come together, and the visit spurred within workshop participants a dialogue that addressed regeneration, the future of cities, and the myriad forces that animate the global through local spaces. We discussed what constitutes community, as well as the value of redevelopment vis-à-vis social context and class. These reflections were integrated and complicated by the testimony of an Australian Indigenous scholar who joined us that day, and whose presence emphasized not only the transnational nature of the workshops, but also the many possibilities engendered by the global in its power to connect localities. The global—in this case London—as a main point of attraction and transition, intersected with not only the local knowledge of an Indigenous scholar who shared his experience in relation to Indigenous pedagogical practices and epistemologies, but also encountered the local knowledges of the participants, themselves originally from India, Mexico, Sierra Leone, Italy, Canada, and other global sites.

Another critical aspect of the theoretical and methodological frameworks was the collaborative and participatory ethos in which they were enacted. Collaboration was key to the development of the activities and for the weakening of hierarchical structures and power relations among participants—workshop coordinators included. In line with scholarship on participatory ethnographic methods (Selener, 1997; Schensul, & Berg, 2004), this case study offers as a way to rethink and revalidate research practices that aim to reduce the distance between researcher and researched (Lassiter, 2005).

Within this context, collaboration comes to signify a very tangible aspect of research; namely, pedagogical praxis which may lead to concrete opportunities, when coupled with partnerships. A good example of this is given by the collaboration established with LSBU, which offered the opportunity to record a hip-hop track at the Elephant Studios. Here students collaborated with staff and with LSBU students, gaining direct experience of how a recording session is organized. Collaboration also entailed critical engagement with urban sites, enabling participants to reflect on their role not only as occupants of urban spaces, but also as creators—through the production of certain social relationships, by taking part in collective activities, and intervening in shaping spaces that reflect their ideas, experiences, and desires.

Through participatory action research (Schensul & Berg, 2004), not only did the students overcome their feeling of homesickness, being far away from their homes, families, and friends, but they also learned to critically engage with different urban configurations, thus reflecting on their positionality in relation to urban space. To feel grounded—with the double meaning of being bound to the earth and feeling a sense of stability—also enhances a sense of one's ability to achieve agency so as to address social injustices (Cammarota, 2007), change one's immediate environment, and potentially influence public decisions.

## WORKSHOPS IN PRACTICE

The workshops were conceptualized to provide students who struggle with academic life with a platform to garner a sense of community in London, facilitating self-expression in a less restrictive way and exploring cogent sociocultural, political, and economic questions. They were promoted through a series of initiatives, such as marketing on digital platforms and through the university's outreach channels (bulletin boards, e-mails, social media, etc.), by word-of-mouth, and via the distribution of flyers. Yet, despite the efforts to reach as many students as possible, the number who expressed interest was low. Ultimately, four graduate students joined every session. Hence, the aims and the outcomes of the workshops had to be modified accordingly. The new challenge was to create a learning space that was stimulating, engaging, but that could also provide some practical outcomes in terms of well-being and the development of transferrable skills.

The students who took part in the activities were international students with varying degrees of expertise in the fields of journalism, media, international relations, and marketing, among others. Their previous experiences, as well as their sociocultural background, thus informed their modalities of learning and the ways in which they experienced inequalities in London.

The internalization of the University is a growing phenomenon and London, as well as many other global (and less global) cities, are witnessing a surge in the number of international students who move to the capital to increase their chances of employability elsewhere (see Hewitt-Dundas & Roper, 2018). London has always constituted a pole of attraction for both career enhancement and acquisition of capital, be it economic, cultural, symbolic, or social. Hence, the pressing requests posed by a growing student body characterized by a high level of heterogeneity in terms of preparation, expectations, and understandings of education constitute a new challenge for university staff. Within this context, and taking into consideration the demands generated by highly globalized societies with their complex patterns of mobility, pedagogical practices should aim to diversify content and approaches to education, as well as promoting sustainable alliances between the university and the industry (Hanna, 1998; Hewitt-Dundas & Roper, 2018). With this in mind, the workshops aimed to strengthen such a connection through the organization of a culminating event, the "Sonic Futures Conference," where representatives from various industry sectors met the students.

The workshops took place on Saturdays and Sundays, lasting three to five hours apiece. Each workshop was taught by the author and by the founder of May Project Gardens, Ian Solomon Kawall. The connection between hip-hop culture and music, gardening, and critical theory was rendered explicit through a playlist and via the combination of theory and praxis. More context was provided through a brief lecture on the history of the area, the history of hip-hop, and the relationship between our practices and the environment. We would ask students to look around and familiarize themselves with the natural environment for that session. Gardening provided the perfect terrain to test teaching methods based on nonhierarchical structures, aiming to infuse self-empowerment and collaboration while strengthening a sense of community (cf. Hoffman, Morales-Knight, & Wallach, 2007).

The first and the last workshop took place in Morden, the official site of May Project Gardens, where Ian lives and runs his regular activities. These two workshops each represented the beginning and ends of cycles, both in metaphorical and more concrete terms: the first workshop was organized in the fall of 2018, at the end of a natural cycle, whereas the last one was scheduled in spring, when a new season of growth begins.

When the workshops began, I was particularly eager, as I had been longing for a more active connection with nature since I moved to London, often touted as the "greenest" city in Europe. Growing up in the Italian Alps, where most of my holidays where spent helping my family work the land, I felt I could contribute to the activities in the garden using my own form of "local knowledge." The first and last workshops were the most active, as we got a chance to get our hands dirty in Ian's garden and greenhouse.

On both occasions, the students were assigned different tasks—from raking to spreading the compost over the winter garden beds and sowing seeds—but, due to the weather conditions we were forced to spend more time inside the greenhouse and in Ian's home.

During the last workshop we mainly worked in the greenhouse, where students learned about planting and about what to grow in different seasons. Ian showed them different seeds and asked each student to guess what they were. Subsequently, after choosing a variety of seeds, they planted them in small pots that would facilitate growth, allowing the shoots to be transplanted successfully. As the students were planting, Ian gave them basic instructions about different methods and on what to do with the seasonal vegetables they had selected. While students were busy in the garden, I encouraged them to think about the links between their courses and what they were doing, reflecting on ways to strike a good balance between their academic commitments and their personal lives. This prompted a discussion about life in London for international students and economies of sharing. At the end of the session, the students said they felt a sense of purpose and connection, as expressed by Rani, a graduate student from India, who explained:

> I really enjoyed all the workshops. I learned so much at every workshop. The workshops also mainly became a space for me to self-reflect and to mentally grow in my views on my role as an international student in London—on how I can contribute to the community around me and learn from the community around me. I found that everyone in the workshops became like family, and the workshops really felt like a safe space to be myself and express my views on our course, and our journeys with Hip Hop. I also learned about certain plants and how they grow, and I particularly loved spending time in Ian's garden and learning what permaculture truly is.

The activities in the garden were also integrated with a complete tour of the garden and lessons on permaculture that revealed its relevance as a tool for regenerative agriculture. Ian would normally take the lead in the garden, asking students to identify all forms of life and guiding them in their explorations. In the first workshop, to test the students' knowledge, Ian pointed to a small pond, which constitutes the heart of his garden, and asked them: "do you see any living creatures in the pond? If yes, would you be able to tell me what they are?" The students' senses were not yet trained. They looked puzzled and his queries remained unanswered for a few minutes. After a while, one student identified frog eggs and replied with excitement: "is this what you are referring to?" Ian nodded in agreement and smiled. The students were starting to open their eyes to the secret life of the garden as their confidence was growing.

Reflection and personal growth were common threads that emerge from the students' observations and are constitutive of participatory research action (Fals Borda & Rahman, 1991; Schensul & Berg, 2004). It is particularly interesting to note that it was through self-reflection that students learned to observe, analyze, and interrogate privilege, as well as those structures that hinder economic, social and personal development. When asked to explain the value of the workshops in a city like London, the same student explained:

> I think in a city like London, the workshops are extremely valuable in addressing issues one doesn't even know they have. In the absence of time or spaces that allow for exploring of this kind, residents work towards productivity every day but this is somehow accompanied with growing mental and physical health struggles. Safe spaces like the one that these workshops tend to become, are so important. I joined the workshops a month after moving to London from India, and they helped me find myself and gave me a support system in a country away from home.

Another student wrote:

> [The workshops] surpassed expectations, becoming spaces where we not just engaged with nature and the world around us, but also looked inwards and got to know ourselves better. Unexpectedly, they became safe spaces for freedom and expression, and I found myself leaving each session feeling peaceful and having learnt more about myself. C. and I. structured the workshops in a way that allowed participants to spend time together exploring an area (Elephant & Castle) or spending time in a garden, and then taking time to discuss personal learnings together, leading to larger questions. Each of the workshops gave me so much food for thought; I don't think anything else could have caused this kind of enrichment.

These remarks provide a very interesting window into the experiences of the students, what they value, their needs and expectations. As international visitors, the students faced some difficulties in navigating London both geographically and socially and the workshops provided a space for them to develop a sense of self within the city, which is often imagined as a symbolic "global," rather than referring to its complexities as many "locals" to which one can learn to belong to and take part in (Harvey, 2003; Holston & Appadurai, 1996).

## CONCLUSION

I conclude this chapter by returning to Lear's notion of "radical hope" (2006) to suggest that emerging community spaces could offer one feasible solution to the challenges posed by financial cuts to cultural and social initiatives.

Moving within the constraints of austerity measures, and the uncertainty of a pending exit from the European Union, London is traversed by a series of contrasting forces that are creating a sense of insecurity, while also promoting forms of resistance.

To be able to navigate the city, with its intricate net of seemingly infinite possibilities, requires a map that modern GPS technologies cannot provide. It is the sensorial world of things and beings that stimulates those who "walk" (de Certeau, 1984) to not simply look for answers, but pose questions in the first place. Space here has been conceptualized as a space of places, as Castells (2005) would put it. In Castells' work, the expression bore a key meaning in relation to the daily practices which define human nature and society. Here, space of places, maintains the same core value but moves beyond this definition as it postulates the element of hope. "Radical hope" as a precondition for equality and equity, can be seen in spaces dedicated to sociality and social activities that incorporate diversity. This is precisely the work of projects such as Sonic Futures, where younger generations can become agents of social change. The workshops encouraged students to embrace a positive attitude in their relationship to the city, thus forging new alliances and alternative forms of citizenry that transcend the national to embrace the realm of the transnational and transcultural (cf. Holston & Appadurai, 1996).

A systematic and concerted effort in the redefinition of the city and its meanings is pivotal, and it can only be successful if promoted by educational institutions that work with the younger generations. Despite the challenges that I have encountered in promoting the workshops, the students who participated seemed to have thoroughly enjoyed the program as their comments and reflections demonstrate.

The creative dimension of the workshops provided the perfect terrain for speculations on urban interventions and place-making, enabling participants to learn and create knowledge, conceptualizing new possibilities for their newly found communities and for themselves. A concrete example of the practical outcomes of the workshops is the possibility to transform the program into a project that can be used by graduate students for employment, thus shifting the leadership and enabling modes of action based on resistance and support. The students who participated in the activities will thus be the leaders of the future, taking ownership of the workshops to support younger generations of students with limited access to resources.

## NOTES

1. An ethnographic approach applied to participatory action research has been carried out through data collection derived from participant observation, written interviews, and field notes. Ethnographic data lend themselves to nuanced narratives

that complicate well-known questions, in particular when it comes to investigating inequalities in contemporary societies.

2. While the workshops have proven to be very positive experiences for the students, there are several challenges that need to be addressed as they raise important questions in relation to inequalities and the role of these activities in tackling questions of participation, attendance, and attainment. Indeed, students from less privileged backgrounds are unlikely to find the time to participate in the workshops, and further limitations to participation likely include transportation challenges, stigma, and socioeconomic need.

3. The Heygate Estate was a large housing complex in Elephant and Castle, South London. The demolition of the buildings was carried out from 2011 to 2014 due to a plan to regenerate the area.

4. With a concertation of ninety-six Latin American businesses, the Elephant and Castle shopping center represents one of the most important hubs for Hispanic communities in London (Cock, 2011).

5. Here, I adopt Arjun Appadurai's (1990) terminology detailing the global dimension of cultural flows as this chapter focuses on the transnational dimension of cultural phenomena and citizenship in the global city.

## BIBLIOGRAPHY


Akom, A.A. (2009). Critical Hip Hop pedagogy as liberatory praxis. *Equity and Excellence in Education*, *42*(1), 56–66.

Appadurai, A. (1990). Disjuncture and difference in the global cultural economy. *Theory, Culture & Society, 7*(2–3), 295–310.

Butler, T. (2007). For gentrification? *Environment and Planning A: Economy and Space*, *39*(1), 162–181.

Cammarota, J. (2007). A map for social change: Latino students engage a praxis of ethnography. *Children Youth and Environments*, *17*(2), 341–353.

Castells, M. (2005). Space of flows, space of places: Materials for a theory of urbanism in the information age. In B. Sanyal (Ed.), *Comparative planning cultures* (pp. 69–88). New York, NY and Abdingdon Oxon, UK: Routledge.

Chang, J. (2005). *Can't stop won't stop: A history of the Hip-Hop generation*. New York: St. Martin's Press.

Cock, J.C. (2011). Latin American commercial spaces and the formation of ethnic publics in London: The case of the Elephant and Castle. In C. Mcllwaine (Ed.), *Cross-border migration among Latin Americans* (pp. 175–195). New York: Palgrave Macmillan.

De Certeau, M. (1984). *The practice of everyday life*. Berkeley, CA, Los Angeles, CA, London, UK: University of California Press.

Dimitriadis, G. (2001). *Performing identity/performing culture: Hip-hop as text, pedagogy, and lived practice*. New York, NY: Peter Lang.

Fals Borda, O., & Rahman, M.A. (1991). *Action and knowledge: Breaking the monopoly with participatory action research.* New York: Apex.

Greater London Authority. (2020, January 12). *Context and strategy: A growing population.* Retrieved from https://www.london.gov.uk/what-we-do/planning/london-plan/current-london-plan/london-plan-chapter-one-context-and-strategy-0.

Hanna, D.E. (1998). Higher education in an era of digital competition: Emerging organizational models. *Journal of Asynchronous Learning Networks, 2*(1), 66–95.

Harvey, D. (2003). The right to the city. *International Journal of Urban and Regional Research, 27*(4), 939–941.

Hewitt-Dundas, N., & Roper, S. (2018). Innovation in UK higher education: A panel data analysis of undergraduate degree programmes. *Research Policy, 47*(1), 121–138.

Hill, M.L. (2009). *Beats, rhymes, and classroom life: Hip-hop pedagogy and the politics of identity.* Teachers College Press.

Hoffman, A.J., Morales-Knight, L.F., & Wallach, J. (2007). Gardening activities, education, and self-esteem: Learning outside the classroom. *Journal of Urban Education, 42*(5), 403–411.

Holston, J., & Appadurai, A. (1996). Cities and citizenship. *Public Culture, 8,* 186–204.

Kolb, A.Y., & Kolb, D.A. (2005). Learning styles and learning spaces: Enhancing experiential learning in higher education. *Academy of Management Learning & Education, 4*(2), 193–212.

Krausova, A. (2018). Elephant and castle: Mapping super-diversity and the 2011 Census. *Centre on Migration, Policy and Society Working Paper No. 142.* Oxford: University of Oxford. Retrieved from https://www.compas.ox.ac.uk/wp-content/uploads/WP-2018–142-Krausova_Elephant-and-Castle-2.pdf.

Lassiter, L.E. (2005). *The Chicago guide to collaborative ethnography.* Chicago, IL: University of Chicago Press.

Lear, J. (2006). *Radical hope: Ethics in the face of cultural devastation.* Cambridge, MA and London, UK: Harvard University Press.

Low, B. (2011). *Slam school: Learning through conflict in the hip-hop and spoken word classroom.* Stanford, CA: Stanford University Press.

Malone, C., & Martinez, G. (Eds.). (2014). *The organic globalizer: Hip hop, political development, and movement culture.* New York and London, UK: Bloomsbury Publishing.

Regelski, T.A. (2005). Music and music education: Theory and praxis for 'making a difference'. *Educational Philosophy and Theory, 37*(1), 7–27.

Rose, T. (1994). *Black noise: Rap music and black culture in contemporary America.* Hanover, NH: Wesleyan University Press.

Sassen, S. (2000). Spatialities and temporalities of the global: Elements for a theorization. *Public Culture, 12*(1), 215–232.

Schensul, J.J., & Berg, M. (2004). Youth participatory action research: A transformative approach to service-learning. *Michigan Journal of Community Service Learning, 10*(3), 76–88.

Seidel, S. (2011). *Hip hop genius: Remixing high school education*. Lanham, MD: Rowman & Littlefield Education.

Selener, D. (1997). *Participatory action research and social change*. Ithaca, NY, USA: The Cornell Participatory Action Research Network.

UAL. (2018/19). *Central planning unit dashboards: Access to key university data*. Retrieved from https://canvas.arts.ac.uk/sites/working-at-ual/SitePage/46264/staff-development-at-lcc#week.

Ulvik, M., Riese, H., & Roness, D. (2018). Action research–connecting practice and theory. *Educational Action Research*, *26*(2), 273–287.

Vargas-Silva, C., & Rienzo, C. (2019). Briefing: Migrants in the UK. An overview. *The Migration Observatory at the University of Oxford*. Retrieved from https://migrationobservatory.ox.ac.uk/wp-content/uploads/2017/02/Briefing-Migrants-in-the-UK-An-Overview.pdf.

Vertovec, S. (2007). Super-diversity and its implications. *Ethnic and Racial Studies*, *30*(6), 1024–1054.

# Conclusion

## *The Power of Breadth and Depth: Urban Ethnography across Geographies*

Angela D. Storey and Jessica Bodoh-Creed

Ethnographic praxis brings together the powers of detail and of scope. As Laura Nader reminds us, "ethnography is never mere description, rather it is a theory of describing" (Nader, 2011, p. 211). Indeed, the impact of ethnography is not only in the thick description of a diverted bus ride during a storm in Maputo, or a conversation with a dancer stringing aluminum beads in Hermosillo, but in the framing of these everyday stories as moments situated within the complexity of lives understood across scales. The dancer in Hermosillo with whom Lucero Radonic converses at the start of chapter 4 knows and acts within layers of history, geography, and political economy that are understood from—but not limited to—that moment sitting on the dusty ground. Each of the chapters in this volume highlights the potential of ethnography as a method that embeds the poignancy of lived experience within the many temporal, spatial, and power-laden scales that shape our world.

This volume intentionally includes the work of scholars from multiple disciplines. Although many are anthropologists, authors include ethnographers within the fields of sociology, geography, communication, and international development. Drawing together disciplines highlights the wide adoption of ethnographic methods and the ways in which these methods integrate with work that may concurrently be archival, historical, participatory, or community-driven. As Chiara Ministrelli suggests, ethnography may be linked to critical and engaged pedagogies to imagine new urban experiences within particular spaces and histories. As Raffael Beier and Cristiana Strava contend, ethnographic research can provide a foundation upon which to argue for necessary shifts in development policies that too often seek one-size-fits-all solutions for individuals embedded in profoundly different social worlds.

The volume's range shows the adaptability of ethnography to speak to diverse social worlds and global problems by situating them within the nuance of everyday life.

Chapters in this volume were selected to traverse geographic confines, identifying case studies from five continents and nine cities. This geographic breadth allows us to focus not on location but on the power of ethnography as a methodological tool through which to understand urban inequality. As cities take on a growing portion of the world's inhabitants, scholars increasingly turn their attention to understanding the specificity of regional urbanization. This has resulted in the development of significant new fields, such as Southern Urbanism, which articulates the necessity of exploring urbanization within the global south through particular postcolonial junctures of economic dispossession, exclusion, and knowledge production (Pieterse, 2015). The geographic scope of our volume is meant to complement the critical nature of such approaches, both theoretically and practically, and to offer possibilities for ethnography to support a diversity of frameworks for understanding urban inequality. We do not argue that cities face the same experiences of urbanization; rather, we note the importance of connecting wider processes to qualitative, narrative details of local experiences. As the daily minutia of urbanization and the reality of city living are laid bare in these case studies, the contributors offer analytical insights that may resonate across geographic confines. This inquiry is, importantly, always situated within the particularity of the local. This is the power and potentiality of urban ethnography—to expose the processes through which diverse social worlds are created.

## ETHNOGRAPHY AS BRIDGE: LINKING RESEARCH AND LEARNING

As ethnography is characterized by a grounding within both the particular and the situated, what might we learn more broadly about urban inequality from these case studies? We see these chapters as ways to learn about ethnography as a method of inquiry into urban inequality, and to read the distinctiveness of situations alongside each other. As such, we read each chapter as possibilities for provocation, translation, and critique; in short, we see them as foundations upon which to ask different kinds of questions about changing cityscapes.

There are many ways to approach these chapters as scholars, teachers, and students. For those who are new to reading academic work, scholarly literature might feel far away, both geographically and conceptually. The ethnographic lenses employed by each author allow us, as readers, to situate specific individuals and places at the center of political, social, and economic processes. This facilitates reflection on disparate sites not as far-flung locales, but as narratives resulting from tangible methodologies. Voices of those experiencing inequalities poignantly illustrate the impacts of global shifts that may otherwise seem nebulous, such as the rise of neoliberal economic policies or the implementation of urban redevelopment plans. For faculty using case studies within courses, or for scholars reflecting upon wider implications, we offer here a few ways in which the volume might serve as a bridge between varied urban sites and broader questions of how inequality can be produced, compounded, or challenged.

As class-based differentiation accelerates within cities in the global north and global south, ethnographers have answered calls to explore inequality by engaging multiple points of view, including "studying up" (Nader, 1972). Hugo Cerón-Anaya, in chapter 8, explores golf courses as urban sites that mark privilege. What other kinds of sites are exclusive, limited, or otherwise seen as elite? How might visibility craft or reinforce the classed status of different spaces or groups within a city? As cities become more segregated along socio-spatial lines, the opportunity to understand and interact with people across critical differences is reduced through what Teresa Caldeira cautions is "the implosion of modern public life" (2000). Megan Sheehan, in chapter 7, discusses how Chilean residents of Santiago perceive migrant use of city space, interrogating the lamination people, places, and stereotypes through spatial associations. What other processes of spatial production mark city sites as those meant for particular kinds of people, or particular kinds of actions? How is this reproduced in everyday actions or in popular sentiment? What unexpected assemblages result from the interaction between lived practices and wider perceptions of places?

With heightened global attention to the pressures of movement, mobility, and displacement, ethnography provides a potent set of methods and questions via which these processes are experienced in particular communities. In chapter 5, Ben Chappell's work in Austin highlights the violence and losses of gentrification, as well as the ways in which memory becomes a tool through which communities claim space and belonging. In what ways do memory-related practices shape other sites, or push back against larger processes? What are the points at which practices such as gentrification, housing discrimination, or redlining meet concerted pressure from coordinated action, or from the confluence of everyday practices? With increasing scholarly attention to the extension of settler-colonial logics into modern sites, such as Radonic's work in Hemosillo in chapter 4, what submerged histories of dispossession or dynamics of power undergird access to land on which we live, work, and study? How do communities push back against municipal and private authority in order to lay claim to sites of memory and of cultural practice?

Many chapters engage with work to counter injustice. Ministrelli explores this through innovative educational endeavors that employ creativity and hands-on labor in chapter 9. Such an approach draws from rich veins of applied and activist scholarship within ethnography (Lyon-Callo & Hyatt, 2003), including a focus on social justice and community-based partnerships (Low & Engle Merry, 2010; Strand et al., 2003). How might justice and equity be created through unexpected alignments of people, places, and actions? What kinds of belonging and knowing might result from approaching city spaces at the intersection of multiple pasts and varied futures?

## URBAN ETHNOGRAPHIC FUTURES

As global urbanization expands, ethnographers will necessarily attend to an evolving set of subjects. How will ethnography understand, imagine, and shape urban futures? We conclude this volume by suggesting a few broad themes we can see urban ethnographers exploring in the years to come.

Ethnographers are uniquely situated to understand the impacts of growing precarity and informality. While informality remains most strongly associated with cities in the global south, increasing socioeconomic precarity affects residents of urban areas worldwide. Crisis-level expansions of homelessness in US and UK cities come as a result of intensifying local inequality (OCPD, 2020; Lucas, 2019) and housing precarity expands through the compounding actions of public and private entities (Desmond, 2016), prompting local and national reactions. Ethnography increasingly addresses the impacts and lacunas of projects meant to produce formality and stability. As Beier and Strava discuss in chapter 1, projects of resettlement like the one explored in Casablanca often emphasize approaches with singular solutions. Statistics detailing the brute number of people resettled into formal housing obscure the varied ways in which displacement impacts households and individuals, reshaping everyday experiences and political possibilities. How can ethnography shape policy and development practices so as to avert the destruction of communities or of individual lives? Informality is not limited to housing. As Christian Reed explores in chapter 3 about Maputo, informality refracts through countless inequalities within a city or region. As residents with less economic capital are forced into more distant sites, this unevenness is compounded through unequal access to roads and modes of transit, and in the need to take on significant everyday risks in the process. As he argues, the riders of informal transit are forged through everyday acts as a particular public, and as one whose actions also reshape the city in form and in demands for resources. What new publics will emerge as precarity expands? What kinds of claims and modes of access will be crafted against urban exclusions and informality?

As ethnographers address the social implications of shifting urban resources and divided access, analyses must explore the effects of emerging or compounding limitations. As pressures from climate change accelerate, urban infrastructures and resources will heighten as sites of sociopolitical contestation. In 2018, Cape Town faced drought and water shortages during which a "Day Zero" was set, in which residential water access would largely be cut off due to a lack of supply (Maxmen, 2018). As Angela Storey discusses in chapter 6, peripheral areas of Cape Town have long faced severe limitations on water and basic services, highlighting the profound unevenness of access to critical resources that is the crisis-laden backdrop for such acute disasters as that of "Day Zero." How will the tools of ethnography intersect with those of other disciplines as scholars, practitioners, and policy makers attempt to understand a global climate shift playing out in specific places and their particular ecological, material, and social worlds?

Developmental aspirations have become platforms for obscuring urban inequality, challenging ethnographers to explore the backdrop of eye-catching projects and their related claims. As increasing populations and global attention spark particular approaches to development and change, cities have emerged as powerful economic and political actors. Seng-Guan Yeoh explores in chapter 2 how colonial and postcolonial trajectories of local development in Kuala Lumpur are framed by the aspirations of Malaysia to make its capital a "World Class" city. Yeoh demonstrates that even amid Kuala Lumpur's dramatic development, the reality of a city without slums does not match its branding. Cities increasingly look to each other comparatively (McCann & Ward, 2011) and are keenly aware of how they are viewed on the global stage. As technologies and policy approaches are borrowed across urban sites with varied histories, what narratives of individual lives and community struggles might illuminate the challenges of urban competition?

Scholarship holds within it the possibility for many interpretations of urban life. In this volume, we hope to have emphasized the importance of ethnography as a platform to amplify the voices of communities and individuals often excluded from development or policy decisions, exploring countercurrents and alterities that exist within the fissures of the city.

## BIBLIOGRAPHY

Caldeira, T.P.R. (2000). *City of walls: Crime, segregation, and citizenship in São Paulo*. Berkeley: University of California Press.

Desmond, M. (2016). *Evicted: Poverty and profit in the American city*. New York, NY: Broadway Books.

Low, S., & Engle Merry, S. (2010). Engaged anthropology: Diversity and dilemmas: An introduction to supplement 2. *Current Anthropology, 51*(S2), S203–S226.

Lucas, S. (2019, December 3). The homeless death statistics are shocking–but the true total may be even higher. *The Guardian*. Retrieved from https://www.theguardian.com/cities/2019/dec/03/the-homeless-death-statistics-are-shocking-but-the-true-total-may-be-even-higher.

Lyon-Callo, V., & Hyatt, S. (2003). The neoliberal state and the depoliticization of poverty: Activist anthropology and "ethnography from below." *Urban Anthropology and Studies of Cultural Systems and World Economic Development, 32*(2), 175–204.

Maxmen, A. (2018). As Cape Town water crisis deepens, scientists prepare for "Day Zero." *Nature, 554*(7690), 13–14.

McCann, E., & Ward, K. (2011). *Mobile urbanism: Cities and policymaking in the global age*. Minneapolis, MN: University of Minnesota Press.

Nader, L. (1972). Up the anthropologist: Perspectives gained from studying up. In D. Hymes (Ed.), *Reinventing anthropology* (pp. 284–311). New York, NY: Pantheon Books.

Nader, L. (2011). Ethnography as theory. *HAU: Journal of Ethnographic Theory, 1*(1), 211–219.

OCPD, Office of Community and Planning Development. (2020). *The 2019 annual homeless assessment report to congress. Part 1: Point-in-time estimates of homelessness.* U.S. Department of Housing and Urban Development. Retrieved from https://files.hudexchange.info/resources/documents/2019-AHAR-Part-1.pdf.

Pieterse, E. (2015). Epistemological practices of Southern Urbanism. In W. Ding, A. Graafland, & A. Lu (Eds.), *Cities in transition II: Power, environment, society* (pp. 310–325). nai010 Publishers.

Strand, K., Marullo, S., Cutforth, N., Stoecker, R., & Donohue, P. (2003). Principles of best practice for community-based research. *Michigan Journal of Community Service Learning*, *9*(3), 5–15.

# Index

Page references for figures are italicized

# About the Contributors

**Raffael Beier, PhD**

Postdoctoral Research Fellow, Ruhr University Bochum, Germany, and University of the Witwatersrand, Johannesburg, South Africa.

Raffael Beier is currently a visiting postdoctoral research fellow at the Centre for Urbanism and Built Environment Studies (CUBES), University of the Witwatersrand, Johannesburg, South Africa. Furthermore, he is the assistant dean and coordinator of the PhD program in International Development Studies (IDS) at the Institute of Development Research and Development Policy, Ruhr University Bochum, Germany. Raffael Beier studied urban geography in Bochum and Grenoble, France. In 2019, he was awarded a joint PhD degree from Erasmus University Rotterdam, The Netherlands, and Ruhr University Bochum. His research mostly relates to topics of urban inequality, housing, and people's resistance, with a focus on the Middle East and North Africa, as well as sub-Saharan Africa. In his PhD, he analyzed the resettlement of shantytown dwellers in Casablanca from the perspective of the people affected. His research was supported by the Ruhr University Research School PLUS, funded by Germany's Excellence Initiative.

**Jessica Bodoh-Creed, PhD**

Lecturer, California State University, Los Angeles, CA, United States.

Jessica Bodoh-Creed is a lecturer in anthropology at California State University, Los Angeles and author of *The Field Journal for Cultural Anthropology* (Sage, 2019). She received her PhD in anthropology from the University of California, Riverside. Her most recent research focuses on female power brokers in Los Angeles and how they form collaborative, supportive, and magnetic networks that contribute politically, socially, and economically. For the past two years, she has been project manager for an NSF

Western Spokes Big Data Grant focused on creating access to LA City Data through open data portals for students, nonprofits, faculty, and community stakeholders through Cal State LA's College of Natural and Social Sciences.

**Hugo Ceron-Anaya, PhD**

Assistant Professor, Lehigh University, PA, United States.

Hugo Ceron-Anaya is an assistant professor of sociology at Lehigh University. He studied history at the National University of Mexico, before completing his MA and PhD in sociology at the University of Essex. His work focuses on social inequalities and privilege, examining how class, race, and gender impact the behavior and perceptions of affluent people. He is particularly interested in the wide array of ordinary and everyday practices that reproduce social inequities. Ceron-Anaya's first book: *Privilege at Play: Class, Race, Gender, and Golf in Mexico*, came out with Oxford University Press in spring 2019.

**Ben Chappell, PhD**

Associate Professor, The University of Kansas, KS, United States.

Ben Chappell is an anthropologist and author of *Lowrider Space: Aesthetics and Politics of Mexican American Custom Cars.* His current research includes a multi-sited ethnography of traditional softball tournaments between Kansas City and Houston, and a critical university studies project on managerialism, algorithmic reason, and neoliberal epistemology. He has served as a consulting scholar for exhibitions with the Kauffman Museum, the Kansas City Museum, the Chicago Urban Art Society, and the Smithsonian Institution; as well as for the photo-history volume *Mexican American Baseball in Kansas City.* He founded and convenes the Ethnography Caucus of the American Studies Association. He is an associate professor of American Studies at the University of Kansas.

**Chiara Minestrelli, PhD**

Lecturer, School of Media, London College of Communication, University of the Arts London, London, United Kingdom.

Dr. Chiara Minestrelli is a lecturer in the School of Media at the London College of Communication (University of the Arts London) and Acting Course Leader of the BA (Hons) Contemporary Media Cultures. She holds a PhD from Monash University where she conducted research on Australian Indigenous hip-hop, identity, culture, spirituality and the role of the media in identity formation. Her book, *Australian Indigenous Hip Hop: The Politics of Culture, Identity, and Spirituality* (Routledge) is an ethnographic study that investigates the discursive and performative strategies employed by Australian Indigenous artists to make sense of the world and establish a position of authority over their identity and place in society. From 2015 to 2016, she was a visiting professor in the Africana Studies and Women, Gender and Sexuality Studies Programs at Lehigh University (Bethlehem, PA, US). Chiara is currently leading a series of workshops (Sonic Futures) that explore the connection between artistic practices, critical theory, hip-hop music, the environment, and local communities in South London.

**Lucero Radonic, PhD**

Assistant Professor, Michigan State University, MI, United States.

Lucero Radonic is an assistant professor at Michigan State University, where she has a joint appointment in the Department of Anthropology and the Environmental Science and Policy Program. Her research examines the intersections of resource governance and urbanization, specifically the cultural politics and everyday engagements with water and infrastructure in cities of Latin America and the US Southwest.

**Joel Christian Reed, PhD, MPH**

Survey Manager, The Demographic and Health Surveys (DHS) Program at ICF.

Joel Christian Reed is a medical anthropologist and epidemiologist from Lexington, Kentucky. He is a Fulbright, Peace Corps, and Doctors without Borders alum. Currently, he manages surveys for the USAID-funded Demographic and Health Surveys (DHS) Program based in Rockville, Maryland. His first book, *Landscapes of Activism: Civil Society and HIV and AIDS Care in Northern Mozambique*, is an ethnography of AIDS activists available from Rutgers University Press.

**Megan Sheehan, PhD**

Assistant Professor of Anthropology, College of St Benedict/St John's University, MN, United States.

Megan Sheehan is an assistant professor at the College of St. Benedict/St. John's University. She received her PhD in anthropology from the University of Arizona. Since 2007, her research has examined Latin American labor migration to Chile, exploring how migration impacts and changes urban areas. Currently, she is examining the urban transformations produced by the unprecedented scale of recent Venezuelan migratory flows to Chile.

**Angela D. Storey, PhD**

Assistant Professor, University of Louisville, KY, United States.

Angela Storey is an assistant professor in the Department of Anthropology at the University of Louisville. Her research examines the politics of the natural and built environment, with a focus on community activism and participatory processes of urban governance. Since 2010, she has been conducting fieldwork in South Africa to explore the intersecting politics of water, sanitation, and electricity infrastructures in informal settlements in the Khayelitsha area of Cape Town. Since 2017, she has also coordinated an interdisciplinary, applied project in Louisville, Kentucky, to examine the expectations and experiences of residents as they engage with city-based participatory projects.

**Cristiana Strava, PhD**

Assistant Professor, Leiden University, The Netherlands.

Cristiana Strava is currently an assistant professor in the School of Middle Eastern Studies, Institute for Area Studies, at Leiden University. She is trained as an anthropologist with a focus on visual media and the built environment (BA, Harvard; MARes, PhD, SOAS, University of London). Her research has been funded by the Wenner-Gren Foundation, the Foundation for Urban and Regional Studies—Oxford, and the UK Economic and Social Research Council. Her work straddles the fields of anthropology, urban studies, and Middle Eastern studies. Her most recent research examines the creation of large infrastructure projects in Morocco as signals for the production of new social and political imaginaries as well as shifts in urban governance.

**Seng-Guan Yeoh, PhD**

Associate Professor, Monash University, Malaysia.

Seng-Guan Yeoh is an associate professor in social anthropology at the School of Arts & Social Sciences, Monash University, Malaysia. Yeoh is an urban anthropologist who has conducted fieldwork in Malaysia, the Philippines, and Indonesia. He also produces ethnographic documentaries. His PhD is from the University of Edinburgh, Scotland.